P T Barnum

GCLS

Gloucester County
Library System

389 Wolfert Station Road
Mullica Hill, NJ 08062
(609) 223-6000

P.T. BARNUM

*America's Greatest
Showman*

by

Philip B. Kunhardt, Jr.

Philip B. Kunhardt III

Peter W. Kunhardt

ALFRED A. KNOPF

New York 1995

This Is a Borzoi Book
Published by Alfred A. Knopf, Inc.

Copyright © 1995 by
Philip B. Kunhardt, Jr.,
Philip B. Kunhardt III,
and Peter W. Kunhardt

Library of Congress
Cataloging-in-Publication Data

Kunhardt, Philip B.
P. T. Barnum : America's greatest showman /
by Philip B. Kunhardt, Jr., Philip B.
Kunhardt III, and Peter W. Kunhardt. —
1st ed.
p.   cm.
"A Borzoi Book"—CIP t.p. verso.
Includes bibliographical references (p.   )
and index.
ISBN 0-679-43574-3
1. Barnum, P. T., (Phineas Taylor),
1810–1891.   2. Circus owners—United
States—Biography.   I. Kunhardt, Philip B.,
[date].   II. Kunhardt, Peter W.   III. Title.
GV1811.B3K85   1995
338.7'617913'092—dc20
[B]   94-42597
          CIP

Manufactured in
the United States of America
First Edition

A NOTE ON THE TYPE

The text of this book was set in Monotype
Century Expanded, a variation of Century,
which was designed in 1894 by Linn Boyd
Benton (1844–1932). Benton cut Century in
response to a request by Theodore Low De
Vinne for an attractive, easy-to-read type-
face to fit the narrow columns of his *Century
Magazine*. Early in the 1900s, Benton's son,
Morris Fuller Benton (1872–1948), working
for his father's American Type Founders
Company, updated and improved Century in
several versions such as Century Expanded
and Century Schoolbook; the bold version of
the latter is used for captions in this book.

Separations and film by Digital Pre-Press
Inc., New York, New York

Printed and bound by R.R. Donnelley &
Sons, Willard, Ohio

Designed by Elton Robinson

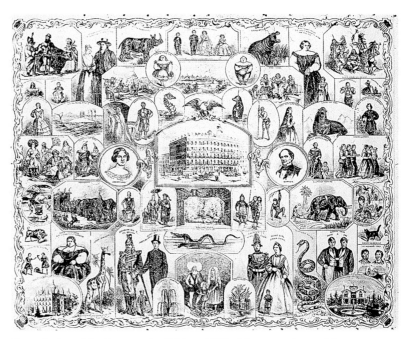

**Commissioned by Barnum in 1864 or 1865, this engraving celebrates
a quarter-century of showmanship and personal success.**

Contents

Preface

ven in his own day, people knew that with Barnum they were dealing with someone bigger than life. "Is it possible you are the showman who has made so much noise in the world?" sputtered Commodore Cornelius Vanderbilt when he first met Barnum in 1851; "I expected to see a monster—part lion, part elephant, and mixture of rhinoceros and tiger." As the 1850s unfolded, no one could define him in ordinary terms. "He represents the enterprise and energy of the 19th century," wrote one admiring contemporary. No, "he represents the material, practical side of our times," wrote another. Still others saw him exemplifying something crass and self-serving in the American character. In his infatuation with the pronoun "I," in his insensitivity as he reached for any prize—no matter how sacred—for his stage, in his constant exaggeration and in his questionable taste, they saw someone they did not think should be helping define the national character. And to this day a negative aura surrounds him. Much of the criticism is unfair. Barnum spent his whole life trying to bring pleasure to others; he had huge respect for his public, and it has been proved that he never even said the phrase he is most often remembered for, "There's a sucker born every minute." But Barnum only rarely bothered to counter his critics. "I am a showman by profession," was his typical response,

"and all the gilding shall make nothing else of me."

For almost 60 years, Barnum saw himself as part of what he called "the show business" (he was one of the earliest to use this phrase). His genius lay in being able to create extraordinary, popular sensations. Hardly a year went by without Barnum's introducing a major new phenomenon. This, combined with a gift for writing in the vernacular, best evident in his oft-revised autobiography, kept Barnum almost constantly before the public eye. One of the country's first millionaires, he was a businessman first and last; his primary goal, as he once put it, was "to put money in my own coffers." To this end he interjected his own self in his work as few had ever done before. His name was blazoned along Broadway in lights, and appeared on posters and billboards all across America. His disembodied face, too, floated—on his museum walls, on his business letterhead, on his circus train cars, on his tent banners. Merchandising not just his business but himself as well, Barnum became the most famous and recognizable man in the world. But money and fame were only a part of what Barnum was after, serving more as signs that he was successfully pleasing the public than as true ends in themselves. His goal was to awaken a sleeping sense of wonder, to help open the eyes of his fellow citizens to the amazing diversity of the human

Using contact prints from his Mathew Brady negatives, Meserve put together a Barnum workbook for his daughter, Dorothy Kunhardt. Shown at right are two pages of giants.

and natural world. To accomplish this, he lifted up the rare, the strange, the beautiful, the awesome—exotic animals, little-known tribespersons, startling new inventions, human oddities. He introduced the rhinoceros to America, brought the first herd of elephants here, pioneered in the display of exotic fish and marine mammals. But he became best known for what he put forth as his "living curiosities." Giants, midgets, thin men, and bearded ladies careened across his stage for decades, and though in some cases there was prejudice or paternalism involved, especially in his display of blacks and the retarded, this went almost entirely unnoticed in an age deaf to such questions. If there was a dark side to Barnum, it was the dark side of his culture at large. "I am not . . . half so cute nor cunning nor deep as many people suppose," Barnum insisted. And it was true.

Barnum's habit of destroying incoming letters each morning after reading them has unfortunately left a one-sided view of his correspondence. On top of this, a succession of fires destroyed key records and papers and personal treasures. Among the losses were numerous daguerreotype and paper images Barnum lovingly collected—of Tom Thumb, of Jenny Lind, of Barnum's mansion Iranistan, of Barnum himself, of the American Museum. Today only four or five photographs exist of Barnum's great emporium on the corner of Broadway and Ann Street, and not one camera image of the vast interiors. Fire alone cannot fully explain this—Barnum seems to have purposely kept photographers out of his museum. Word of mouth, after all, was his best recommendation, along with written ads and color lithographs and illuminated banners that could exaggerate the features of what he had to offer.

By the late 1850s, there was a new reason to encourage photographs—the demand for carte-devisite images of his famous exhibits promised lucrative rewards. And so, one by one, or sometimes in groups, Barnum's unusual performers made their way to the 10th Street studios of Mathew B. Brady to have their pictures taken. Many of the resulting portraits are known to the world primarily through the efforts of a man who was grandfather to one of the triumvirate of authors of this book, great-grandfather of the other two—Frederick Hill Meserve.

Best known for his pioneering work on the photographs of Abraham Lincoln and the Civil War, Meserve had a special interest in P. T. Barnum as well. Back in the days when photographs were not yet prized, Meserve was able to search out and acquire the pictures of hundreds of 19th-century American performers. Many more turned up in Meserve's most important discovery, a cache of thousands of

The 15,000 Mathew Brady glass negatives Meserve discovered in 1902 had been ignored for years, stored in a New Jersey warehouse in their original wooden boxes. This one, marked "Barnum," contained Brady images of some of the showman's most famous performers.

Mathew Brady original glass negatives found in a New Jersey warehouse. Among the scores of Brady's dark wooden boxes he found there were a number marked "Barnum Negs." Inside were hundreds of glass negatives revealing in startling detail many of Barnum's unique and most memorable characters—fat ladies and thin men, giants and midgets, albinos and Circassian Beauties, even the original Siamese Twins. Taken together, they amounted to a kind of Victorian-era peepshow. In his attempt to order and identify these pictures, Meserve enlisted the aid of anyone he could find who had been part of the Barnum era. Tom Thumb's widow was the most helpful. Lavinia Warren Stratton was remarried to Count Primo Magri when, early in the century, Meserve sought her out at Coney Island, where she was performing. He brought with him pictures of her friends and contemporaries at Barnum's American Museum, most of which she could identify, even though her memory had begun to cloud. Thereafter the two corresponded and traded information.

But it was Meserve's daughter, Dorothy Kunhardt, who shed the most light on the Barnum collection as she spent years researching its pictures as well as searching out and acquiring Barnum pamphlets and flyers and other memorabilia. As a New York City child, she had been entranced by The

Ringling Brothers, Barnum and Bailey Circus, Barnum's best-known legacy. In the sideshow, she actually met "Zip, the Missing Link," who had been hired by Barnum himself way back in 1860. In the 1930s, now married with children of her own, Meserve's daughter became a successful author of children's books, her second being a circus story with her own illustrations inspired specifically by the Barnum collection.

The Meserve pictures, along with many later additions to the collection, account for more than half of the 554 illustrations in this book. The rest come through the courtesy of 40 other collections, public and private. Preeminent among them are those of the Bridgeport Public Library, in Bridgeport, Connecticut; the Barnum Museum, also in Bridgeport; and Circus World Museum, in the Ringling Brothers' hometown of Baraboo, Wisconsin (see acknowledgments).

As early as the 1880s, Smithsonian chief Spencer Baird recognized Barnum's work as an important precursor of the great scientific institutions that followed. A bust of Barnum he commissioned for the Institute Gallery was to stand among those of Americans "who have distinguished themselves for what they have done as promoters of the natural sciences." But, unlike the scientist, Barnum could never let evidence speak for itself. He liked to dress it up, give it

In 1934, inspired by her father's pictures and Barnum's circus exploits, Dorothy Kunhardt wrote and illustrated *Now Open the Box*, a now classic children's book that employed the showman's fixation with size to tell the poignant story of a circus dog.

a spin all his own. The tiny man was not allowed to be just plain tiny, he had to be a comic, too, a dancer, singer, mimic, quick-change artist, bon vivant, and lover-boy all rolled into one. It made a better story that way. Convinced that the chief defect of American civilization was a "severe and drudging practicalness," Barnum set out to transform the culture. "Amusement [may not be] the great aim of life," he conceded, "but it gives zest to life and makes a grand improvement in human character." Through his circuses he offered extravaganza galore, a cacophony of sound and light and dazzle, packed with so much action that people had no choice but to sit back exhausted and wallow in confused delight. But it was the American Museum that was the great love of his life, and herein lay Barnum's most extraordinary contributions. There was less hubbub here, more focus than in the circus. You knew what floor the whale tank was on, when the snakes were being fed, where Anna Swan the giantess was going to heft the Lilliputian King. You could walk the floors at your own pace, take some potshots in the shooting gallery, gawk all you wanted to. He liked gawkers. He padded around the floors himself and took pleasure in people taking pleasure. That was part of his homely luster. Though driven and quirky and at times thin-skinned, it was the light side of the man that most

often shined through. Inspired by a robustly held Universalistic faith, he refused to worry, living life as it came. He acted impulsively, on first instinct, rarely stopping to consider the consequences. He brushed away the past—what was done was done. And more often than not, his instincts were on target.

Barnum once wrote that he "preferred to be kicked to not being noticed at all." He needn't have worried; no one could ever forget him. If Lincoln was the great moral force of the day, infusing the young democracy with a hallowed conscience, Barnum was the great liberating force, chasing out old puritanical inhibitions and letting in the light of joy. Over the course of his long lifetime, through both struggle and triumph, he came to embody an important part of the American spirit.

Philip B. Kunhardt, Jr.
Philip B. Kunhardt III
Peter W. Kunhardt

P. T. Barnum

CHAPTER

1

1810–1839

Phineas Taylor Barnum
at mid-life, the product
of his early years.

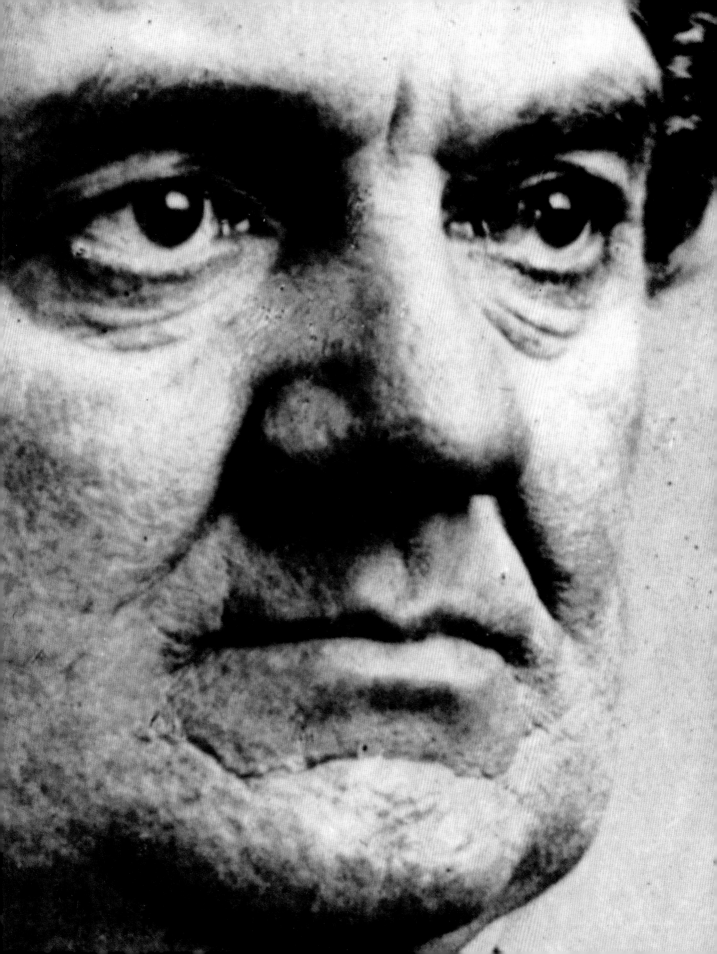

In Connecticut Yankee Country, A Practical Joker Is Born

Phineas Taylor Barnum was born in Danbury, Connecticut, a thriving community of comb- and hat-makers an ancestor had helped settle five generations before. "Taylor" his family called him; "Tale" he was to his playmates. Tale just missed making his first appearance on his country's 34th Independence Day and had to settle for July 5 instead. Typically, he always celebrated this mistake in timing by claiming he had planned it that way; he was just giving the people a chance to settle down after the 1810 festivities so they could better relish his coming.

Taylor was the first child of his father's second wife, Irena Taylor. Philo Barnum had already had five children by his first wife, Polly Fairchild, who died at 27, and he was to sire five more with Irena, one brother for Tale and three sisters. Philo was a farmer, a tailor, a tavern-keeper, a grocer, a livery-stable operator, and he ran a small freight business between Norwalk and Danbury, too, but he wasn't much good at any of his trades. It was Irena's father who was the star of the family. Phineas Taylor was the chief wag in a town of wags. Uncle Phin, as he was known to everybody, was a cunning, sharp rogue who always kept a jump ahead of the next man with his never-ending cascade of wit and practical jokes. Loud, competitive, sometimes close to cruel when he stalked new victims, he had fought in the Revolution, represented Danbury in the state legislature, was one of the town's chief landowners, its census taker, justice of the peace, and top lottery schemer. Upon his little namesake he lavished zesty attention and became the most important and long-lasting influence in the boy's life.

Bethel Village was the section of Danbury where the Barnums presided, and although it had not yet been incorporated into a separate town, it was the territory Barnum remembered when, later in his life, he reminisced about his boyhood. He recalled how pigs ran free in the streets and what a treat it was to be given a sausage link to take to school to roast and eat. He remembered that most everybody, whether sick or not, was bled by the county doctor each spring. He could see in his mind the spots in and around town where many of his young friends lived, where he had played tag and hide-and-seek—Wolfpits, Wildcat Road, Plum Trees, Toad-Hole, and Grassy Plains. He recalled how cut off from the world his life was back then, how newspapers only arrived once a week and punishments were harsh. At school he was banished to the "dungeon" in the basement when the hard swats from a ruler didn't work. Adult transgressors were dealt with at the whipping post. "I can see as if but yesterday our hard-working mothers hetchelling their flax, carding their tow and wool, spinning, reeling, and weaving it into fabrics for bedding and clothing. The same good mothers did the knitting, darning, mending, washing, ironing, cooking, soap and candle making, plucked the geese, milked the cows, made butter and cheese.... Our candles were tallow, home-made, with dark tow wicks. In summer nearly all retired to rest at early dusk without lighting a candle."

Young Barnum ate well—boiled or baked beans, rye bread, applesauce,

AUTOBIOGRAPHY OF P. T. BARNUM.

INTRODUCTORY.

PHINEAS TAYLOR

Young Barnum admired his maternal grandfather so much he started off his 1854 autobiography with this picture of him. "As I was his pet," Barnum wrote, "[I] spent probably the larger half of my waking hours in his arms. . . ."

"hasty pudding eaten in milk." There was plenty of fish and big clams, peddled from Norwalk or Bridgeport, and enough meat for the elders to indulge themselves twice a day. "Uncle Cabot Morgan, of Wolfpits, in Puppytown, was our only butcher. He peddled his meat through Bethel once a week." There were few wagons or carriages; horseback was the chief means of transportation, feet for youngsters. Barnum had no love for his early farm work—plowing for ten cents a day, the same as he got for scraping 100 cow horns for a comb-maker. "Like most farmer's boys, I was obliged to drive and fetch the cows, carry in firewood, shuck corn, weed beets and cabbages," and then he quickly added, "but I never really liked to work." That was not completely true, for, from the beginning, young Barnum enjoyed "head-work"; it was the physical kind he hated. In his sporadic schooling, he was always adept at arithmetic, so much so that once his teacher woke him up in the middle of the night to win a bet that his young pupil could calculate the number of feet in a load of wood in five minutes—Barnum did it in two. It was an aptitude that would serve him well in the entrepreneurial days which lay ahead.

Barnum's was a good, full, boisterous childhood, peopled with a herd of playmates, many of whom proudly wore the same names as the original founders of the town—Taylor, Hoyt, Beebe, Benedict, Barnum. It was a close-knit town. Its young people had been marrying each other for so many generations now, everybody seemed to be related to everybody else, and it was not only local custom that, whenever a young man greeted an elder, the name called out was preceded by an "Aunt" or an "Uncle."

This woodcut of Barnum's birthplace and childhood home was used in the early editions of his autobiography.

Conflicting Forces Help Shape the Showman-to-Be

Colorful storytelling, quick wit, a certain disregard for the truth, and the inventive practical joke were all part of the fabric of life in Barnum's boyhood community. Watching grown men hoax each other out of their shoes delighted the child. To be able to leave a fellow man in an awkward position and the object of laughter displayed rare ingenuity to these Connecticut Yankees, and the process was the best entertainment in town. To young Barnum, the joke of all jokes was pulled off by his grandfather on a voyage to New York which had been prolonged to a full week by fickle wind. During the trip, Uncle Phin and 13 friends from Bethel let their beards grow. Finally, the ship arrived on Sunday, when all the barbers in the city were closed. Owner of the only razor on board, Phineas managed to get his friends to shave off half their beards; on the second go-round, the other half would be removed. But, as it turned out, there was no second go-round. Once clean-shaven, Uncle Phin "lost" the razor overboard while he was stropping it, and his friends were forced to face the city looking like half-beard freaks.

Alongside the freewheeling, fun-loving, often boisterous influence of Barnum's grandfather and his friends, the boy was subjected to a diametrically opposed force—the dour hopelessness and severity preached by the Christianity he was taught in the hard, cold pews of Bethel's meeting house. The Congregational Church was still the official religion in Connecticut, handing down a puritanical and frightening set of tenets. The word of God Barnum learned from Sunday school and the pulpit was the basic Calvinism of former ages—that man by nature was depraved; that it had been decreed by God at the beginning of time who would and who would not be saved; that good works had no effect for those already designated to an eternal hell; but that people had better work hard at being good anyway, because if they didn't that proved they were not among the "Elect." Such a faith was described graphically by the Congregational and Presbyterian preachers of the day, including the famous Lyman Beecher from nearby Litchfield, who fought hard against any move to democratize the church.

Instead of letting it crush him, Barnum ultimately refused to accept the stern teaching of such a church and, guided by the example of his grandfather, gravitated instead to a gentler set of beliefs based on redemption for all men and women of faith. As a 13-year-old, he wrote a Sunday-school paper that planted the first seeds of the count-your-blessings, all-things-are-possible, never-look-back philosophy he would come to live by. "The one thing needful is to believe on the Lord Jesus Christ, follow in his footsteps, love God and obey his commandments, love our fellow-man, and embrace every opportunity of administering to his necessities. . . . In short, the one thing needful is to live a life we can always look back upon with satisfaction."

The spirited influence of doting Grandfather Taylor was complemented by Irena, Barnum's quiet, kindly, self-reliant mother. She had no desire for the riches her son would later achieve, nor his love of mansions, and quietly lived on after she was widowed in the plain house where she had borne her children. She loved the town of Danbury and its gaggle of relatives.

A Tapestry of Vivid Childhood Memories

In his autobiography Barnum pictured himself startled by the snakes and disappointments of Ivy Island (above), a gift of real estate Phineas Taylor made to his grandson when the child was two years old (right).

Laurens P. Hickok, who operated his own private school in Bethel, was one of Tale's early teachers.

Nathan Seeley's son Ransom (above) was a boyhood playmate of Taylor's whose brother, Seth, later sued Barnum and sent him to jail.

As he aged, Barnum cherished his childhood more and more. Memories of it—the good as well as the bad—came floating back, and he not only wrote about it but gave interviews and made speeches on the subject, traveling back to Bethel after a serious illness to reacquaint himself with long-ago sights and sounds before it was "too late." One of his earliest recollections was his fascination with the town bully. Even though "John" beat him up, left him in tears, and brought on reprimands from his mother for keeping such bad company, young Barnum was infatuated with this undisciplined, fearless boy who was always at the center of trouble—whether jumping off a bridge naked in front of churchgoers, stealing a comb-maker's horns and selling them back to him, or getting knocked silly by a horse. Tale, in turn, avoided trouble whenever he could, even ran away from it, claiming that if he were ever forced to go to war, "the first arms that I should examine would be my legs." His attraction to the town bully suggested that young Barnum didn't dare break the rules himself but loved being a party to the fun and excitement.

Early on, as a tiny child, Taylor had been made a landowner when Uncle Phin had presented him with a tract of land called "Ivy Island." "My grandfather always spoke of me (in my presence) to the neighbors and to strangers as the richest child in town," wrote Barnum, "since I owned the whole of 'Ivy Island,' one of the most valuable farms in the state. My father and mother frequently reminded me of my wealth and hoped I would do something for the family when I attained my majority." Finally, at ten, he got to see what he owned. The "promised land," the "mines of silver and gold" he had dreamed of turned out to be worthless, snake-infested swampland. "The truth flashed upon me," Barnum remembered later. "I had been the laughing stock of the family and neighborhood for years." A strange kind of hazing, the incident had been meant to strip Barnum of his boyhood dreams and turn him, like all the rest in Bethel, into a true, hard-boiled Yankee. Still, it was an unusual sort of practical joke for a family to play on its child, and the resolution not only hardened the boy to life but seemed to help compel him to bamboozle others.

Five years later, saying goodbye to his dying grandmother was a memory of quite a different nature—a softening, spiritual one. "I never can forget the sensations which I experienced," he wrote, "when my turn came to approach her bed-side, and when, taking my hand in hers, she spoke to me of her approaching dissolution, of the joys of religion. . . . She besought me . . . to pray to our Father in heaven . . . to use no profane or idle language, and especially to remember that I should in no way effectually prove my love to God, as in loving all my fellow-beings. . . . When I received from her a farewell kiss, knowing that I should never behold her again alive, I was completely overcome."

And then there was Hackaliah Bailey. "Hack" was a born showman, the second American ever to own and exhibit an elephant. Wide-eyed Barnum listened to Hack hold forth whenever he visited Bethel. It seems the owner had taken on a partner who now refused to share the profits made by "Old Bet." Hack's solution was to point a loaded rifle at the elephant, stating, "You may do what you please with your half of the elephant, but I am fully determined to shoot my half." It was another important lesson for young Barnum—learning how to call an adversary's bluff with a threat that could not be ignored.

This painting is purportedly of Hackaliah Bailey (spelled without the "e" back then), who helped popularize the elephant and other wild animals by importing them and taking them on tour. On his visits to Bethel, Hackaliah charmed young Tale with his early circus stories.

Bethel looked like this during Barnum's boyhood. The structure on the left, behind the Revolutionary War–era liberty pole, was built by Barnum's maternal grandfather, Phineas Taylor, who at one time owned most of downtown Bethel. In the center is the Congregational Church, steepled in the late 1820s, and unheated by even a stove because religious passion was considered warm enough. The building at the far right, next door to the home of Nathan Seeley, was Tale's parents' store and tavern, where liquor flowed freely. Drinking was as much a part of Bethel life as breathing, Barnum recalled. "Every sort of excuse was made for being treated. . . . Even at funerals the clergy, mourners, and friends drank liquor."

Nurturing His "Organ of Acquisitiveness"

Before he was five years old, Barnum "began to accumulate pennies and sixpennies." When he was six, his grandfather informed him that all his "little pieces of coin amounted to one dollar." The revelation of what that meant would stun Barnum and stay with him forever. At the village tavern his little handkerchief-full of coins was exchanged for a silver dollar. "Never have I seen the time (nor shall I ever again) when I felt so rich," wrote Barnum, "so absolutely independent of all the world, as I did when I looked at that monstrous big silver dollar, and felt that it was all my own. . . . I believed, without the slightest reservation, that this entire earth and all its contents could be purchased by that wonderful piece of bullion, and that it would be a bad bargain at that."

From that moment on, bullion was the boy's obsession. On the local military-training grounds during the War of 1812, Barnum, hardly out of diapers, began hawking his own concoction of molasses candy to the troops, and since he "always had a remarkable taste for speculation," his stock soon included gingerbread and cherry rum. It was not long before the young capitalist owned a sheep and a calf, and he would have been even wealthier if his father had not dictated that from then on he purchase his own clothes.

In the years ahead, the fledgling financier, with the reputation for laziness when it came to "gaining bread by the sweat of the brow," was put to work in his father's country store. "Like many greenhorns before me, this was the height of my ambition," Barnum recalled. "I felt that it was a great condescension on my part to enter into conversation with the common boys who had to work for a living. I strutted behind the counter with a pen back of my ear, and was wonderfully polite to ladies, assumed a wise look when entering charges upon the day-book, was astonishingly active waiting upon customers. . . . Ours was a cash, credit and barter store; and I drove many a sharp trade with old women who paid for their purchases in butter, eggs, beeswax, feathers, and rags, and with men who exchanged for our commodities, hats, axe-helves, oats, corn, buckwheat, hickory-nuts, and other commodities. It was something of a drawback upon my dignity that I was compelled to sweep the store, take down the window-shutters, and make the fire; nevertheless the thought of being a 'merchant' fully compensated me for all such menial duties."

As time went on, Barnum worked in a variety of country stores, and his further education in the deceptions of the trade, how to haggle over price and strike a hard bargain and pull the wool over a purchaser's eyes, would serve him well in the profession he finally would choose. "[M]any of our customers were hatters," he recalled, "and we took hats in payment for goods. . . . The

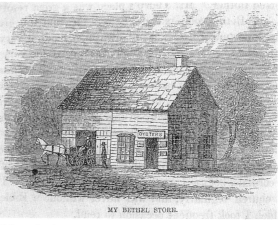
MY BETHEL STORE.

For his autobiography, first published in December 1854, this is how Barnum depicted his own Bethel store, where the specialty was oysters.

At 19, Barnum was in the grocery business with his uncle and guardian, Alanson Taylor. Already having caught on to advertising, the partners bragged of their produce in the local paper.

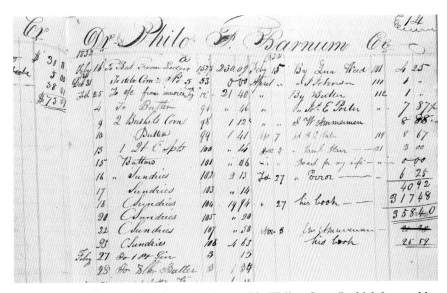

Barnum kept a large leather-bound ledger at his "Yellow Store," which he would start in the spring of 1831 across the street from the old family store of his grandfather. Opened to the account of Barnum's half-brother, Philo F. Barnum, the ledger contains reckonings for almost every family in Bethel.

Approaching his 21st birthday, Barnum had become extremely successful as a lottery-ticket salesman. He had his own office and pretended to be the sole agent of Dr. Strickland, a fictitious name he thought added scale and believability to his operation.

hatters mixed their inferior furs with a little of their best, and sold us the hats for 'otter.' We in return mixed our sugars, teas, and liquors, and gave them the most valuable names. It was 'dog eat dog'—'tit for tat.' Our cottons were sold for wool, our wool and cotton for silk and linen; in fact nearly everything was different from what it was represented. The customers cheated us in their fabrics; we cheated the customers with our goods. Each party expected to be cheated, if it was possible." It was an atmosphere not so much of dishonesty as of trickery, with wealth less a sign of a trader's social status than of his cleverness and daring. In the dullness of life in rural Connecticut in the 1820s and '30s, trickery acted as a form of Yankee entertainment, a harsh but widely practiced method of testing wits, in the tradition of Downeast and New England humor.

At 12, Barnum began selling lottery tickets, and for the next four years he was actually concocting "schemes" and conducting his own lottery offerings to the hat and comb workers of the community. Of the morality involved, Barnum remembered that "one of our neighbors, a pillar of the church, permitted his son to indulge in that line, the prizes consisting of cakes, oranges, molasses candy, etc.; and the morality of the thing being thus established, I became a lottery manager and proprietor."

After leaving the profession while still a boy, as a young man he returned to the lottery business anew, working not for himself but as an agent for nationwide offerings, calling his office the "Temple of Fortune" and opening branches in neighboring towns. Using the press liberally, he "issued handbills, circulars, etc. by tens of thousands" as well. His take grew huge: "I sold from five hundred to two thousand dollars' worth of tickets per day." Over the years, money poured in as Barnum learned that tireless work, crafty ideas, and fast headwork paid big dividends. Looking back at those times, he had to admit that "humbugs certainly existed long before I attained my majority."

In "York" He Learns to Be His Own Boss

Barnum was only 15 when his father died of a "severe attack of fever." All of a sudden his childhood was over, and "the world looked dark indeed." After the burial, he and his siblings "returned to our desolate home, feeling that we were forsaken by the world, and that but little hope existed for us this side of the grave." The future looked darker still when it was discovered that Philo Barnum had died insolvent and his eldest son by his second wife was on his own now—Taylor even had to borrow the money to pay for his new funeral shoes. In due course, however, it became clear that the world had not forsaken the young man. He would be rescued from despair by the glamorous city of "York," as New York was then known to country folk. He had been offered the position of clerk in a Brooklyn grocery store by a former resident of Danbury.

It was not the first time Barnum had visited the big city. Back in January of 1822, at 12, he had once helped drive cattle to market there, where "a new world was about to be opened to me." Free of parental guidance, he roomed at the Bull's Head Tavern for a full week; learned to "swop" in a toy shop; roamed through Bear Market, where he was astonished by the enormous quantities of beef for sale; watched windmills at work; visited the State Prison; and finally, basking in his newfound freedom, returned to Bethel by sleigh.

Now he was 16—"neither boy nor man," as he later put it—but endowed

The Brooklyn grocery store where the 16-year-old clerked was located at Sands and Pearl streets. From a perch in Brooklyn Heights near the busy East River, this was the view of the great city of 200,000.

Across the East River from Brooklyn where Barnum was working was the institution that would one day be central to his life—the American Museum, located at the corner of Broadway and Chambers Street. Established originally as the Tammany Museum in 1790, it would be moved in 1830 to a larger Broadway building at Ann Street, its home when a still-brash but not-quite-so-young entrepreneur named Barnum acquired it 12 years later.

nevertheless with enormous resolve to succeed in the world. Drawn by the New York stage, he entertained friends from Connecticut at the latest plays and with his own sharp critiques of the performances. Crucial to his progress was the day when all purchasing for the store where he worked was placed in his hands. "I bought for cash entirely," he later recalled, "and thus was enabled to exercise my judgment in making purchases—sometimes going into all sections of the lower part of the city in search of the cheapest market for groceries. I also frequently attended the wholesale auctions of teas, sugars, molasses, etc. so that by watching the sales, noting the prices, and recording the names of buyers, I knew what profits they were realizing, and how far I could probably beat them down for cash."

No matter how stimulating the buying game, Barnum learned something beyond numbers during this period, something basic about himself—that he was not temperamentally suited for a job at a fixed salary, that his very nature longed for speculative ventures in which he could sink or swim according to his own merit. He had concluded that any line of work was wrong for him "unless it is of such a nature that my profits may be greatly enhanced by an increase of energy, perseverance, attention to business, tact, etc." Following his instincts, the teenage entrepreneur quit his job, opened a bar on his own hook, made a success of it, and within months sold it for a profit. An offer from Uncle Phin—half a carriage house rent-free on the main street of Bethel if he would start a business there—seemed too good to refuse.

Before heading home, Barnum made arrangements with several city fruit dealers to fill his future orders. He had decided to test his new resolve to be his own boss by trying his hand at the retail fruit-and-confectionery business.

The Teenage Storekeeper and Lottery Lord Marries

ne rainy Saturday evening, after the death of his father but before his New York experience, Taylor Barnum came upon the person with whom he would share the next half-century. Clerking at a store in Grassy Plains, a mile west of Bethel, he had a chance meeting with a striking young woman almost two years older who moved him as had no other. "The brief view that I had of this girl by candle-light," he later recalled, "had sent all sorts of agreeable sensations through my bosom. I was in a state of feeling quite new to me, and as unaccountable as it was novel." Riding with her home to Bethel in the dark, "I opened a conversation with her, and finding her affable and in no degree prim or 'stuck-up' . . . I regretted that the distance to Bethel was not five miles instead of one. A vivid flash of lightning at that moment lighted up the horizon, and gave me a fair view of the face of my interesting companion. . . . That girl's face haunted me in my dreams that night."

Temporarily home from New York while recovering from a case of smallpox during the summer of 1827, Taylor took the opportunity to further his acquaintance with Charity Hallett, who had grown up in Fairfield before taking a job as a tailoress in Bethel—the "fair, rosy-cheeked, buxom-looking girl" with the pretty laugh and flashing white teeth who had unknowingly kindled his first strong attraction for the opposite sex. Home for good in May of 1828, and dividing his time between his store and the lottery business, he at first tried to keep his feelings from "Chairy," as people called her, but it was not long before a proposed move to Tennessee that would have insured him a huge area of exclusive lottery territory was nixed because he "feared the distance was too great to meet the approbation of a certain tailoress in Bethel" whose wishes Barnum felt he must take into account "for special reasons."

The budding romance was not good news to Barnum's mother, who had been running the family tavern since her husband's death and now felt that her ambitious son could do better than a poor tailoress. On the other hand, some of young Barnum's friends thought Charity was actually too good for the big, fast-talking, round-faced pun-lover. Finally, in the summer of 1829, convinced she was "one of the best women ever created," the 19-year-old proposed to the girl he now considered his "sweetheart"—and was accepted. To avoid family friction, they held the marriage in New York City, at the house of Charity's uncle, the bride's family attending but the groom's kept in the dark. Irena Barnum was hurt that her eldest had married in secrecy and without her presence, but after a month of coolness she softened and welcomed the couple into her house. "From that day," Barnum surmised, "I am sure neither she nor any other person ever said or believed that I had not been extremely fortunate in the selection of my companion."

Pretending he was going to New York on business, Barnum got married there instead. Among those attending was the bride's mother, Hannah Hallett (above), whose sense of fun rivaled that of Barnum himself.

The fair young neighbor Barnum described marrying in 1829 looked more forbidding in this portrait than she actually was. Painted by American artist Frederick R. Spencer 18 years after the wedding, it is the earliest known picture of Charity.

When Barnum denounced Bethel church elder Seth Seeley as a "canting hypocrite" in his paper, he was sued for libel, tried, convicted, and sentenced to 60 days in the Danbury jail. Barnum's highly publicized incarceration made him known throughout the state.

From jail, Barnum wrote his friend Gideon Welles, the 30-year-old editor of the Hartford *Times*, that he had been sent "within these gloomy walls . . . for daring to tell the truth."

unning his recently constructed "Yellow Store," which dispensed everything from Bibles to brandy; dabbling in real estate; auctioning books purchased in New York to eager-to-read country people; checking his lottery agents and branch offices sprinkled now across the state—all of these activities together were not enough to satisfy the pent-up energies of the young husband. Pinched by the limitations of a Bethel existence, Barnum began to widen his scope by throwing himself into the religious and political controversies of the day. He had long since determined what kind of God to follow; his religion was to be joyful—a "cheerful Christianity," as he put it. It was a concept in direct opposition to the old-time Calvinist and evangelical forces at work in Connecticut, which hoped to control the political scene as well as the very soul of the populace. Especially abhorrent to Barnum was the clergy-sponsored "blue law" movement, aimed at squelching not only travel and entertainment, but lotteries as well, Barnum's bread and butter. When a Danbury newspaper refused to publish Barnum's writings on the subject, he started his own paper in retaliation. The weekly, entitled *The Herald of Freedom*, was a radical, democratic sheet in the tradition of Gideon Welles' Hartford *Times*. With Barnum as its main voice, and a message of "equal rights" in the face of the Sabbatarian reformers, the *Herald* went on record as opposing "all combinations against the liberties of our country." Boldness and vigor helped the new paper acquire a liberal audience that was almost national in range, but, "impelled by the vehemence of youth," Barnum later wrote, "I repeatedly laid myself open to legal difficulty under the law of libel, and three times, during my three years as editor, I was prosecuted." When the fledgling editor wrote that a church dignitary had "been guilty of taking usury of an orphan boy," he ended up in jail. Because of his growing power in the community and the strong support of most of its people, it wasn't any ordinary prison term. From his newly papered and carpeted cell, Barnum kept right on editing his paper, as well as receiving friends, for the two months of his confinement. Upon his release, he was celebrated at a dinner held in the very Danbury courtroom where he had been convicted. Odes were sung, orations given, toasts made by several hundred of the editor's supporters, after which he was driven back to Bethel by a six-horse coach in a festive parade that included music, songs, and the roar of cannon. The adulation was intoxicating, and a resulting appetite for public attention would be with Barnum for the rest of his life.

Charity had brought him happiness with the birth of their first child, Caroline Cordelia, on May 27, 1833. But when the Connecticut Legislature finally banned lotteries outright in 1834, thus shutting down Barnum's gambling empire for good, Bethel could no longer hold this restless, rambunctious, ambitious, many-sided man. Bored with grocery stores, Barnum sold his interest in the "Yellow Store" and later in the year severed himself from his paper. Then, in a move that winter, Barnum pulled up stakes and headed with his family for the place where any American with his potent personality and powerful initiative had to be—New York City.

A Jail Sentence Helps Arouse a Lust for Fame

Still intact is the front page of an early issue of Barnum's weekly paper, *The Herald of Freedom* (above). The paper got Barnum a jail sentence. On release (right), the prisoner was greeted by his supporters before being given a grand parade back to Bethel.

Hard Times in a Big City Where Hoaxes Flourish

nstead of welcoming him with open arms, the big city gave Barnum the cold shoulder. He had hoped to find a position in a mercantile firm where he could share in the profits, but when no such opportunity materialized, out of desperation he tried to make ends meet by drumming up business for several stores. Up until now, Barnum had been sloppy with money, spending whatever he made and saving nothing. "I had learned I could make money rapidly and in large sums," he recalled. "I acquired it so readily, that I did not realize the worth of it. . . . To be sure, I thought that at some future time I should begin to accumulate by saving, but I cared not for the present, and hence I scattered my means with an open and unsparing hand." Now that present was at hand, as every morning at sunrise he scoured the want ads in the New York *Sun*. There were plenty of medicinal pills and mousetraps to be peddled, plenty of rickety stairs to be climbed, and, at their end, plenty of for-

Unknowing dupe of the Moon Hoax was the great British astronomer Sir John Herschel, who, it was reported, had spotted pelicans and winged creatures on the moon through a new superpowerful, seven-ton telescope set up in Africa that could magnify distant objects 42,000 times. When he focused the lens, Herschel could clearly see, said the story, that the wings of the four-foot-high yellowish creatures were made of thin membranes "without hair, lying snugly upon their backs, from the top of the shoulders to the calves of the legs."

The corner of Broadway and Ann Street, shown here as it looked in 1831, would in the future be made famous by P. T. Barnum, still only an apprentice hoaxer. The American Museum he would acquire was now located in its new, five-story marble building (far left), opposite St. Paul's Church. Later in the decade, the buildings at right would give way to the grand new Astor Hotel.

Perpetrated by Edgar Allan Poe, the Balloon Hoax made the crossing of the Atlantic seem real in a detailed description of the apparatus and flight accompanied by passages from the bogus journal of phony passengers. "We have flown at a great rate during the day, and we must be more than half way across the Atlantic. We have passed over some twenty or thirty vessels of various kinds, and all seem to be delightfully astonished. . . . At 25,000 feet elevation the sky appears black, and the stars are distinctly visible."

tunes to be made—but only if the job-seeker had money to invest. Always on the lookout for something he personally could exhibit, Barnum answered an ad of John Scudder's American Museum, an institution that featured oddities. To his dismay, for a mere $2,000 a device called a Hydro-oxygen Microscope could be had. No real work was forthcoming all winter long and into the spring, but still the future showman kept honing his considerable skills. In a tavern one evening, he got a friend to persuade the local jokester to play a particular trick on him. "Come, Barnum," he was challenged, "I'll bet you hain't got a whole shirt on your back." Well aware that only half of the shirt he was wearing was on his back, Barnum had taken another shirt from his suitcase "and nicely folding it, placed it exactly on my back, fastening it there by passing my suspenders over it." After the wager was made, to the delight of the crowd Barnum stripped down and showed that, indeed, he did have a whole shirt on his back. Hoaxing coursed through his veins like a disease.

It was not only the tall, handsome young man from Connecticut who was afflicted. The ruse, the prank, the fraud, was everywhere, especially New York, which seemed to be the epicenter of deception. The down-to-earth, skeptical Yankees who came crowding into the city shouldn't have been such easy prey for duplicity, but they were. It was a fact that the common man, no matter how sharp and tough, actually enjoyed having the wool pulled over his eyes, and made it easy for the puller. Extraordinary stories, amazing-sounding evidence, outlandish claims were all part of the game. Barnum watched and listened and learned. One of his most telling lessons occurred the very year he arrived in the city, when one of the truly great hoaxes was pulled off. A long, detailed article in the New York *Sun* told how the world's most famous astronomer had discovered life on the moon. Filled with elaborate, technical-sounding descriptions of the powerful new telescope that supposedly had been used, along with eyewitness accounts, the tall tale was taken as truth, and the Moon Hoax, as it came to be called, made the *Sun*, at least temporarily, into the best-selling paper in the country. Later, Edgar Allan Poe, who tried to legitimize the idea of ruses in a story entitled "Diddling," himself perpetrated an equally outrageous scam by publishing a supposed "news" story about a highly believable but completely bogus trans-Atlantic balloon flight. For better or worse, Barnum was learning by osmosis.

Barnum Embarks on a Hoax of His Own

It wasn't that he deliberately set out to hoax the public. In fact, it isn't clear even today how aware he was of what he was doing. What is clear is that Barnum did not yet know that his lifework would be in the amusement field and that, by his own admission, he "fell into the occupation." By the spring of 1835, a few lottery debts still owed him had been paid off, enabling Barnum to open a little New York City boarding house for old Connecticut neighbors, along with a grocery store. It was in the store one late July morning that he first learned from Coley Bartram, a Connecticut friend, that a bizarre "exhibition" currently showing in Philadelphia was for sale. Joice Heth was, by the account of her owner, a 161-year-old slave who had tended George Washington at his birth and was still alive to tell about it. The vision of a stars-and-stripes Methuselah danced in Barnum's head as he caught the next stage south. By August 6, he had had a cordial meeting with Heth, confirmed his instinct that this shrunken, black ancient was a potential gold mine, inspected the original bill of sale, dated February 5, 1727, which bound a 54-year-old Joice Heth to George Washington's father, talked her present owner down from $3,000 to $1,000, and clinched the deal. By fall, Barnum had his remarkable relic on display in New York, lying on a high lounge in the center of a large, packed room. Handbills and posters plastered the city, and two ingenious, back-lit, out-of-doors Joice Heth transparencies two by three feet in size marked the slave's whereabouts in the city and helped bring in an average of $1,500 a week. To introduce his "astonishing curiosity" and induce her to answer questions, sing hymns, and tell stories about "dear little George," Barnum hired Levi Lyman, a shrewd, amiable half-lawyer, half-barker. The press reaction to the spectacle was astounding. The New York *Sun* called Joice a "renowned relic. . . . [A] greater object of marvel and curiosity has never presented itself." The New York *Star* found her appearance "very much like an Egyptian mummy just escaped from the Sarcophagus." And the New York *Commercial Advertiser* ventured that, "since the flood, a like circumstance has not been witnessed." In the past, Barnum had used the press to help exploit his lottery schemes, but he had never manipulated the institution so effectively. Nor had he ever so clearly realized that the truth, the whole truth, and nothing but the truth was not a necessity. In fact, whenever there was a whiff of doubt about the authenticity of what the public crowded to see, so much the better. Sometimes that very doubt was a necessary ingredient and had to be manufactured. With ticket sales tapering off in Boston, Barnum employed a subterfuge he would repeat over and over during his career. In an open letter to a newspaper signed "A Visitor," he

If one were to believe it, Joice Heth had a long and complex history. Originally acquired by the Washington family as a 54-year-old domestic, she had helped raise "little George," was transferred to the Bowling family and taken to Kentucky, then moldered in an outhouse for decades before her original bill of sale was rediscovered. In fact, she was a slave woman belonging to John S. Bowling, who had leased her for exhibition to fellow Kentuckian R. W. Lindsay. Now even Lindsay was losing interest in his questionable exhibit, and was amenable to a transfer of rights when Barnum entered the picture.

THE GREATEST
Natural & National
CURIOSITY
IN THE WORLD.

JOICE HETH,

Nurse to Gen. GEORGE WASHINGTON, (the Father of our Country,)
WILL BE SEEN AT

Barnum's Hotel, Bridgeport,

On FRIDAY, and SATURDAY, the 11th, & 12th days
of December, DAY and EVENING.

JOICE HETH is unquestionably the most astonishing and interesting curiosity in the World! She was the slave of Augustine Washington, (the father of Gen. Washington,) and was the first person who put clothes on the unconscious infant, who, in after days, led our heroic fathers on to glory, to victory, and freedom. To use her own language when speaking of the illustrious Father of his Country, "she raised him." JOICE HETH was born in the year 1674, and has, consequently, now arrived at the astonishing

AGE OF 161 YEARS.

With the help of handbills like this, Barnum cashed in on Joice Heth in New York, Providence, Boston, Albany, and shorter stops all over New England, including Bridgeport, where he exhibited his "living skeleton" in a relative's hotel (above). Whereas Heth had not stirred much excitement before, under Barnum she became a sensation. With extravagant claims, picturesque language, and skillful use of the local newspapers, "the greatest curiosity in the world" drew customers by the tens of thousands.

This portrait of Barnum was painted by Frederick R. Spencer in 1847 as a companion to his oil of Charity (page 14). Saved from a fire in Barnum's first mansion, the two paintings hung side by side in the parlors of his subsequent homes.

charged that Heth was a fake, that she was a "curiously constructed automaton, made up of whalebone, India-rubber, and numberless springs," and that the exhibitor was "a ventriloquist." Crowds thronged again to see if this could possibly be true. It all led to a breakthrough discovery for Barnum—that the public actually enjoyed being deceived, as long as they were, at the same time, being amused. And as for Joice Heth, as Barnum wrote in an 1841 satire, "she began to take great delight in the humbug, which was a profitable one to her."

This first success in the field of show business for the overjoyed Barnum was short-lived. By late fall, Joice Heth was ill and had to be sent to the home of Barnum's half-brother, Philo, in Bethel. There, cared for by a black lady hired in Boston for the purpose, Joice steadily failed, and died on February 19, 1836. Conveyed by sleigh back to Barnum in New York, the pathetic little body was turned over to a distinguished surgeon who had earlier been promised the opportunity to perform a postmortem. It was executed with much fanfare, with Richard Adams Locke, author of the Moon Hoax the year before and now editor of the New York *Sun*, present in the large audience. At the end of the autopsy, the surgeon announced there had surely been some mistake about Joice Heth's age—instead of being 161, she was, in his opinion, no more than 80. "Dissection of Joice Heth—Precious Humbug Exposed" was the *Sun*'s headline the next day.

Nor did the weird tale end there. Deciding to play a practical joke on the New York *Herald*'s editor, Barnum's fun-loving assistant, Levi Lyman, called on James Gordon Bennett in his office and informed him that Joice Heth was not really dead, she was performing in Connecticut at that very moment, and as a joke the postmortem had actually taken place upon the body of a recently demised old Harlem "Negress." "Bennett swallowed the bait, hook and all," Barnum recalled. "He declared it was the best hoax he ever heard of, eclipsing Locke's 'moon hoax' entirely, and he proceeded to jot down the details as they were invented by Lyman's fertile brain," and within days published them.

Bennett, of course, was furious when he found out that it was he and not Locke who had been duped, but somehow the credulous editor was still gullible enough to fall for yet another of Lyman's concoctions, the "absolutely real and true exclusive" story of Joice Heth, which was also duly published, in four long articles. They told how Joice had been discovered in a Kentucky outhouse, how her benefactors extracted all her teeth, then taught her the George Washington story, while aging a bill of sale with tobacco juice, and increasing her age from 110 in Louisville, and 121 in Cincinnati, finally to 161 when she arrived in Philadelphia.

All in all, it was not only an eccentric way for Barnum to have entered what would soon become his chosen profession, but an unfortunate one as well, for, like it or not, from that time on his name would be associated with humbug and not taken as seriously as it should have been. What Barnum did and did not know of the Joice Heth hoax is still disputed. Even he made opposite admissions. In a letter he wrote years later concerning Lindsay, the man from whom he'd bought Heth's services, he protested: "I never had anything to do with him except to buy from him, in perfect good faith and pay him the money for, an old negress which he falsely represented as the 'nurse of Washington' and which he imposed on me as such by aid of a forged bill of sale purporting to have been made by the father of George Washington. I honestly believed all this and exhibited accordingly. . . ." In the same letter, having always publicly claimed pleasure at his "humbug" reputation, Barnum finally acknowledged the "stigma" he had "ever since borne" after being accused of "originating" the Joice Heth "imposture." But, then again, when he was younger and flushed with early success, Barnum had made fun of himself by fictionally describing how he had forged the documents and trained Joice in her routine. And on his first trip to England, in the 1840s, he flamboyantly described himself as the perpetrator in the Heth "imposture" to an English journalist.

Who knows? It was a hoax certainly, whether a carefully conceived and calculated one or not. More important, for Barnum it opened the door to the field he would flourish in and eventually influence so greatly.

Struggling to Make It As an Itinerant Showman

BRILLIANT Attraction!!

SIG. VIVALLA,

The celebrated Professor of EQUI-LIBRIUM and PLATE DANCING, has the honor to inform the Ladies and Gentlemen of Bridgeport, that he will give his wonderful entertainments at *M. Hinman's* Hotel, on *Friday* and *Saturday* evenings, 1st & 2d *April*.

While exhibiting Joice Heth, Barnum stumbled onto a juggler named Antonio, whom he renamed Signor Vivalla. Among Vivalla's many talents was his ability to balance an array of plates and other china objects on the tops of sticks which in turn were balanced on his hands, feet, forehead, nose, and chin. Then, to lively music, he made all the crockery simultaneously spin and dance.

Although Barnum had found a calling, he still lacked a stage on which to play it out. For the rest of the decade, he tested several, the Franklin Theater in New York being one of the first. Here he brought a colorful juggler and plate spinner named Signor Antonio, whose act he had caught in Albany when on tour with Joice Heth. "The daring feats of Antonio upon stilts," Barnum recalled, "his balancing guns with the bayonets resting on his nose, and various other performances which I had never seen before, attracted my attention." Leaving his assistant, Lyman, to exhibit Joice Heth, Barnum made the little Italian take a much-needed bath, changed his name to the more foreign-sounding Signor Vivalla, promised him $12 a week for a year, and put him on stage to great acclaim, acting himself as prop man and spokesman. During a subsequent performance in Philadelphia, at the Walnut Street Theatre, Vivalla was hissed by a local juggler named J. B. Roberts and his fans. Instead of dismay, Barnum showed his native ingenuity by publishing a challenge the next day—$1,000 to anyone who could reproduce all of Vivalla's feats. Of course no one could, but Roberts took the bait and it was not long before Barnum was, characteristically, making a silk purse out of a sow's ear, cooking up and publicizing a bogus rivalry between the two performers. Well rehearsed right down to their fiery exchanges, the competition was a big draw, and Barnum repeated it to enthusiastic audiences in other cities. When the crowds finally thinned, and with Joice Heth now dead, Barnum turned to a Danbury neighbor named Aaron Turner who ran a highly successful traveling circus. Barnum and Vivalla signed on for a six-month tour with Turner's Old Columbian Circus, Barnum getting a piece of the profits in return for acting as secretary, treasurer, and ticket seller. Wagons, carriages, tents, horses, a band, and around 35 men and boys set off from Connecticut, where the circus was still outlawed, and wound north to Massachusetts, where performances began. Over the next months, the show leisurely wended its way down to South Carolina, with Turner's two sons giving exhibitions of equestrian skill; Joe Pentland, a famous performer of the day, doing double duty as both clown and magician; and Barnum often holding Bible readings on Sunday for the cast. Barnum considered the proprietor, Aaron Turner, "an original genius" who had amassed a fortune and liked to talk about his philosophy of life. "Every man who has good health and common sense is capable of making a fortune, if he only resolves to do so," Barnum quoted Turner. "As proof of it, look at me. . . . I never had any education; I commenced life as a shoemaker. . . . You see what I am now. I have become so by industry, perseverance, and economy. . . . There is not such a word as 'cannot' in the English language. Never say you 'can't' do a thing—and never cry 'broke' till you are dead."

When the six months he had committed to were up, in October 1836, Barnum took his $600 profit and formed his own troupe, which included Vivalla, Pentland, a blackface singer, and a few musicians, and the group commenced performances throughout the South in a variety show he called "Barnum's Grand Scientific and Musical Theater." Filling in for defecting performers over the winter of 1837, Barnum became an acceptable blackface singer and a better-than-fair magician. Once, as Pentland's assistant in "several tricks of legerdemain," Barnum squeezed himself into a tiny spot under the magician's table. Articles were passed down to him through a small trapdoor and he, in turn, passed others up to Pentland. One of them was a live squirrel which promptly bit Barnum. "I shrieked with pain," he recorded in his diary, "overthrew the table, smashed every breakable article upon it, and rushed behind the curtain. . . . Pentland was struck speechless, but if there ever was hooting or shouting in a mass of spectators, it was heard that night."

It was a ragtag show that Barnum sponsored. Written years later, his description of another magician mystifying his hayseed audience in Alabama caught the spirit of such easygoing country entertainment. "He first exhibited several dexterous tricks with cups and balls—swallowed apparently a pound of tow—blew fire from his mouth, and then drew many yards of various-colored ribbons from the same receptacle. These were followed by wonderful tricks with iron rings, strings and keys; he apparently swallowed a watch, and pulled an unknown quantity of cabbages, turnips and onions from the bosom of a verdant young countryman who volunteered to 'assist' at the performances."

Meanwhile, Charity and young Caroline were deposited on the second story of the Yellow Store in Bethel for the duration of their breadwinner's travels. Twenty-six years old, filled with the same unquenchable energy of his youth and still learning the ins and outs of the frustratingly difficult business of entertaining people, Barnum disbanded his show in May of 1837 in Nashville, Tennessee, turned his horses out to grass, and returned to "home, sweet home," in order "to spend a few weeks with my dear family."

Circus owner Aaron Turner was typical of the show-business people young Barnum was beginning to amass as his friends. Enormously successful, irreverent, fun-loving, and a practical joker like Barnum, Turner taught him that the nature of any publicity made little difference—"all we need to insure success is notoriety."

Joe Pentland was one of the supreme clowns of his day. Barnum, who employed Pentland in the 1830s, described him as "a capital ventriloquist, balancer, comic singer and performer of legerdemain." On tour he helped Barnum play tricks on other performers.

Swindled by Bootblack and Bear Grease

Barnum's first 30 years saw enormous technological advancements, making the world seem more manageable, more welcoming. Formerly dark and forbidding cities were being lit up by gaslights. Steam had been harnessed and now steamships crossed seas and locomotives moved produce and passengers in both Europe and the U.S. Electromagnetism had been discovered, the telegraph invented, as many of the previously inviolate principles of life were collapsing. No wonder this was an era of hoaxes—a new invention such as photography in 1839 seemed so impossible to most, so absurd, that it was surely another link in the long chain of humbug.

After visiting his wife and daughter in the summer of 1837, Barnum returned to the South to try again as a showman. Nothing went right. When his little caravan of horse-driven carriages was dogged by adversity, he sold them and purchased a steamer at Vicksburg, heading south by river to play the towns along the Mississippi banks. Not even a week's performances at New Orleans could change his luck, and pretty soon he was back in New York, "thoroughly disgusted with the life of an itinerant showman." He was sure he could eventually succeed in that line, although he "always regarded it, not as an end, but as a means to something better in due time." Trying to find that "something better," Barnum now made the mistake of advertising for a partner and dangling $2,500 as seed money for some new venture. He received 93 propositions. Every would-be pawnbroker, patent-medicine salesman, and crazy inventor in the city seemed to apply; even a counterfeiter saw him as an able partner, hoping to get his hands on Barnum's money to buy new paper, ink, and "dies." Finally, the promised cash went to Mr. Proler, a manufacturer of bootblacking, waterproof paste for leather, Cologne water, and bear grease. To Barnum, now at 101½ Bowery, his new business seemed to move smoothly. He kept the accounts and ran the retail store while Proler manufactured the goods and sold them at wholesale around the country. But Barnum's cash began to dwindle as Proler taught him the subtleties of "the credit system." His partner was "a fine-looking man, of plausible manners," but Barnum began to experience sleepless nights as the due day for notes in the bank crept closer. Eventually, Proler agreed to buy him out, but the catch was that he never paid. Instead, Proler skipped the country, leaving his former partner practically destitute.

Almost simultaneously, Barnum, along with all other New Yorkers, was being swept into the worst financial depression in decades. Virtually overnight, following the terrifying Panic of 1837, New York real-estate values plummeted 50 percent, long-standing businesses disappeared, and the entire city seemed to screech to a halt. What a stunned Barnum could not yet see was the unusual opportunity that was about to open up for him and his kind. For decades, New York businesses had been in the hands of Old Family elites; only those born to wealth or able to parlay capital into riches on

Wall Street could afford to own the large concerns of the day. But the crash of '37 and the three-year-long depression following it opened up large businesses for the first time ever to members of the true middle classes. Now, as a new decade dawned, penny newspapers, publishing houses, theaters, even museums were suddenly all possible entities for a man like Barnum to reach for and make his own.

So here, after 30 years on this earth, was an engaging man of superior energies with a flair for entertaining people and an instinct for promotion, but a man who had not yet found his role. Here was a fast-talking, appealing, impetuous scallywag of a fellow with a lightning mind for figures, a gambler's nerve, a hard bargainer on the one hand, but still naïve enough on the other to be easily taken in and fleeced. Here was a tall, handsome, curly-haired chap, with a lot of self-discipline and an adman's vocabulary, a fun-loving character who wallowed in pranks and spewed puns and jokes, a bright-eyed optimist with plenty of moxie, who was coming closer and closer to knowing the ins and outs of human nature, what caught people's fancy, what tweaked their curiosity, exactly what made them come to the ticket window, reach in their pockets, and smack their money down.

On March 19, 1838, the New Orleans paper reported that "Captain Barnum" had arrived on his steamer *Ceres* "with a theatrical company." On reaching the Mississippi, Barnum had abandoned his carriages and horses for a $6,000 boat and traveled south on the river, putting in at little ports and setting up his tent show close by. Almost the last stop before disbanding was New Orleans. Photography had not yet been invented, but this daguerreotype of Canal Street, taken 20 years later, is close to what the showplace of Louisiana looked like when Barnum first hit town.

Barnum and
the boy who
made him
rich—
Charles
Sherwood
Stratton,
alias Tom
Thumb.

Learning Lessons Out on the Road

Horace Greeley attacked her life of "wantonness and shame," but studying how Fanny Elssler was promoted in America was one of Barnum's most important lessons.

Under the artful ministrations of her debonair manager, Chevalier Henry Wikoff, the great Austrian ballerina Fanny Elssler danced 208 times in the U.S. and Cuba and earned an astonishing $140,000.

As the decade of the 1840s opened, Barnum was diligently plying his showman's trade in the big city, but when a song-and-dance act which he sponsored in the saloon of Vauxhall Gardens flopped, "I determined once more to endure the privations, vexations, and uncertainties of a tour in the West and South." Putting together a little company with John Diamond, a remarkable rubber-legged dancer, as his main attraction, along with a singer, a fiddler, and an advance man, Barnum headed north into Canada, and then south again to Detroit, Chicago, St. Louis, and points between, and then by steamer directly to New Orleans—"my company of performers having been reduced, by deserters, to Master Diamond and the fiddler." By February of 1841, even John Diamond had deserted. Barnum wrote theater managers in the vicinity not to employ his runaway dancer if he were to show up. "Diamond has overdrawn the money due him to the amount of $95 and has during the last week expended a hundred dollars in brothels and other haunts of dissipation and vice." A few days later, in New Orleans, Barnum sent a message to local theater manager Sol Smith—"Master Diamond has at last come to his senses and has voluntarily returned to me. . . . [I]f you wish a little dancing as an offset to the 'divine Fanny,' I offer you Master Diamond's services. . . . On each night, if you wish, he will dance the Black Bayadere a la Elssler. . . ."

"Divine Fanny" and "a la Elssler" referred to the vivacious Austrian dancer and entrancer Fanny Elssler, who was touring America and happened to be playing New Orleans the very weeks Barnum was stopping there. Her much-ballyhooed presence allowed Barnum to witness firsthand what a success could be made of a little-known European superstar, even in a small, remote city.

Fanny Elssler was the world's first true international star. In Europe she reigned alongside two other matchless talents of the mid-century—Rachel, the daughter of a Jewish peddler who became the greatest actress of her time, and the incomparable Swedish opera singer Jenny Lind. Fanny was the first of the three to allow her talents to be imported to the U.S.

The pristine, classical, almost spiritual perfection of traditional European ballet had given way to a romantic era to which Fanny Elssler's talents were perfectly suited. She was earthy and voluptuous, and her graceful, exotic movements across a stage were filled with intoxicating, primitive passion. But how many Americans had ever heard of Fanny Elssler? And what red-blooded Yankee would pay good hard-earned money to watch a foreigner prance and tiptoe about a stage? The answer would be forged by the innovative skills of Elssler's manager, a strange, dandified American known as Chevalier Henry Wikoff. Barnum would learn more from this controversial young man about promotion than he ever dared admit.

Harry Wikoff had three fancies in life—journalism, the stage, and women. He satisfied the first through his friendship with James Gordon Bennett of the New York *Herald*, who made him a floating correspondent. Through his best friend, the American actor Edwin Forrest, Wikoff was able to brush elbows with stage personalities. And Paris amply gratified his third whimsy. While luxuriating in a life of Parisian leisure, he befriended the great Elssler, helped persuade her to perform in the U.S., and agreed to be her manager, publicist, and confidant for her trip abroad. As many an admirer had done before him, Wikoff also became Fanny's lover.

A master of "puff"—that was the name in newspaper circles for stories that were designed to inflate reputations and stimulate enthusiasm— Fanny's cosmopolitan manager was able to transform her upcoming tour from a mildly interesting ballerina visitation into a frenzied 19th-century media event. When she finally stepped off the boat and into America's waiting arms, New Yorkers knew all about Fanny's sorceries. An hour after she had disembarked, a *Herald* "extra" was on the stands, describing how Fanny's final performance in London was attended by Queen Victoria, and how the Queen's newly wed consort, Prince Albert, at the tumultuous finale of Elssler's goodbye appearance, had stood up in the royal box and publicly bid the great dancer a safe passage.

With a guarantee of $500 a performance against half the receipts from the tour, Fanny had the promise of a fortune—if anyone came to see her, that is. Wikoff saw to it they did. Through his considerable social contacts, Fanny was invited to event after event by the city's elite, each function reported on ecstatically in the papers. Pretty soon Fanny had first New York, then the whole country at her feet. The Chevalier had literally masterminded a new kind of American insanity—"Elsslermania." All this acclaim and fascination for a foreign import was not lost on Barnum as he watched the New York excitement repeat itself in New Orleans, the little river city which had somehow guaranteed the dancer $1,000 a night for each of 12 performances. Nor was Barnum unimpressed by Wikoff's novel, crowd-drawing publicity stunts, including the auctioning of opening-night tickets, the first of which in New Orleans went for the princely sum of $61.

"I thought the price enormous," Barnum recalled, "and gave her manager the credit of doing what I had considered impossible, in working up public enthusiasm to fever heat."

Even though Barnum was back in New York by April, and for the next six months selling Bibles, putting on acts again at Vauxhall's, and writing ads for the Bowery Amphitheater, he had learned lessons he would never forget from Chevalier Wikoff and his imported star. Other European greats would follow Elssler across the Atlantic, but for a decade none of them swept America off her feet as Fanny had. There was a simple reason. None of these subsequent tours until Jenny Lind's was orchestrated by a well-organized, well-connected, publicity-savvy, daring impresario like Wikoff—and such as Barnum was destined to become.

Barnum first got acquainted with the Western theater owner and impresario Sol Smith in 1841, during a trip to New Orleans, where Fanny Elssler was performing. The two became fast friends and confidants. Nine years older than Barnum, "Uncle Sol" is shown here posing with his second wife, Elizabeth Pugsley.

A Shrewd Deal for a Prime Showplace

The city that Barnum had returned to was, in 1841, the third largest in the world, its population approaching 300,000. At its heart and center, by almost any measurement, was Broadway, "The Great Avenue," which ran more than three miles in a straight line from the Battery north until it finally trickled off into an unpaved country lane. By far the busiest street in the city, far busier in fact than any boulevard in London or Paris, Broadway seemed continually awash in a sea of carriages, horses, wagons, and pedestrians, all part of the restless, money-oriented, mercantile fury which was New York. Also, it was dirty. "If there is one thing in the world of which our city authorities should be heartily ashamed," commented Barnum in the early 1840s, "it is the abominable filthy streets which we have." Visitors routinely agreed, describing badly managed sewers, the disgusting, very American habit of public spitting, and the sight of scavenging pigs and horse manure left on the streets for weeks at a time. And yet, despite the dirt, here on this avenue was the height of American fashion and the single most promising location for commercial success. And here, a half-mile north of the Battery, at the busiest, most important intersection of the entire city, where upper-class and lower-class neighborhoods came together at City Park, was a ten-year-old, five-story building destined to change Barnum's life, John Scudder's American Museum. Overseen by trustees since the death of its founder, this New York institution had been hit hard by the financial crash of '37, just barely escaping the bankruptcy that swallowed up other institutions whole. With a public losing interest in its unchanging array of shells and minerals and stuffed birds and fossils, receipts had fallen off precipitously for three years in a row. "Although valuable," Barnum later commented, it had become almost "unknown"; though "interesting," it was now "unnoticed." For many months now, Barnum had been wracked with anxiety about his future. Realizing that after ten years of hard labor he was still nowhere in life, he now determined that the time had come to make one immense "grand effort" to succeed.

In the fall of 1841, Barnum learned that the contents of Scudder's museum were up for sale. The asking price of $15,000, far below what the collection was worth, was still $15,000 more than Barnum possessed. He decided to approach the owner of the museum's building, Francis Olmsted, and convince him to buy the collection on Barnum's behalf. Arguing that he alone could make the place profitable once again, Barnum maneuvered cannily, successfully outwitting a competing buyer, and finally obtained the collection and building for himself. The success revealed a man now at last coming into his own: a master deal-maker whose personality alone could conquer kingdoms.

New York City was now the country's most important center, with Broadway the spinal column of the sprawling, humming, uniquely irreverent and independent metropolis.

Scudder's American Museum Is Renamed Barnum's

In Hill's original engraving, Barnum's Museum can be seen as it looked during the decade of the 1840s—not yet having expanded into the space of the Chemical Bank building, immediately to its south.

W ithout gold or silver," Barnum boasted, he had obtained the American Museum using only his "own brass." That, plus several items of collateral—pieces of Connecticut real estate, including—and this always made Barnum smile—a choice parcel known as Ivy Island. The first of hundreds of other grand efforts to come, the American Museum would always be to Barnum his "ladder to fortune."

Here it stands, at the far left in the picture above, proudly displaying its new owner's name. We are looking across Broadway to the south, toward the harbor. To the north of the museum, just outside our view, is City Hall and its impressive grounds, known simply in these early days as "The Park." Opposite Barnum's, its rooftop just seen from the vantage point of its high steeple, is St. Paul's Church, the oldest parish in Manhattan. To the north of St. Paul's, on Broadway, kitty-corner to the museum but again out of our view, is New York's most famous and important hotel, the Astor House. Built during Barnum's Joice Heth days, the six-story, granite-walled, 600-bed building was larger than any hotel in either Paris or London. Behind the museum, to the east, lies the city's newspaper district, where the New York *Herald* and *Tribune* and *Sun* had their large enterprises, so important to Barnum now. Here also is bustling Chatham Street with its laundries and shops, and the Bowery, with its inexpensive entertainments, working-class saloons, and tenements from which many of Barnum's future customers

would stream. And farther to the north is the poorest, roughest section of the entire city, clustered about a confluence of streets known as "Five Points."

Now Barnum's life centered around the museum. He and his family even lived in it, in a ground-floor apartment which had previously been used as a billiard hall. Beneath the museum, on Ann Street, was Jim Grant's barber shop, within weeks of Barnum's arrival nicknamed "Philosopher's Hall" because of the regular gatherings there of local store-owners and merchants, including the young showman—"a literary nucleus unequaled in intelligence," he affectionately called it. For his own hairdressing needs, however, Barnum bypassed Grant's and walked a block farther east, to number 2 Beekman Street and the tonsorial talents of a Mr. Ciprico. For meals, when Barnum wasn't feasting on cold sandwiches to save money, there were two affordable eating establishments within close walking distance. For breakfast there was Seelye's Eastern Pearl Street House; for lunch or dinner Barnum's favorite was Sweeney's Restaurant on Ann Street, where he could obtain a full meal for as little as 15 cents. Also in the neighborhood, and visited regularly by Barnum, were Lorin Brooks' boot shop on Fulton Street, Tice's hat store on Bowery, and Tom Bell's auction house on Spruce Street. And for daguerreotype pictures, something along with the telegraph that Barnum admired more than any other developments of the century, by 1844 it was just a few steps across the street to the galleries of Mathew B. Brady.

What Barnum Did to Make His Museum a Landmark

Above is the back cover of an 1847 publication that was sold inside the museum.

A visitor to the city couldn't miss Barnum's Museum at night; the huge light on the roof revolved and lit the streets below and the buildings across Broadway with a light unlike any other in New York.

The museum Barnum now presided over had long since lost its sparkle. To create charisma and crowds, its new owner developed a threefold plan: renovation, a massive publicity campaign, and the injection of sheer personality. He began by concentrating on the huge, drab, marble building itself. His first innovation was a lineup of colorful world flags along his rooftops, their flapping visible from over a mile away as they gave the museum an international air. Along the second floor of the building's exterior, Barnum installed a wraparound balcony, upon which guests could take in the air and at the same time inadvertently lure other customers in. Always interested in the latest technology, Barnum went on to install a huge lighthouse lamp on his rooftop, the city's first spotlight. Retractable and stored inside a parapet by day, the diamond-shaped "Drummond Light" possessed a powerful, moving reflector beam designed to sweep up and down Broadway by night, lighting the whole area, Barnum liked to boast, "with unaccustomed glare."

But the most striking transformation of the building's exterior occurred following weeks of secret preparation. Then, on a single night, Barnum's crew installed a series of large oval color paintings between all of the nearly 100 windows along the museum's upper stories. Suddenly, from the front of the museum, loomed polar bear and elephant, ostrich and giraffe, tapir, pelican, eagle, and gnu. Here was a lion, a kangaroo, a peacock, and an elk, a rattlesnake, a tiger, a fur seal, and a cormorant. The impact was startling, transforming a large but ordinary building into a dreamlike emporium. According to Barnum, the paintings alone increased his revenues by $100 a day—close to 20 percent.

By May of his first year in operation, 1842, the showman was working hard on his newest idea, to transform the rooftops of his building into "a splendid, aerial garden." Completed in early June, the garden offered what became known as "the finest view of the city, harbor and surrounding county of any public building in the city." Here customers could stroll among planted gardens, or sit beneath awnings and eat ice cream on comfortable chairs while listening to Barnum's own brass band, the "Columbian." Here balloon ascensions were scheduled by day, and giant, illuminated balloons were often sent up by night. Fireworks displays, in an age before fire marshals required permits, added romantic flair. And by Barnum's second year, a new luxury had arrived as well—Croton water, running all the way up to the museum's top floor, where it erupted in an extraordinary, 100-jet fountain.

In its former days, the museum's main feature had been its taxidermy collection. In contrast, and aiming to build up all-important repeat business, Barnum now began to emphasize live acts, a bewildering array of them. Hardly a week went by without some new performers being added. There was Benjamin Pelham, "the great Paganini whistler," and Yan Zoo, the Chinese juggler. There was J. Nathans, the serpent charmer, and Signor Vivaldi with his moving mechanical figures. There were ropedancers and glassblowers and ventriloquists and jugglers. There was a mysterious and beautiful gypsy girl fortune teller with whom customers could consult privately for an additional fee. And there were the amazing "industrious fleas," trained in Germany to submit to tiny harnesses and to pull vehicles "several thousand times their weight." There were Indian chiefs from the Rocky Mountains demonstrating war dances and hunting techniques. There were Mother Cary's trained chickens, and Mr. Cole's "wonderful dog," and a 20-foot-long python, and the country's first Punch and Judy show. There was a real, live orangutan, and a knitting machine operated by a dog, and a professor of phrenology who could read a customer's future by feeling the bumps on his or her head. And there was a host of ever-changing inanimate features as well. Children and adults were fascinated by the bald-eagle skin, and the set of medieval armor, and the plaster cast of Vendovi the cannibal chief, and the huge, organlike musical instrument called the Melodean. And then there was the painstakingly accurate model of the city of Paris containing 40,000 individual wooden buildings; and the series of animated tableaux, including scenes like the "conflagration of Moscow" and "A Moonlit View of Spain"; and the special gold-plating apparatus powered by batteries which the public could make use of for a small additional fee.

To tout such wonders widely, Barnum turned aggressively to advertising, making use of it on a scale unheard of before now. He placed oversized

The country's first great museum was in Philadelphia and was owned and operated by Charles Willson Peale, the painter (above), who is raising the curtain on the wonders of his establishment in this 1822 self-portrait. Peale's high-minded approach set the tone for the U.S. museum, making art, music, history, nature, and scientific and industrial invention the main attractions, but allowing for certain oddities as well.

Most famous of all Barnum's fat children were his "Highland Mammoth Boys," three broth-ers named Stewart procured in mid-decade and appearing regularly throughout the rest of the 1840s. Encouraged by their employer to fatten up even bigger, the Stewarts enriched their act by giving "soirees mysterious," in which they demonstrated powers of mesmerism. In an era of scarcity and competition, perhaps all these large boys symbolized a kind of well-fed, happy security. Just as likely, they offered a simple escape into the ludicrous.

banners on the outside of his building, and for nighttime hung huge illuminated transparencies and projected a "boiling and bubbling illusion" on the museum walls—anything to break with its hypnotically dull reputation. To carry his message about the city, Barnum invented the country's first "bulletin wagons," traveling advertising carts bearing posters and signs. And in newspapers like the *Herald* and the *Sunday Atlas* he touted his "marvelous novelties," his "breath-taking splendors," and his "wilderness of realities."

Barnum's New York was actually two towns split along class lines, with upper-crust families migrating ever northward along Broadway, while working-class families remained associated with the Bowery. The fashionable preferred uptown opera houses and gardens, while the more numerous members of the working class turned toward the entertainment halls and theaters which were now targeting them as audiences. With his museum and lecture hall situated at the juncture of these two worlds, Barnum early on made it his intent to capture both kinds of audiences. The low door fee of 25 cents allowed access to almost anybody, and Barnum courted the Democratic, working-class Irish, for example, by offering up regular Irish performances and songfests, by exhibiting a large model of the city of Dublin, and by initiating special events on St. Patrick's Day. At the same time, he carefully sought out patronage from the Whiggish upper classes as well, advertising the Virginia dwarf Colonel Chaffin, for instance, as a "favorite with the fashionable elite at . . . popular watering places throughout the country." When politicians tried to find out where his sympathies actually lay, and whether he would vote Democrat or Whig, Barnum liked to answer, "I vote for the American Museum." To change the museum's stiff, unpopular image and reach out to "the millions" Barnum was after meant not only exhibits aimed at immigrants, but also, for the proprietor, human oddities—"representatives of the wonderful," he called them. One after another they appeared: an "Albino Lady" of striking beauty, a tattooed man named O'Connell, a hairy child named Caspar billed as "The Wild Boy," a giant and giantess couple, the Randalls, and a German midget named Raddo Schauf— "all that is monstrous, scaley, strange and queer," as Barnum liked to put it. And then there was the highly touted so-called Wonder of the World, a four-and-a-half-foot-high, 26-year-old armless man named Mr. Nellis, who could use his feet to load and fire a pistol, wind up a watch, cut paper airplanes and valentines, and play musical instruments.

But if there was one type of act that recurred again and again on Barnum's stage, it was that of the giant boy. "I must have the fat boy," Barnum wrote to a fellow showman in early 1843, and after the arrival of Master J. F. Reed, Barnum was almost never without one. From his "Carolina Fat Boy" of 1844 to the "New York Giant Boy" of 1845, from his "Great Wisconsin Boy" of 1846 to the "Infant Hoosier Giant" of the end of the decade, Barnum tapped into a curious public fascination with overweight children. And as it turned out, the fascination crossed all class lines.

Selling the Public a Bogus Mermaid

n his assault upon museum fame and success, almost from the very beginning, Barnum had the help of a powerful ally. Far enough away not to threaten, but close enough to allow regular contact and cooperation, Boston's Moses Kimball had opened his own museum just six and a half months before Barnum acquired Scudder's. Like Barnum, Kimball had come up the hard way, sweeping floors, doing odd jobs, hawking goose quills, and then trying his hand more or less successfully at a variety of businesses from dry goods and men's apparel to small-scale publishing. Only after going bankrupt in the crash of 1837 had Kimball finally stumbled upon his real calling. More than any other museum in the country, the Boston Museum and Gallery of Fine Arts was Barnum's sister institution, an eclectic mixture of paintings and curiosities, live acts and zoological exhibits, all presided over by a showman who was Barnum's born soulmate.

In the late spring of 1842, having heard stories of a strong rival to his south, Moses Kimball traveled to New York to meet Barnum in person, and to make him an irresistible proposal. Traveling with him, in a large oblong box, was the most unusual curiosity that had ever fallen into Kimball's hands—an embalmed mermaid purchased at great price near Calcutta by a Boston sea captain in 1817. Or, if it wasn't a real mermaid, it was the cleverest fabrication anyone had ever seen—an ingenious sewing together of a large fish's body and tail with the head, shoulders, arms, and rather pendulous breasts of a female orangutan and the head of a baboon. Startled at the

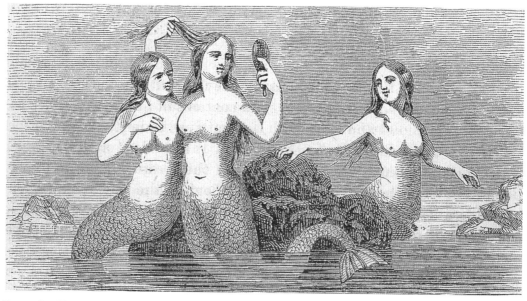

Preparing New York for the grand arrival of "the Fejee Mermaid," as he spelled it, Barnum got woodcuts of bare-breasted, fish-tailed beauties engraved, conned the influential newspapers into printing them, and had them also inserted into a pamphlet he had written and subsequently sold for a penny apiece.

object's appearance and size, and certainly recognizing it as fraudulent from the start, Barnum was nevertheless impressed. Even close examination could not reveal obvious marks of artifice, and though Barnum's own museum naturalist, Emile Guillaudeu, rejected it instantly on the basis that "mermaids do not exist," Barnum quickly decided that keeping a more open mind could pay. After all, weren't scientists learning that nature was more mysterious than ever suspected, that it held wonders unimaginable to skeptics—for example, the newly discovered duck-billed platypus, still widely considered a fabrication? In Edwin Chapin's words, quoted now by Barnum, was it "not only an arrogant but a shallow philosophy that says the existence of this or that [is] impossible [or] contrary to the laws of nature"? Clearly there was money to be made here—at least as much as the Joice Heth hoax had brought in.

On June 18, Barnum and Kimball entered into a written agreement to exploit jointly their "curiosity supposed to be a mermaid." Kimball would remain the creature's sole owner, and Barnum would act as lessee, paying $12.50 a week for the privilege of showing her at profit. In the course of doing so, Barnum was to "take all proper and possible care" of the mermaid and to "exert himself to the utmost" to make it popular, a benefit that would of course spill over and help Kimball's ensuing efforts in Boston. After each showman had had his own individual run, the mermaid was to hit the road on what would amount to a true partnership. After deducting expenses for a full-time manager, Barnum and Kimball were to split the remainder, 50/50.

And so Barnum launched out on his newest hoax. Deciding that no place sounded more exotic than faraway Fiji, Barnum christened his new object "The Fejee Mermaid," and began laying plans to "puff" her to the skies. With his own reputation still in question because of the Heth affair, Barnum's plan called for divorcing his name from all public discussion of the mermaid. Letters authenticating her were arranged to be mailed to New York papers from distant cities, unrelated to Barnum. The mermaid itself was assigned its own "proprietor," presented as a visiting English naturalist connected with London's Lyceum of Natural History. In actuality, "Dr. J. Griffin" was Barnum's old co-conspirator Levi Lyman, the very man who had earlier exhibited Joice Heth, now disguised with new costume and accent. As interest in the mermaid mounted, 10,000 pamphlets introducing her were distributed in the streets, and an eight-foot-high color transparency was strung outside New York's Concert Hall, where the curiosity's debut was to be held. Depicting a full-sized, bare-breasted, seductively beautiful creature rising out of blue waters, the giant banner added whole degrees to what Barnum called the city's rising "mermaid fever."

Finally, on August 8, the big day arrived. Unaware that Barnum had any involvement with the debut, thousands of citizens and a host of prominent naturalists poured into Broadway's Concert Hall to see the "wonderful specimen of creation." But instead of the living beauty depicted for weeks in the city papers, what the public discovered, to its shock, was an "ugly, dried-up, black-looking" thing all covered with stringy black hair that looked, Barnum admitted, as if it had "died in great agony." But it was too late for revolt.

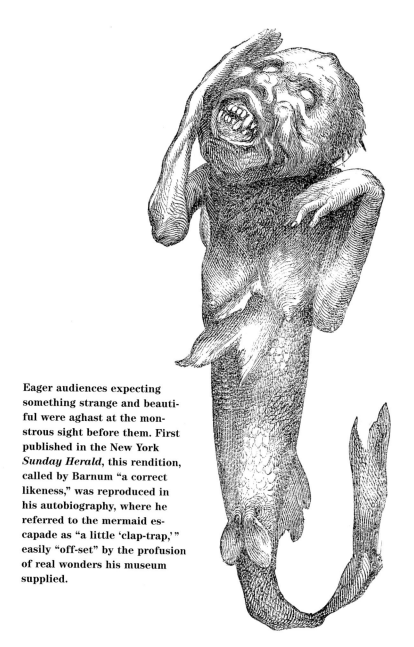

Eager audiences expecting something strange and beautiful were aghast at the monstrous sight before them. First published in the New York *Sunday Herald*, this rendition, called by Barnum "a correct likeness," was reproduced in his autobiography, where he referred to the mermaid escapade as "a little 'clap-trap,'" easily "off-set" by the profusion of real wonders his museum supplied.

Too many people had been too aroused for the spell to be broken. The dissonance between expectation and reality, instead of hurting the act, served only to enhance it, as amateur skeptics and believers alike over the next days jostled to gain entrance, that they might tender their own opinions.

Within a week, the mermaid had been moved, where else but to Barnum's Museum, brought there, the ads said, "at a most extraordinary expense" for the benefit of Barnum's "discerning public." Though the exhibit was initially billed for "one week only," her stay stretched on for over a month; Barnum's mysterious "lady fish" almost tripled the gate, bringing it close to a phenomenal $1,000 a week. In the nationwide tour which followed, led by Barnum's uncle and former store partner, Alanson Taylor, the mermaid made big money, shown alongside a host of natural wonders and curiosities, most of them authentic. Then, suddenly, in the South, the act ran into controversy. In South Carolina a clergyman-naturalist named Bachman became incensed not only by the fake mermaid but by what he considered its obviously fraudulent partner, the "ornithorhinchus," or duck-billed platypus. With Bachman threatening to undo the "humbug," and with an angry public about to make "mincemeat" of the mermaid, Taylor shipped the object back to Barnum's Museum, where it was secreted in a box on a high shelf in Barnum's private office. Writing to Kimball, Barnum said, "The bubble has burst."

In the months ahead, Barnum briefly considered ways they might bring "the critter" back. One idea was to mount a lawsuit against her detractor, Pastor Bachman, an act which "just might," Barnum wrote privately, "breathe the breath of life into her nostrils again." Even simpler was his idea to acknowledge the controversy and then challenge the public to make up their own minds. "Who is to decide when doctors disagree?" ran Barnum's hypothetical ad. But the Fejee Mermaid was never to be shown again.

For many, the whole affair was Barnum's most shameless scam upon the American public—proof of an innate greed and lack of ethics and of an outright disdain for the public. Barnum himself soon admitted that his "wonder of creation" was in reality nothing but a "questionable, dead mermaid," and to the end of his life he would say he was "not proud" of the entire incident. In fact, never again did Barnum resort to quite such outright quackery—increasingly he insisted that his exhibits possess real merit. But when all was said and done, there had been something wondrously funny about the mermaid affair as well, something that redeemed it from the condemnation of moralists. In it Barnum had proved how many people actually liked being fooled, how "the pleasure often is as great of being cheated as to cheat," as Barnum liked to quote the obscure poem "Hudibras." If nothing else, the whole affair revealed a true advertising genius at work—Barnum's ability to take a questionable act and through clever management turn it into the most exciting, talked-about event of the year. "Thus was the fame of the Museum . . . wafted from one end of the land to the other," wrote Barnum by way of epitaph some years later. And in truth, by the close of 1843, with the help of a museum man from Boston and a dried-up old mermaid, Barnum had become the most famous showman in America.

It has been claimed that Barnum's original mermaid found its way back to Moses Kimball in Boston and thence to the Peabody Museum at Harvard. But this mermaid (at the Peabody) is one of the many imitations that appeared in rival exhibits across the country.

To One Man Barnum Reveals His Inner Self

Over the course of the Fejee Mermaid affair, Barnum and Moses Kimball became fast friends. By 1843, they were writing each other every three days on average, at least during the busy season, in what evolved into the most affectionate, unguarded, and irreverent correspondence of Barnum's whole life. Here the two men traded secrets, laid plans for exchanges of key performers and curiosities, negotiated joint business arrangements such as for poster work and woodblocks, and listened patiently to each other's problems. After a time, almost nothing was off limits between them—the letter-writers could be playful or complaining, businesslike or intensely personal, vulgar or even unabashedly angry with one another. "You have a right to be cross," Barnum wrote Kimball in March 1843. "But don't eat a fellow up now without giving him a chance for his life!" When Kimball later wrote suggesting that an infatuation existed between Barnum and a scandal-ridden magician named Mary Darling, Barnum snapped back that he had not "taken an especial fancy in that quarter," and "the Darling" was "only so-so." When Kimball offered to send his New York friend a performing pony, Barnum declined: "I have now a goat, but he *shits* so I can do nothing with him. I fear the same objection would spoil the pony business."

As the friendship progressed, Barnum chose more and more affectionate and humorous ways to address Kimball, calling him "my boy," and "my dear fellow," and "friend Moses," and even once "dearly beloved Moses." Posing as a kind of older brother, even though they were almost exact contemporaries, Barnum loved to offer advice to his friend, including his own homemade, four-point business philosophy: "drive ahead, don't spare the steam, make all the noise possible, and by all means keep down the expenses." It was a friendship strong enough to last well into old age, one that could survive ups and downs, even crises of confidence. In the mid-1840s, feeling avoided, Kimball once threatened to end the relationship, until Barnum snapped back, "If you get on your high heeled shoes and talk of 'not wishing to continue friendship or advice when it is not needed,' you are greener than I take you for." Indeed, as Barnum became more and more famous, the two men did begin to drift apart, though Barnum always insisted it was only because he was so incessantly busy. "You know better than that," he wrote Kimball in the mid-1850s after being accused of having found better friendship. "I am always proud to number Moses Kimball as the first." But in the early 1840s such apologies were not needed—everything was still fresh and new. And toward the close of 1843, a year in which the two men had written each other more than 50 times, Barnum scrawled, "Your letters do me a vast deal of good," admitting to his newfound partner just how important the friendship had become to him.

No man in show business pierced the shell of privacy Barnum built around himself as thoroughly as did his soulmate in Boston. Like Barnum, Moses Kimball (above) had owned his own newspaper before acquiring, in 1841, the stuffed birds and animals, paintings and Greek sculpture of the old New England Museum. Adding to them his own assortment of oddities plus a stage disguised as a "lecture room," he presented the entertainment-starved citizens of Massachusetts with the Boston Museum.

Shown here is the new museum building Kimball moved into in November 1846. Two months after the opening, Barnum wrote his friend, "I hope you may prosper as such *really daring* enterprise so richly deserve[s]."

What follows is a sampling of Barnum's letters to Moses Kimball from the year 1843. Because of Barnum's tendency to throw away mail and a succession of fires destroying his files, no Kimball letters to Barnum remain. Brackets indicate damaged, unreadable areas in the originals, with guesses often added by the letters' editor, A. H. Saxon.

American Museum, 8 March 1843
Oh Temperance! *Oh Moses!!!*

What a big oat you must [have] swallowed crossways when you wrote me those [letters.] That of the 7th came early this morning—that of the 6th . . . hours afterwards. Well, you are in rather bad luck just [now] and you have *a right to be cross*: the armour was wrong, [the] Indian men were contrary, Harrington was wiffling, Barnum w[as] greedy and was keeping Tommy longer south than he promised, yo[ur] business was bad, you generously advanced that "*bitch*" $12 a[nd] got her the situation, and all that like a devilish clever fellow as [you ?are.]

And you may get cross once in a while, and [you] may write me cross letters, and I'll bear with [it like] a man; but you *must* permit me to *laugh* when I read your bitter effusions, for I know just how you feel, having felt exactly so a thousand times. But *don't* eat a fellow up now without giving him a chance for his life—pray don't! . .

Do you want a pretty good-sized *bald eagle* skin? I bought two yesterday—shot on Long Island. . . .

As ever thine,
Barnum

American Museum, 1 September 1843
Dear Moses,

I am grieved, vexed, and dissappointed [to] hear of the sickness and *death* (for I know she will die) of the Ourang Outang. D——n the luck! I have puffed he[r] high & dry, got a large transparency and a flag 10 [by] 16 feet painted for her, besides newspaper cut engraved, [&c.]—and now, curse her, she must up foot and die. [This] is *peculiarly distressing* from the fact that Tom Thumb, Cole, his dog, & Great Western all leave this week to [make] room for *her*—& she can't come! But some p[ork] will boil that way & I must grin & bear it. The Par[k,

Olym]pic, & Amphitheatre all open next Monday—and of course catch me with my breeches down. . . .
Barnum

American Museum, 26 September 1843
Dear Moses,

. . . You must either get a [?building] near the museum for the Indians to sleep and cook their own victuals [in] or else let them sleep in the museum on their skins & have victuals sent them from some *Sweeny* shop. I boil up ham & potatoes, corn, beef, &c., *at home* & send them at each meal. The interpreter is a kind of half-breed and a decent chap; he must have common private board. The lazy devils want to be *lying down* nearly all the time, and as it looks so bad for them to be lying about the Museum, I have them stretched out in the workshop all day, some of them occasionally strolling about the Museum. D——n Indians *anyhow*. They are a lazy, shiftless set of brutes—though they will *draw*.

N.Y. Nov. 8th 1843
Dear Moses,

Harrington pretends that *Weeks* is about to buy a share of his dioramas—I don't quite believe it however.

You *will* lick me bad this week—the Shaws are the worst *suck* I ever had. . . .

Monday I took $78—last night only $35—ain't that horrid!

. . . I send Hitchcock to Baltimore this afternoon to get those dirty lazy and *lousy* Gipseys—I expect they are too d——d low for me to do anything with them. However I *must try*—if I don't do better than at present I am sure to bust.

As ever thine
Barnum

The Art of Humbug Was Part of His Business

"The titles of 'humbug,' and the 'prince of humbugs,' were first applied to me by myself," Barnum insisted. "I made these titles a part of my 'stock in trade.' "

By claiming to be in possession of a very strange-looking horse captured by John C. Fremont, Barnum took advantage of the public's hero-worship of the great explorer and its hunger for news of him after he had been lost in the Rockies.

Barnum's reputation as a "humbug" was now firmly established. Besides the big hoaxes, Joice Heth and the Mermaid, he had become known for a constant stream of lesser humbuggeries as well—his so-called Great Model of Niagara Falls with Real Water, for example, which turned out to be an 18-inch miniature operated by a single barrel of recirculating liquid. Or the famous "Captain Cook Club," the very weapon, supposedly, that had killed Captain Cook, but which looked suspiciously like one of the innumerable Indian war clubs inherited from the museum in Scudder's day. Possessing no qualms about mixing the spurious with the genuine, Barnum believed his task was "to arrest public attention; to startle, to make people talk and wonder; in short to let the world know that I had a Museum." As for the recurring accusation of humbug, "it never harmed me," Barnum insisted, for he would "much rather be roundly abused than not to be noticed at all."

On June 17, 1843, while in Boston to hear Daniel Webster speak at Bunker Hill, Barnum discovered his latest fodder for deception: a herd of scrawny, docile, undersized buffaloes being displayed under a tent by a certain Mr. Fitzhugh. Purchasing the whole lot for $700, Barnum developed an ingenious scheme. The scene of the new humbug was to be Hoboken, New Jersey—a favorite summer excursion point just across the Hudson for New Yorkers eager to escape the crowded city. Advertising a "Grand Buffalo Hunt, Free of Charge" to take place at Hoboken on August 31, Barnum portrayed his animals as dangerous beasts from the New Mexican prairies, to be presented behind double-rail fencing so as to prevent any possible risk to the public. The unheard-of, tantalizing word in these ads was "Free." Barnum's goal was to create a phenomenon, to excite an entire city to make the crossing to Hoboken. The crux of his business plan lay in a secret arrangement with the ferryboat companies to receive half of their net revenues for the day. "If it doesn't rain tomorrow I expect to have 16,000 persons visit the ferriage," Barnum scrawled to Moses Kimball on August 30. At 6 cents per person each way, he anticipated a profit of close to $1,000, not including extra moneys he expected from the refreshment stands. According to his final accounts, Barnum had underestimated the numbers; some 24,000 persons made the crossing, boatload after boatload of them, representing profits of almost $3,400 by the end of the day. The show itself was an absurdity. The skinny, frightened animals refused to cooperate, the Indian lasso acts were a disaster, and when the audience hollered out in laughter and disbelief, the poor beasts became so disoriented they stampeded, breaking through Barnum's flimsy fencing and escaping into the New Jersey swamplands. Some papers reported that people were hurt in the melee and buffaloes killed. In fact, all had been harmless. The weather was beautiful, the price was right, and no one thought to suspect Barnum's involvement in the affair.

Five years later, in a subterfuge often linked in Barnum's mind to the Hoboken hoax, the showman would stumble upon and purchase a small, maneless horse, freakily covered with curly, thick, wool-like hair. The opportunity for putting his new horse to use would come in less than a year, as Barnum decided to play to an intense public excitement surrounding the disappearance and resurfacing, deep in the snow-covered Rockies, of the great

An admitted purveyor of humbug, the youthful, vigorous Barnum looked down on true con men.

American explorer John C. Fremont. Again remaining anonymous and behind the scenes, Barnum placed stories touting his "wooly horse" as the "extraordinary nondescript," captured by Fremont "near the river Gila," an "astounding animal" made up of part "elephant, deer, horse, buffalo, camel and sheep"—"the most astonishing specimen" ever received from "California!" Once again the public responded—this time pouring into a huge, retrofitted drygoods store at the corner of Broadway and Reade Street that Barnum had leased for the purpose. "The public appetite was craving something brought from Col. Fremont," wrote Barnum later. "The community was absolutely famishing. They were ravenous. They could have swallowed anything, and like a good genius, I threw them, not a 'bone', but a regular tid-bit, a bon-bon, and they swallowed it in a single gulp."

All this would seem rather cynical, except that for Barnum the title "humbug" described two very opposite characters. On the one hand there was the outright swindler—the snake-oil salesman, the con man, the fraud, and the charlatan. No one was more critical of such operators than Barnum; he ultimately wrote a whole book on them entitled *The Humbugs of the World*, detailing the underhandedness of medical quacks, real-estate schemers, spiritualists, religious frauds, and unethical sales people. On the other hand, there was his own type of playful humbug, developed in order to increase what he called his "notoriety." This consisted of "putting on glittering appearance," he wrote, "by which to suddenly arrest public attention, and attract the public eye and ear." Though such methods might be inappropriate for physicians, lawyers, bankers, or the clergy, there were "various trades and occupations which need only notoriety to ensure success, always provided that when customers are once attracted they never fail to get their money's worth." This last rule, throughout all his long life, was essential to Barnum. If the public was not well served by a showman, then he deserved to fail. And so, in Barnum's mind, his hoaxes were justifiable aspects of an honorable business strategy. "The Mermaid, Woolly Horse . . . etc. were . . . used by me as skyrockets," he insisted, "or advertisements to draw attraction . . . to the *Museum*. . . . I don't believe in 'duping the public', but I believe in first *attracting* and then pleasing them." Furthermore, "the greatest humbug of all is the man who believes . . . that everything and everybody are humbugs."

A Tiny Four-Year-Old Is the Find of a Lifetime

The document that Barnum hastily drew up hiring tiny Charlie Stratton was signed in the name of both Stratton parents. Sherwood did the actual writing, with his illiterate wife Cynthia adding her mark.

Had it not been so cold in Albany that November day in 1842, the Hudson River would not have frozen over, compelling Barnum to return home from his business trip by train. And had the train not stopped in Bridgeport, Connecticut, where half-brother Philo managed the Franklin House hotel, Barnum might never have passed the night there. And, later that evening, had he not remembered hearing of an amazingly small boy in Bridgeport and asked Philo to fetch him, the 32-year-old showman might not have encountered that miniature concoction, who was to make him rich beyond belief and famous beyond his wildest dreams.

Four-year-old Charles S. Stratton was no bigger than a doll. All at once at seven months, measuring 25 inches and weighing 15 pounds, the child had simply stopped growing. "Nature [had] put a veto on his further upward progress," a Barnum booklet later described the phenomenon, "and ordered him for ever afterwards to remain in statu quo." Upon seeing him, Barnum instantly recognized the extraordinary possibilities that the boy represented—that is, if Charlie didn't suddenly start to grow again. Sherwood Stratton, the boy's carpenter father, was only too happy to rent his little son out for a trial month at $3.00 a week plus room, board, and travel expenses for the boy and his mother, Cynthia. Barnum whisked the youngster away to New York City, where speedily printed museum posters testified to the thorough Barnumizing Charles Stratton underwent; the four-year-old carpenter's kid from Bridgeport had been transformed overnight into General Tom Thumb, an 11-year-old marvel just arrived from Europe and engaged at "extraordinary expense." It was basic Barnum that the end justified the means. "Had I announced him as only five years of age, it would have been impossible to excite the interest or awaken the curiosity of the public. The thing I aimed at was, to assure them that he was *really a dwarf*—and in *this*, at least, they were not deceived. It was of no consequence, in reality, where he was born or where he came from.... I had observed ... the American fancy for European exotics; and if the deception ... has done any thing towards checking our disgraceful preference for foreigners, I may readily be pardoned for the offense I here acknowledge."

There was room for the Strattons on the fifth floor of the museum, where two giants already lived across the hall from each other. The converted billiard hall next door to the museum where the Barnums dwelt was already full—Charity had given birth to three daughters by now—but it was here, beside the living-room fireplace, that General Tom Thumb's education began. Barnum himself was the schoolteacher, training his small charge first in manners, then in memorizing little quips and speedy comebacks, finally in

Charles Sherwood Stratton looked like this when Barnum discovered him in late 1842. In his earliest known portrait, the tiny boy appears with his father, Sherwood Edward Stratton, a Bridgeport carpenter who was embarrassed to have a dwarf for a son.

Sherwood Stratton
Cynthia her mark Stratton
Phineas T Barnum

the words and actions for a number of dress-up roles he would play. With the help of costumes, props, a few dance steps, and some songs, Tom, who was a natural mimic, would strike poses and in other ways imitate well-known individuals, including Cupid, Samson, a Highland chieftain, Hercules, an English fox-hunter, Frederick the Great, and Napoleon. Realizing right off that Tom had "native talent and an intense love of the ludicrous," Barnum coached the boy hour after hour, both day and night, until his routines were down pat.

The next step was to introduce his prodigy to the editors of New York's papers. He knew them all, and Barnum was not above barging into their private homes at dinnertime, as proved by a story in the *Courier and Enquirer* by its editor, Colonel Webb. "While quietly discussing our dinner, we were honored with a very unceremonious visit from no less a personage than the distinguished General Thomas Thumb. We were somewhat annoyed at the interruption at first, but discovering its cause, and the honour conferred upon us, very quietly proceeded in the operation of carving a turkey, which the companion of the General assured us weighed more than his Grace. . . . We admitted the truth of the assertion, and placed the General alongside of our plate to superintend the operation of carving. He took his station with great sang froid, and, amid the roar of our little ones, quietly kicked aside a tumbler of water, which he considered dangerous in the event of his falling into it."

New Yorkers, therefore, were already familiar with the General and his tininess when he was sufficiently prepared to take the stage. At first, Barnum himself appeared with him as interlocutor and straight man—this role was commonly known as "the Doctor." From later-published scripts we know how the Doctor usually started things off: "You being a general, perhaps you will tell us what army you command?" "Cupid's artillery," the General would reply. "But there are so many generals in the army," the Doctor continued; "perhaps you will tell us whether you are a major general, a brigadier general, or an adjutant general?" "I'm a quartermaster general." "You are? How do you make that out?" "Because," squealed Tom, "I look out for the quarters." To Barnum's liking, the script was peppered with puns and double entendres, a fast-paced, good-humored repartee the expressionless "Doctor" and the impish, gleeful mite brought off to perfection. The General was no instant smash, but superior word of mouth and strong advertising about his "chemical synthesis, in which manhood had been boiled down," soon brought in packed houses. When the trial month was over, Barnum raised Tom's weekly take to $7.00, $3.00 of which went to his father, Sherwood, who was now on the scene and doing odd jobs for the museum. Barnum made up for that by soon raising Tom to $25, "and he fairly earned it," said the showman. "I frequently exhibited him for successive weeks in my Museum, and when I wished to introduce fresh novelties there, I sent him to numerous cities and towns in many of the States, accompanied by my friend Fordyce Hitchcock."

As part of his tutoring of Tom Thumb, Barnum placed a mirror on the floor of his living room so the little mite could see himself as he practiced strutting and saluting.

Tom Thumb had been the hit of Barnum's for almost a year when this typical billboard ad appeared.

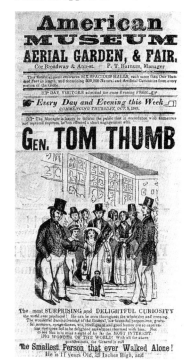

Of the many roles diminutive Charlie Stratton was asked to imitate, his most famous was Napoleon. This daguerreotype, made probably in 1843, shows how early Tom assumed the role.

Instead of being bitter over his littleness, Tom seemed to glory in it, almost as if it were his own special blessing. He loved to strut out on the stage and show what he could do to an audience. Barnum fashioned the basic show, but it was Tom who took the raw materials and turned them into art. Of course, Tom's childhood suffered from his full-time occupation as an adult. At five he learned to drink wine at meals, at seven to smoke cigars. His attempts to be only a child were feeble and never lasted long. He laughed hysterically when Barnum and his father pretended to fall on their faces tripping over traps of twine Tom had set. He loved money and hoarded it. He loved to be carried around holding on with both hands to a cane, and he loved to be read to, something that his illiterate mother couldn't help with, but which Barnum did often. "[I] never had any childhood, any boy-life," the usually effervescent Thumb once ruefully reminisced. "[He was] very fond of me," Barnum summed up their relationship, "[and] I was . . . sincerely attached to him." When the two were on stage, Barnum would often turn to the audience and ask for a little-boy volunteer to come up and contrast his size with Tom's. "I'd rather have a little miss," a squeaky voice piped up, and the audience howled. Even at his tender years, Tom knew that women had a strange urge to touch him, hug him, kiss him. It was as if he could be both child and lover to them at the same time. Tom learned early to take advantage of his strange appeal, and as his career progressed, he began selling kisses along with his booklet at 25 cents apiece. Later, as part of his show, he would estimate out loud that he had imparted over a million kisses to his fair admirers.

Having conquered America, Barnum decided to try out his "dwarf" on England and Europe. With dreams of visiting Queen Victoria herself as well as the royalty of France and Spain and Germany and Belgium, Barnum put his museum in the hands of his trusted friend Parson Fordyce Hitchcock, and in January 1844 he and the General set sail. The New York *Sun* reported that "several thousand persons joined in procession yesterday to escort this wonderful little man on board of the ship Yorkshire. . . . The procession passed down Fulton Street, preceded by the city brass band. The General was in an open barouche, and bowed very gracefully to the myriads of ladies who filled the windows on each side of the street, and who testified their delight in seeing him, by the waving of thousands of white handkerchiefs." The moment of departure afforded Barnum one of the few instances of true emotion he ever recorded. "The 'melting mood' was upon me, for the pathway of the ship was toward the wide sea with its deep mysteries, and my heart clung to my family and home. I successively grasped for the last time the hand of each parting friend as he passed the tow-boat, and I could not restrain my emotion; and when the band struck up 'Home, Sweet Home!' my tears flowed thick and fast."

So that Thumb would look even smaller, the artist who made this engraving in 1844 put his subject on a desktop and filled the scene with other little objects for comparison—a seal, a feather, a spoon, a bottle, books.

An old friend of Barnum's from Bethel and a Universalist minister, "Parson" Fordyce Hitchcock often shepherded the General when he toured outside New York. Despite a history of nervous breakdowns, Hitchcock was Barnum's choice to run the museum in what turned out to be a long but lucrative absence.

Thronged with masts and rigging, the New York waterfront was the new country's foremost port when Barnum and Thumb set sail for the old country.

"The Golden Shower Was Beginning to Fall"

A pleasant, wily, carefree rogue, neatly decked out and looking self-satisfied—that is how the artist portrayed the "foreign correspondent" for the New York *Atlas* as he quilled away at his London desk.

The carriages of the rich were usually stacked up three deep in front of London's Egyptian Hall during the General's performing hours. Soon Barnum saw to it Tom had a carriage, too, a specially made miniature one, shown here waiting for its trifle of a passenger outside the hall.

fter an uneventful 18-day crossing, the General had an unusual entree to the city of Liverpool. While his parents and tutor, along with Barnum and Professor Guillaudeu, the museum's French naturalist, made their way to the Waterloo Hotel on foot, Tom was smuggled past the crowds posing as a babe in his mother's arms—the showman was determined that no one would get a free view of his "pigmy-prodigy." He was also determined to have the General meet the Queen. Hoping to go straight to London to "set up headquarters at Buckingham Palace," Barnum was dismayed that the death of Prince Albert's father had thrown the royal family into mourning, with all entertainment at the palace curtailed. In typical fashion, Barnum plunged ahead anyway. In London he rented a mansion in the most fashionable district and sent invitations to the rich and famous to come visit his charge. Barnum's new friend Horace Greeley had written a letter of introduction to the American ambassador, the famed Edward Everett, and upon its delivery Everett came calling. Yes, he would help arrange a meeting with Her Majesty Queen Victoria. In fact, it was not long before the showman was breakfasting with the Master of the Queen's Household at Everett's house. Barnum engaged the Egyptian Hall in Piccadilly and put the General on its stage, and the rush was on. Money started pouring in.

The showman had thought of everything, even keeping his name before the American public for what might turn out to be an extended absence. Before leaving, he had signed up to write a series of articles on his travels for the New York *Atlas*. These turned out to be chatty, filled with observations on the first visit abroad of a perceptive Yankee, as well as an often colorful documentation of the General's adventures. But on the subject of a hoped-for meeting between Tom and the Queen, Barnum offered only small talk to *Atlas* readers. "It is well known that she has the smallest pony in the world, and the General is fully determined to tell her that he thinks it is just about large enough for him."

For Barnum it was a memorable evening when Baroness Rothschild, wife of the richest banker in the world, sent her carriage for the General in hopes of a "little" command performance. Barnum and Tom were treated to a reception amid 20 lords and ladies in a "glare of magnificence" so stunning that the man who could conjure up extravagant, tongue-twisting portraits of the most meager exhibits felt he could not find adequate words to describe the Rothschild grandeur. He could describe, though, a happy occurrence as the evening came to an end. "On taking our leave, an elegant and well-filled purse was quietly slipped into my hand, and I felt that the golden shower was beginning to fall." Even more exciting was the placard Barnum left one night on the door of the Egyptian Hall: "Closed this evening, General Tom Thumb being at Buckingham Palace by command of Her Majesty."

An early daguerreotype of Tom Thumb in his traveling clothes.

A "Command Performance" Is Arranged

The hour had arrived. Who shall tell of it? The Queen? Tom? Barnum? Let the showman proceed. "On arriving at the Palace, the Lord in Waiting put me 'under drill' as to the manner and form in which I should conduct myself in the presence of royalty. I was to answer all questions by Her Majesty through *him*, and in no event speak directly to the Queen. In leaving the royal presence I was to 'back out,' keeping my face always towards Her Majesty, and the illustrious Lord kindly gave me a specimen of that sort of backward locomotion."

Barnum and his miniature meal-ticket now mounted an enormous flight of marble steps. Suddenly the doors to the Queen's Picture Gallery were thrown open and there was Victoria herself at the far end of the room, smiling in anticipation. Although she was surrounded by a circle of royalty in resplendent suits and gowns which sparkled with gems, the Queen wore a plain black dress and not a flicker of jewelry. "The General toddled in," Barnum continued, "looking like a wax-doll gifted with the power of locomotion. . . . The General advanced . . . and exclaimed, 'Good evening, *Ladies and Gentlemen*!' A burst of laughter followed this salutation. The Queen then took him by the hand, led him about the gallery, and asked him many questions, the answers to which kept the party in a constant strain of merriment. The General familiarly informed the Queen that her picture gallery was 'first-rate' . . . then gave his songs, dances, imitations, etc."

That night the Queen made an entry in her diary. "After dinner we saw the greatest curiosity I, or indeed anybody, ever saw, viz: a little dwarf. . . . He made the funniest little bow, putting out his hand & saying: 'much obliged, Mam.' One cannot help feeling very sorry for the poor little thing and wishing he could be properly cared for, for the people who show him off tease him a good deal, I should think. He was made to imitate Napoleon and do all sorts of tricks, finally backing the whole way out of the gallery."

To Tom, what seemed like teasing was all part of the act. Of his second meeting with the Queen, eight days later, he remembered only respect. "Her Majesty called me to her and asked me a great many questions. The Duke of Wellington remarked, 'Their royal highnesses are head and shoulders taller than Tom Thumb.' Her Majesty heard it and turning to the old Duke said '*General* Tom Thumb.' The Duke bowed and with a military salute to me repeated '*General* Tom Thumb,' and everybody bowed."

After this second audience, Barnum was in rapture as he took pen and addressed his audience back in America. "If I was not a remarkably *modest* man, I should probably brag a little, and say that I had done what no American ever before accomplished; but being 'remarkably modest,' I shall say *nothing*, but wait for an American to appear who has visited the queen at her palace *twice* within eight days."

Edward Everett, the famous Massachusetts statesman, educator, and orator, who was currently the American minister to the Court of St. James, helped arrange an appearance before Queen Victoria for Thumb and his guardian. Usually reserved and unhelpful on matters he considered beneath him, this time Everett was all cooperation, because of a letter from Horace Greeley that Barnum came bearing. Queen Victoria was only 25, the same age as her consort, Prince Albert, whom she openly worshipped.

Tom Thumb's glove fits well with the miniature chair being readied for the General in this contemporary engraving of his audience with the Queen and Prince Albert.

When Queen Victoria sent her "command" for Thumb to appear before her, the almond-eyed, moon-faced monarch had been married to Prince Albert for four years and was the proud mother of the Princess Royal and the Prince of Wales.

Exit from the audience was strictly by protocol, with the guests backing out of the Queen's Picture Gallery and bowing all the way. Because of his size, the General couldn't keep up and every few steps had to turn his back on the Queen and run. But, as Barnum described, "running was an offence sufficiently heinous to excite the indignation of the Queen's favorite poodle-dog."

Now Barnum Explores the City of Lights

n late June of 1844, with H. G. Sherman, a former museum singer, arrived from New York to take over the day-to-day management of the General, Barnum was free to travel to Paris and attend the Great Exposition, where he hoped to find new tricks and treasures for his prize museum back home. A once-every-five-years event to show off worldwide products of industry, the enormous fair was rich in "artists of curiosities," among them automatons, and it was at their exhibits that Barnum picked up 87 individual cards of the most talented geniuses and followed up personally on every one of them. The merchandise was so bizarre and desirable, its purchase soon used up the $3,000 allocated for the purpose. Still Barnum bought on. He was too happy to start cutting corners, for, during this first whirlwind trip to the Continent, the showman was falling head over heels in love with Paris. He was conversant in French, and it was with relish that he reported back to America that he ate at a restaurant with no fewer than 443 dishes on its

A dapper Barnum, and Paris as it looked back then.

Palace was lit at night, and then discovering the Duke of Buckingham had spent $7,500 for candles alone to illuminate a grand party at his palace, Barnum promised himself never to chintz on lighting up his beloved showplace in New York.

Tom Thumb was the most popular exhibit in London, but when Barnum attended a private performance of a group of bell ringers, he claimed they might even outstrip his dwarf. It was the "most extraordinary and beautiful musical exhibition I ever saw or heard," he wrote to the *Atlas* readers. "A long table is placed in front of these novel musicians, on which are ranged some forty to fifty common hand bells of various sizes. With the bells the 'band' perform a great number of difficult and celebrated overtures, besides waltzes, quadrilles, and indeed any tunes they please, with an accuracy, precision, softness and harmony unsurpassed by any orchestra in the world." Barnum suggested that an American showman could make a fortune by hiring them. He did not mention, though, that he himself had already signed them up, as he confessed to his friend Moses Kimball by letter. "I have hired the 'Bell Ringers' at a roaring price—much too high to think of putting them in our museums at present. I have made them '*Swiss*,' procured *Swiss dresses*, got out a lithograph representing them in *Swiss costume*. . . . [T]he public are to suppose that the *Ringers* go to America *on their own hook*." The plan was for the "Swiss" ringers to play the best theaters at high ticket prices before moving to more common-man surroundings at Barnum's and Kimball's museums.

In that same letter, Barnum mentioned having sent along for exhibition a dress the Queen had worn at her levees and drawing rooms. "It is positively *true, on my honor, so help me God!*" Barnum also mentioned that "the Indians will be here tomorrow." Upon arriving in London, he had found the famous American painter of Indians, George Catlin, already ensconced in Egyptian Hall, showing, at great profit, an exhibit of his paintings along with artifacts, weapons, costumes, and a huge Indian wigwam set up in the middle of the room. Now, six months later, Catlin and Barnum were in partnership to bring to London a whole troupe of live American Indians. Warning his pen-pal Kimball against letting his plate get too full, Barnum, who sometimes was unable to follow his own advice, wrote again to describe *his* overflowing platter. "I now have got the Indians under full blast, and what with them and Tom Thumb, my automaton writer exhibiting at the Adelaide Gallery, the Bell Ringers, Am. Museum and Peale's, giants, dwarf, etc. I guess I have about enough on hand to keep one busy."

Barnum's stay in Britain was not without its controversial turns. To the outrage of every Englishman, the showman actually tried to buy the house

Almost from the beginning, Barnum had had problems with Tom's parents, shown here in the only picture of the three of them together. "I'll blow the concern to hell before I'll allow anybody else [to gather] up the fruit which I have shaken from the tree," Barnum wrote after discovering that the Strattons were planning to break free from his management. As Thumb's profits in Europe increased, the parents wanted more and more of a share in them, eventually convincing Barnum to make them full partners in the operation. "I can do business with blockheads and brutes when there is money enough to be made by it," Barnum wrote Kimball in January 1845, "but I can't be tempted by money to associate with them nor allow them to rule."

in which Shakespeare had been born. His plan was to disassemble it and ship its carefully packed parts back to New York, where it would be reassembled for public exhibition. And Barnum almost got away with it. Had not at the last moment some wealthy men stepped in to buy the house and present it to a newly formed Shakespeare Association, he might have actually smuggled the national treasure out of England for a song. Or at least made a lot of money trying. For he was subsequently assured that the British people, rather than part with Shakespeare's house, would have bought him off for at least twenty thousand pounds. "I do not doubt," wrote Oliver Wendell Holmes much later, "that he would make an offer for the Tower of London, if that venerable structure were in the market."

While in England, Barnum went into partnership with the American artist George Catlin, who specialized in painting American Indians. "I find him a very kind, sociable and excellent gentleman," Barnum wrote home, "and am most happy to add that he is making a fortune here."

Barnum now was in a buying frenzy. He tried and failed to acquire relics associated with Guy of Warwick, the fabled English giant. He tried for some huge elk horns that had been dug out of an Irish bog. He was struck by a Rubens portrait of St. Ignatius. And he spent $2,500 for a large cage-full of diverse animals whose contiguous living arrangement was curiously peaceful. Success was not always without consequence. Checking out a Canadian giantess at the Warwick races, Barnum bent down and lifted her skirts to see if she was standing on a platform. She was, but in an instant Barnum was sent sprawling.

Once, another more serious sprawling almost put an end to the Thumb enterprise. Barnum and party were out driving the countryside in an open carriage, with Mr. Sherman and the General seated on the driver's box. Descending a steep hill, the frightened horse stampeded into a stone wall and killed itself. Barnum was terrified that Sherman and the General had been crushed. "Our fears were readily dissipated, however, upon hearing the tiny voice of the General," Barnum told the story soon afterward. "Mr. Sherman saw the approaching danger, and, with a remarkable self-possession, held the General firmly in his arms, and the moment the concussion occurred, he gave a tremendous leap, cleared the wall . . . and landed safely in the adjoining field, preserving his little charge perfectly harmless."

At the start of 1845, Barnum allowed the Strattons to become full partners in the Thumb adventure. Even though this still permitted the showman to clear a healthy annual profit of $25,000 for himself, it stirred up trouble. "The Strattons are crazy," he wrote Kimball at the end of January, "—absolutely deranged with such golden success. At first they were inclined to take airs, carry high heads, and talk about what *we* were doing; but when Mrs. Stratton began to be too inquisitive about the *business* and to say that she thought expenses were too high and that I spend too much for printing etc., I told them both very *decidedly* that I was the *manager* and that unless the *whole* was left to my direction [I] would not stay a single day. Their horns were hauled in very suddenly, you may depend, and they are now down to their *old level*, where you may be sure I will keep them."

In late July 1844, Barnum discovered a talented group of Lancashire musicians whose specialty was performing with as many as 40 or 50 handbells. Within days he had convinced them to don Swiss costumes and become known to Barnum's readers—and soon to his museum audiences as well—as "The Swiss Bell Ringers."

Herr Faber's talking machine, which Barnum exhibited in London, could squeak out in three languages while the lips and eyes on its face moved at the same time. Faber considered it so valuable he "always took off the head and neck," observed Barnum, "placed it in a tin box, and took it with him whenever he left the Egyptian Hall." Accused of being fraudulent, a mere ventriloquist's dummy, Faber's machine actually worked. "It is operated by means of a foot-bellows," Barnum explained. "While the bellows operates as the 'breath of life', the glottis is moved in exact imitation of the human tongue by a delicate combination of little springs, connected with keys similar to those of the piano-forte." Barnum exhibited later versions well into the 1870s, with a sign offering $10,000 to anyone who could match the device. When he first heard rumors of Edison's talking machine, Barnum quickly took down the sign.

A Command Performance for the King of France

After performing in almost every town in England and Scotland as well as in Belfast and Dublin, Barnum's tiny General headed for France. Again the royal carpet was out. The General appeared before King Louis Philippe four times at the Palace of the Tuileries as well as visiting his family in their private quarters. Receipts in Paris made London's pale as the City of Lights went crazy over the midget. Parisians could attend the General's regular levees or see him in a French play written for him—*Le Petit Poucet*, in which he popped out of a pie and slid through the legs of a line of chorus girls. A tour of France led to Belgium and thence to Spain, where Tom appeared before Queen Isabella at Pamplona and Barnum rejoiced over the marvels of a bullfight. One of the reasons for the continued success of the entourage was Barnum's willingness to do anything and everything. For much of the time, he acted as the General's advance man, keeping days or even weeks in front of the caravan, hiring halls and arranging for advertising as he went. Still filled with boyish energy, Barnum was absorbed with the notion of making things happen himself.

The imposing Tuileries (below), where Tom Thumb was presented, and their royal occupant, the gracious and unassuming monarch of France, King Louis Philippe (above). To outdo the English, Louis Philippe ordered four command performances from Tom and asked him into the family's private chambers.

"Dash Ahead and Damn the Expense"

Jean-Eugene Robert-Houdin was a legend in France when Barnum arrived, the world's greatest "conjurer," as he liked to be called, as well as the most ingenious inventor and builder of mechanisms that could baffle and outwit humans. Houdin befriended Barnum and sold him the automaton that had won him a gold medal at the Paris exposition—a little figure that could answer questions and draw pictures upon request.

From almost the beginning of his trip, Barnum had been highly critical of Britain's stuffy class structure and its reliance on wealth instead of brains and hard work as the measure of worth. It was different with France. His affection for Paris, especially, was immediate and complete. Once, midway through 1845, taking leave of the city, he wrote of his deep feeling for its charms and enchantments. "I have at last torn myself away from the glare and brilliancy, the beauties and gaieties, the enjoyments and enchantments of the gayest city in the world—Paris. Never did or could I spend four months more happily than the last four months have been spent in the French metropolis."

As he had done in England, Barnum wrote copiously of his times in France, some of his words revealing as much about himself as insight into the French mystique. One of his earliest observations concerned Jean-Eugene Robert-Houdin, the celebrated magician, "who was not only a prestidigitateur and legerdemain performer," as Barnum put it, "but a mechanician of absolute genius." The first time Barnum visited the great Houdin at his suburban Paris home, he described his house as being like one big mechanical toy. "When a visitor rang at the gate, a plate dropped, politely inquiring 'What name?' A card, slipped into a slit and drawn pneumatically to the house, was followed by another plate 'Enter,' when, lo! the locked gate opened mechanically. Indeed, all the doors in the house were opened and shut by unseen servants. After greetings and chat with Houdin in his library, he touched a knob, and through the floor rose a table laden with luncheon." No wonder Barnum was spellbound by automatons and other mechanical devices and shipped so many examples from Paris back to his museum.

Along with a steady diet of charms, Barnum was exposed to at least one Parisian terror, through a prank played on him that bared the supposedly hardened showman's distaste for the morbid. One day a friend led him to a small building on the Seine where, he was told, he was in for a delightful surprise. "We entered, and, horror of horrors! four naked dead bodies lay before us. We were in the *Morgue*, a place in which are deposited for three days the bodies of unknown persons who are drowned, or meet with accidental death. They were laid upon inclined planes, open to the inspection of the public, in order that they may be recognised by those interested in their fate. Their clothes are hung up near them, as an additional means of recognition." Barnum readily admitted that the surprise visit to "this house of the dead" pained him and he could scarcely laugh for the rest of the day.

From village to French village, Thumb's entourage included Barnum, Thumb's parents, H. G. Sherman (Tom's sometime manager and tutor), Mr. Howard (the pianist), a groom, a coachman, two footmen (one doubled as a crowd organizer), two servants, and Monsieur Pinte (the interpreter). On top of this there was a carriage for six drawn by six horses, a springed transport for Thumb's ponies and miniature carriage requiring an additional four horses, and a baggage car for the sets and props, including the elegant house and furniture used in Tom's plays. All this elaborate entourage was part of a carefully crafted business plan, invented by a Barnum more and more willing to spend money in order to make it. "It is necessary always to *put on the appearance of business*," he explained, "in order that the *reality* should follow. . . . [P]ersons catering for the public amusement must dash ahead and damn . . . the expense."

It had taken a lot of persuasion to get Monsieur Pinte to join the tour as interpreter. A college professor, he was sure the post was beneath his dignity, especially when, at the Belgian border, Barnum referred to him as a showman. What exactly are the qualifications of a good showman? Pinte wanted to know. The first, Barnum replied, "was a thorough knowledge of human nature, which of course included the faculty of judiciously applying soft soap." And what is "soft soap"? "I told him it was the faculty to please and flatter the public so judiciously as not to have them suspect your intentions." At the customhouse a large quantity of books and lithographs of the General were subject to duty, but when Barnum passed out free samples to the customs officials, the rest were quickly waved through duty-free. "Is that what you call 'soft sup'?" inquired Professor Pinte. "Exactly," Barnum replied.

After launching the General in Brussels, Barnum took on the job of *avant-courier*, or advance man for the tour. His first duty was to approach the mayor of a town to be invaded and get his backing. After a theater or saloon was chosen, placards were nailed up which announced the date and time of Tom's appearance. According to Barnum, none of the usual "puffing" one might now expect was ever needed for Thumb. "All my energies are devoted to *keeping the public quiet*, and begging them *not to get excited*, for we will endeavor to give them all a chance to see him—of course, provided they 'down with the dust!'. . . The consequence is that, when the General arrives, we have a great deal of trouble in taking the money and finding places for all the people to get a look at him; but a man can stand almost anything when he gets used to it, so we bear our troubles with the calmness and fortitude of philosophers and Christians."

Barnum was enamored with the French. He approved that places of amusement in France had to pay a percentage of their receipts for the support of hospitals; it was the right of the poor. And he was sure that the way Frenchmen laughed betrayed their true character. "Give me a man who can laugh, and laugh heartily—not one who 'grins horribly a ghastly smile,' but one who laughs in earnest, as though it came from the heart—and a hundred to one that is a whole-souled, liberal-minded and charitable fellow."

Bewitched by Vineyards and Fleshpots

Barnum's Paris experience included watching the great tragedian Rachel perform at least three times and meeting "that little bag of bones with the marble face and the flaming eyes," as Edwin Forrest once described her.

Among his many calls in Paris, Barnum paid several intriguing visits to George Sand, one of the foremost writers of her day but, Barnum felt, completely misunderstood by Americans.

For most of his three years abroad with Thumb, Barnum was a free-wheeling bachelor. But for one stretch of eight months in 1844–45, his nervous, cloistered wife, Charity, joined him in what turned out to be a revealing time for her, a frustrating period for him. Straitlaced and often sickly, Charity took a dim view of the very things her liberal-minded, investigative, inquisitive husband had come to love. She found the amusements of London all "vanity and wickedness," and the English, as a group, "miserable misguided beings." "They are a wretched nation of drunkards and gamblers," Barnum reported her as saying. "The very first dinner party we attended, every person drank wine—even the ladies—and I am sure that some of the gentlemen drank a quart apiece. . . . The poorer classes, seeing these examples, think they must do the same; but as they can't afford to drink wine, they guzzle down the ale." As for Paris, Barnum's "paradise," it was "the most vulgar place I ever visited; and every one of the half-naked trollops who come out upon the stage to show their legs and expose their nakedness, ought to be horse-whipped and kept on bread and water till they are willing to work and gain an honest and a decent livelihood!" Pregnant now for the fourth time, Charity was anxious to return to what she called "the happiest land in the world—the land of Sabbaths—America." And so she sailed for home, leaving Barnum to his own pursuits and a host of new acquaintances, including the actress Rachel and the female writer George Sand. Wherever he went Barnum had a quick eye for female beauty, as his *Atlas* articles attested. In England, he had observed the bright-eyed "gipsey girls" at a fair, had admired their "long black hair and beautiful teeth," but had been reluctant when one had tried to sell him a kiss. "I never kissed a lady in my life, and never expect to," Barnum told her. "Ah, you need not tell me that," the girl replied, "for I can see a little devil in your eye." Realizing that keeping the conversation going would cost him half a crown, he turned away and got a good scolding for his "meanness." In France, the peasant girls, in Barnum's opinion, left something to be desired. "The upper lip . . . almost invariably bears a light mustache, and I have frequently seen females who had a heavier beard than I ever yet could cultivate! Ye gods! but this is a damper to a man's admiration of the softer sex." In Spain, at a bullfight, at a time of pause, Barnum noticed in the women's gallery "such a cooing and cawing in this rookery of turtle-doves—. . . such a rustling of silks—such telegraphic workings of fans," that he was left almost speechless. "I had intended to describe the beauty—the fascination of Spanish ladies, but the taste is too overpowering for me, or, indeed, for any mortal man. Suffice it to say, this is a dangerous country to any except those who, like myself, have lived long enough to resist all temptations!"

In wine country, Barnum was not so abstemious. "Here, day after day, have I revelled and run riot among thousands of acres of ripe luscious grapes, the very sight of which is enough to make anybody but an infernal, cold-hearted rascal drop on his knees, and offer up sincere thanks to Heaven for its unbounded munificence!

"Upon a square wooden trough stands three or four men with bare legs, all stained with purple juice, dancing and trodding down the grapes as fast as they are thrown in, to the tune of a violin. The labor of constantly stamping down the fruit is desperately fatiguing, and, without music, would get on very slowly. A fiddler, therefore, forms part of every wine-grower's establishment, and as long as the instrument pours forth its merry strains, the treaders continue their dance in the gore of the grape, and the work proceeds diligently. . . .

"I made a barrel or two of wine yesterday, having taken off my stockings, rolled up my trousers, and joined a couple of others in treading down the grapes to the tunes of the violin. The fiddler gave us the Polka, but we soon found that we were getting too much of a good thing, and that dancing the Polka was not what it is cracked up to be, especially when the dancer is up to his knees in ripe, bursting, bleeding and delicious grapes! . . . I can truly say I never was so happy in my life as I have been in attending the vintage at Médoc!"

Broken away from the Thumb tour, never so free or alive, he felt, as now, Barnum traveled back country roads like a regular bohemian, wearing a slouched hat and with the stub of a pipe in his mouth, stopping off at restaurants in Brittany for fresh bread and butter and always local wine. His drinking was now heavy, and he didn't mind admitting it. "I fear that my temperance friends would have rolled up the whites of their eyes, in amazement and horror," Barnum wrote to the *Atlas* in September 1845. "It is certainly wicked, in these days of temperance, to drink brandy . . . but any man who can resist the oily, delicious, charming and enchanting temptations of a glass of real Cognac . . . can resist the devil."

It was in this devil-may-care mood that Barnum left the General during a "farewell" tour of England for a whirlwind return to New York, but the trip was not a happy one. On board ship he was argumentative and quick-tempered with fellow passengers, and the condition must have continued back home, for, before he had got his business done, he had quarreled badly enough with his wife, who had just given birth to a fourth daughter, that he headed back to England earlier than he had planned. There potential disaster awaited. The General had been performing once again at Egyptian Hall at the same time that a British artist named Benjamin Robert Haydon was exhibiting his latest historical paintings there in a desperate attempt to keep out of debtors' prison. When the crowds flocked to see Thumb and left Haydon's exhibit deserted, the distraught artist killed himself. Arriving to find that the British press was making him the villain in the sad affair, Barnum turned a hardened cheek, fortified by his oft-proven theory that any publicity, no matter what the complexion, was better than none at all.

Living in Paris, the Irish playwright and actor Dion Boucicault befriended Barnum at several dinner parties, showed him the haunts of the city, and introduced him to Frenchmen who could open doors.

After touring the General in France, Belgium, and Spain, Barnum brought his midget back to England, where he outdrew another current exhibit 100 to 1—the paintings of Benjamin Robert Haydon (above). The entries in Haydon's diary told the story of the grievous outcome. "They rush by thousands to see Tom Thumb. They push, they fight, they scream, they faint, they cry help and murder! and oh! and ah!" The artist's answer was to scratch a last entry— "God forgive me, Amen. Finis of B. R. Haydon"—and then kill himself, first firing a bullet into his head, and then, having failed to deliver the mortal blow, finishing himself off with a razor slash across the neck.

Finally, Home to His Beloved Museum

In the three years Barnum had been away in Europe, his thoughts had seldom strayed far from his beloved museum. Presided over in his absence by the Universalist clergyman Fordyce Hitchcock, in many ways the museum had never really been left by him at all. From afar, Barnum kept close watch on its weekly receipts as well as those of his competitors, pelted Hitchcock with a spray of regular mail, and shipped off a steady supply of new-found performers and curiosities, as well as boxloads of European profits for Hitchcock to invest. He even made two on-the-fly trips home to attend to business personally.

As early as 1842, he had begun to enlarge his holdings, buying out

This is how Barnum's section of Broadway looked after his return from three years abroad. At the left, with flag flying atop, is the museum itself, with an immense poster of one of Barnum's giant serpents as the main decoration. At the right is the Astor House, then the columns of St. Paul's, and farther south the building that houses the Mathew Brady gallery. The scene, made from a lithograph of an original drawing by August Kollner, is viewed from the northeast corner of Broadway, looking downtown.

Ruben Peale's New York museum and, after running it anonymously as a phony rival to the American, finally merging it with his own collections at Ann Street. Throughout the decade, he would continue to consume other institutions, first the Baltimore Museum in 1845, then New York's Chinese Collection, and finally the mother-lode of Peale's famous Philadelphia Museum, its spoils divided equally with fellow vulture Moses Kimball, and landing Barnum the country's premier mastodon skeleton.

During the years abroad, he added more and more elements to the museum: a bowling alley in 1844; in 1845 a large "camera obscura," mounted on the museum roof and allowing visitors to see live images of Broadway street

H. & PUB. BY CURRIER & IVES

152 NASSAU St N.Y.

"Signor" Antonio Blitz was an accomplished magician and ventriloquist on Barnum's stage throughout the 1840s. When Barnum attended a performance of the more famous "Wizard of the North," John Henry Anderson, and saw no trick that was not obvious in its execution, he wrote, "I think Signor Blitz far his superior."

Child prodigies Kate and Ellen Bateman performed for Barnum in *Richard III* and were later sent abroad under his auspices. "Aside from the absurdity of seeing children playing tragedy," wrote actor Harry Watkins, "there was too much straining of the voice." Barnum, however, adored them.

scenes projected onto a huge tabletop for an additional charge of 6 cents; and in 1846, the year he reintroduced the mysterious "Hydro-oxygen Microscope," his first large expansion of the lecture room, an increase from one to two stories in height, and considerable improvements to the interior.

Over the course of his career, Barnum never depended primarily on original ideas, but borrowed freely from many sources. His peculiar talent was to know instantly what he liked when he saw it, and then to go after it. In Paris, after discovering that theaters there issued checks to patrons for their hats and umbrellas, Barnum decided he would be the first to introduce the custom in America. In London, watching in awe as Buckingham Palace was lit up for Queen Victoria's birthday and her initials were actually spelled out in light by a myriad of gas lamps, Barnum got the idea to illuminate his museum as no other American building had ever been lit. And in Regent's Park, where he discovered a theater with a series of curtained stages surrounding the auditorium, which was then rotated on a moving floor as one after another of the curtains was raised, Barnum decided that versions of these so-called "dioramas" would be employed by his museum as well. "Although I can make more money with General Tom Thumb in two months than I can in the American Museum in a year," Barnum wrote to the *Atlas* at one point from England, "yet my whole pride lies centered in the museum. . . . I am determined to [make it] . . . the most attractive and valuable establishment of the kind in the world . . . and am prepared to make every kind of improvement that could suggest itself to my mind."

In late 1846, Barnum received word that Fordyce Hitchcock's wife had died suddenly, and that the good parson had been thrown into the second profound mental collapse of his life. Bringing his long tour to a close, in early 1847 Barnum headed home to take the helm. Fabulously rich, his museum having spilled by now into the upper stories of three adjoining buildings and pulling in close to 400,000 visitors a year, Barnum proceeded to secure a 25-year lease from the building's new owners.

Currier & Ives executed this rendition of one of the museum's most popular exhibits, 257-pound, seven-year-old Vantile Mack. His 24-year-old mother proudly shows off her baby with the 61-inch chest.

Helping Pioneer the Minstrel Craze

Minstrelsy was invented in the late 1820s by the comedian Thomas D. Rice, a regular at Barnum's in the late 1840s (above). Hard put for a new act, Rice blackened his face and did a shuffling dance to lyrics which ended, "[E]very time I turn about I jump Jim Crow."

"Uncle Frank" Brower (center) was one of the four original "Virginia Minstrels," America's first blackface group, and appeared at Barnum's as early as 1843.

James A. Budworth, who performed blackface as part of "White's Original Serenadors," was at Barnum's in the early 1850s.

In the 1840s, a curious new form of entertainment took the country by storm, and as usual P. T. Barnum could be found on the scene. The new craze was minstrelsy—white performers wearing blackface and offering up a medley of humor, melodrama, song, and dance. Pioneered by Thomas D. Rice, who had combed the South during the 1820s and '30s in search of Negro storytellers, dancers, and singers to borrow from, full-blown minstrelsy burst on the American scene in 1843, in New York City. In February of that year, four unemployed actors—Frank Brower, Billy Whitlock, Dan Emmett, and Frank Pelham—successfully repackaged themselves as the "Virginia Minstrels" and parlayed a languishing season into a massive box-office success story. Barnum, who had included one-man minstrel shows on his stage ever since acquiring the museum, rushed in to capitalize. When the Virginia Minstrels left town for a whirlwind tour of England, Barnum made sure that another hot group, the Boston Minstrels, would be performing at his place.

The appeal of minstrelsy, popular primarily among the huge, lower-middle-class audiences that were Barnum's bread-and-butter clientele, lay in its devastating portrayal of American blacks. Though drawing on legitimate humor and music and storytelling traditions, and often creating endearing portraits, by definition minstrelsy was denigrating and racist. Its stock images of "Old Zip Coon" and "Jimmy Crack Corn" were based on a portrayal of the fun-loving, ignorant slave who loves "de plantation" where he "belongs." Northern white audiences found it hilarious. President Tyler dignified the art form with a special White House performance. And, like most of his contemporaries, Barnum was all but oblivious to any moral questions raised by the new craze. After all, it was not so many years since he himself had performed in blackface, and before that leased the slave Joice Heth from her owner. Worse still was a new admission, made in 1845, that while on the road in the South in the late 1830s Barnum had actually owned slaves—a woman and child at one point, and, earlier, a personal valet. Suspecting the "nigger" of having stolen from him, Barnum wrote, he "gave him fifty lashes, and took him to New Orleans where he was sold at auction."

"I ought to have been whipped a thousand times for this myself," Barnum later lamented. Routinely referring to black people as "darkeys" and "colored gemman," and boldly publishing such slurs as "niggers always like jewels," Barnum in the 1840s was as prejudiced as almost any other white person in the country. He argued for the necessity of ongoing slavery and remained adamantly opposed to the growing moral cause of the abolitionists, so that he could write, "[I]f the blacks were . . . set free and there was no army to protect the whites, the blacks would murder them and take possession of their property." And even though his point of view would change dramatically and totally in the decades ahead, in the 1840s catering to the public's prejudices was something it would not occur to him to question.

The elaborate costume and makeup that came to characterize minstrel acts is worn by Oscar Willis, an "Ethiopian" comedian of the 1850s.

One of Barnum's stars in 1849 was 576-pound Susan Barton, who boasted a 69-inch bust and hips seven feet three inches in diameter.

A great American acrobat, minstrel, and clown, Dan Rice got his start as a jockey boy for Henry Clay on his Lexington farm. Appearing at Barnum's as early as 1842 as a 20-year-old "American Hercules," and then throughout the decade, Rice went on to an eminent career and riches, before losing it all in the 1870s.

Here costumed in leopardskin leotards, these brothers were members of the celebrated Martinetti Family, which went through a long engagement on Barnum's lecture-room stage beginning on September 14, 1849.

Billed as a former elder, an overseer, and a doctor from the Shaker Society at Canterbury, New Hampshire, three gentlemen who had recently seceded from the ranks of the faithful and their "beautiful ladies" gave an exhibition of "singing, dancing and whirling" as the "Shaking Quakers." As one newspaper observed, "[T]he 'Whirl' of Miss Willard, is truly wonderful. . . . She goes around like a top 1,000 or 1,500 times without stopping."

BARNUM'S
AMERICAN MUSEUM

Corner of Broadway and Ann-street, opposite St. Paul's Church and the Astor House.
Contiguous to the Park, Fountain, City Hall, &c.
P. T. BARNUM....Manager & Proprietor   J. GREENWOOD, Jr.....Assist. Manager.

RARE ATTRACTIONS!
WONDERFUL CURIOSITIES!!
AMUSING ENTERTAINMENTS!!

EVERY DAY & EVENING this WEEK!
Commencing Monday, August 27th, 1849.

☞ The Museum is kept open every day in the year, except Sundays, from 7 o'clock in the morning till 10 o'clock in the evening, for visitors to examine the various curiosities, the splendid collection of WAX SCRIPTURAL STATUARY, the NATIONAL PORTRAIT GALLERY, GRAND COSMORAMA, &c. &c.

The Manager desirous of affording every possible accommodation to his patrons, and anxious that every visitor should witness the entertainments in the Lecture Room, has made arrangements to RE-ADMIT MORNING VISITORS TO THE AFTERNOON PERFORMANCES FREE.

Magnificent Performances and Exhibitions!
In the Afternoon at 3½ o'clock, and in the Evening at 8 o'clock.

ADMISSION to the WHOLE 25 CENTS.

The Manager has re-engaged for Exhibition, the
LIVE MAMMOTH

CROCODILE

Which arrived in this city a few days since from the River Nile, and which, without exception, is the LARGEST OF THE SPECIES that has ever been seen in this country. This Enormous

Monster of the Deep
Which is 10 feet in length, and weighs nearly **300** Pounds· is in all probability the

LEVIATHAN OF SCRIPTURE!
Ah has been visited during the past few weeks by THOUSANDS OF PERSONS, who all agree in pronouncing it the most wonderful and truly astonishing animal in existence.—It can be seen at all hours both day and evening.

Mr. Jerry Merrifield,   **Miss Stanhope,**
THE POPULAR COMIC SINGER.   The Favourite and Accomplished Actress.

Miss Barton,   **Miss Josephine West,**
The Talented and much admired Vocalist.   The beautiful Danseuse.

Mr. Higgins,   **Mr. A. Delapierre,**
The well known Comic and Fancy Dancer.   The celebrated and unrivalled performer upon the Fluting Accordeon

Mr. George Clark,   **Mr. Bleeker and**
Mr. Oakley.

All of whom have been long and favourably known in this city, are engaged and will appear, both Afternoon and Evening, in a great VARIETY OF ENTERTAINMENTS; also in

TWO FARCES
Of the most amusing and laughable Character entitled

PERFECTION
or the Maid of of Munster. and

THE OMNIBUS,
or a Convenient Distance.

Straight from the River Nile came this ten-foot-long, 300-pound "Monster of the Deep" to frighten customers in 1849.

The Orpheon Family of outstanding gymnasts first appeared at Barnum's in October of 1846.

The ubiquitous actor and magician Barney Williams shared Barnum's stage in the spring of 1846 with a five-year-old New York Drummer Boy, a living sloth, Bini "the unrivalled guitarist," and the Glass Blowers.

The Antics of a Questionable Husband

Barnum had never been much of a family man. He had been off on the road in the late 1830s, preoccupied with work whenever home, and the eight-week excursion with Thumb to Europe he had planned had turned into a three-year disappearance. Absent during the illness and sudden death of his two-year-old daughter Frances, absent again beside his "treasure of a wife" when she herself suffered a serious illness, Barnum, at least in the mid-1840s, seemed happier when off on his own. In contrast to the thousands of words that poured out of his pen concerning actresses and singers and friends, Barnum had almost nothing ever to say about Charity. Opposed to the theater, strictly moralistic, and possessing only a thin sense of humor, Barnum's wife was intensely critical of many of the things he himself relished, among them opera, card-playing, cigar-smoking, and alcohol. "Her ideas of morality and propriety," Barnum wrote in a thinly disguised parody, "savored too much of the old blue law school of Connecticut." Though he portrayed himself as a "good natured guy who takes things remarkably easy," Barnum described Charity as a woman "exceedingly nervous and given to hysterics." After agreeing to include her and his two daughters in a bit of Thumb's tour in Europe, and taking her abroad on the steamship *Great Western*, Barnum had proceeded to ridicule her mercilessly. In a published article, he described her as a sickly, carping hypochondriac, and spoke of her "piteous moaning about the danger of shipwreck," and of how he had joined in with a ship-wide mockery of her which kept everyone aboard "in a half-suffocation of concealed laughter." When Charity finally lashed out, "Why did you let me come?," Barnum had replied, "Now Charity, you know if I had objected . . . you would have said it was because I did not want you." Clearly he did not.

In Europe, Charity had complained almost incessantly. All Barnum could say was that his wife's "prejudices" were of "quite too long standing" for him to be able to reform. And so he preferred humor as his way of coping with Charity, humor that smacked at times of the almost cruel family variety that had once tricked him with Ivy Island. After his first absence in Europe of nine months, for example, he had made an unannounced trip to New York. But instead of heading straight home to their new apartment in the city, Barnum had gone directly to the museum, where he forced manager Hitchcock to inform Charity that an English messenger was waiting to see her at once in the museum with important news concerning her husband. Terrified, Charity had rushed over to receive the dreaded announcement, only to discover Barnum himself, in the flesh, tickled by the ingenious hoax he had just played on her. Charity's reaction "ended my sky-larking for that day," Barnum soberly concluded his account of the incident.

The interminable European tour had been followed by other long ab-

This portrait of the three Barnum girls was painted by the fashionable New York artist Frederick R. Spencer, known for his treatments of Washington Irving and Stephen C. Foster. Executed in 1847, the same year he rendered oils of Charity and P. T., it shows Caroline (left) and Helen flanking baby Pauline, Barnum's fourth daughter and his favorite. A third-born daughter, Frances, had died on April 11, 1844, just shy of her second birthday.

Instead of awe and inspiration, Niagara Falls was the site of fear and humiliation for Charity.

sences, as Barnum and Thumb cashed in on new markets all across the U.S. and Cuba. Finally, on the last leg of these circuits, as his new house in Fairfield was receiving finishing touches, Barnum invited his wife and daughter Caroline to come along for what he promised would be a real family vacation. Their destination was Niagara Falls, with stops along the way in Albany, Utica, Montreal, Quebec, and Buffalo. But even now, Barnum was restless. Often frustrated by how long it took the ladies to get ready, he would sometimes impatiently break away on his own without them. Fifteen-year-old Caroline in many ways was now closer to Barnum than was Charity. Possessing her father's wry sense of humor, delighting in being mistaken for Thumb's mother when she carried him publicly in her arms, Caroline could see right through her mother's "episodes." In a diary kept throughout the trip, she chronicled Charity's recurring illnesses and flare-ups of hypochondria, describing a series of almost humorous sudden reversals in health; she even observed at one point, "[S]he was so frightened she forgot to be sick." Knowing that her father read her daily entries and often added his own written comments and corrections, Caroline described how he took pleasure in his wife's seasickness, told her disgusting stories to make it worse, and refused to change plans even when Charity begged him to do so.

Old-fashioned, nervous, and proper, though also kindly and caring, Charity was often bedeviled by her heavy-drinking, practical-joker of a husband.

And then the worst came as the trip reached its climax. Upon arriving at Niagara Falls, and discovering the massive 250-step staircase that led down to the river, Barnum not only forced a terrified Charity to descend the stairs with them, but, when she became dizzy halfway down and refused to go farther, he and Caroline decided to leave her there alone and continue without her. "We found when we got home," Caroline recorded that night, "that she had fainted on the stairs and was obliged to be conveyed up by some men." Like so many experiences that Barnum seized hold of and that Charity simply missed, the sight of Niagara seemed well worth having abandoned her once again. Caroline, always her father's daughter, agreed. "What could be more sublime than they?" she wrote of the falls. "To see such an immense sheet of water continually falling in such tremendous mass seeming as if it would overwhelm you in its waters. While the roar comes like distant thunder . . . the spray arises in high clouds and presents a . . . brilliancy . . . as if it was some misty veil covering beauties unseen to the human eyes."

Taking Hold of His Life by Swearing Off Alcohol

It is not known precisely when Barnum renounced alcohol for good, but it is clear that by the mid-1840s drinking had become an increasingly destructive force in his life. The problem seems to have got out of hand while Barnum was in Europe, carousing through wine country without Charity. With his ego at an all-time high, and his "appetite for liquor," he admitted, growing stronger "month to month," Barnum had never felt happier in his life. At home, a pregnant Charity was beside herself. The more her husband caroused, the meaner he seemed to get toward her, and the more unpredictable. His ridiculing letters to the New York *Atlas*, lumping her among the "old maids" of New York City, stung. And then came his sudden trip home to New York in the spring of 1846, one month following the birth of their new daughter, Pauline. But instead of paying attention to his family, Barnum was now planning the building of a giant Oriental palace, and talking about yet another year in Europe. Something bad seems to have happened between Charity and Barnum during this visit, for suddenly, without warning, he cut his stay short by three full weeks and disappeared back to England, where his heart was. "I never before experienced so much trouble, nay misery . . . as I was forced to endure during my stay in the States," Barnum confessed in a letter to Moses Kimball at the time. "If I believed I should be obliged to go through the same vexations and annoyances when I returned, I would never go back, by God!" Though these "vexations" and "annoyances" were never clearly spelled out, Barnum as usual keeping key cards close to his vest, a third sentence in the Kimball letter offered at least a hint. "So here I am, and although hard at work and not very happy, I have less troubles than when I was home." With a wife who felt lonely and mistreated and afraid, and with Barnum yearning for freedom, to all appearances it was his home life he could no longer endure.

Charity's chief concern, in fact, was Barnum's drinking. Alcohol was changing him, she felt, "deluding" him. Terrified that his drinking was leading "to a drunkard's path," she routinely cried herself to sleep now, fearing for their future together. In the fall of 1847, seven months after having finally returned from Europe, Barnum took a first halting stab at confronting his problems. While he was exhibiting Thumb at a New York State Fair in Saratoga Springs, the sight of widespread drunkenness among the crowds suddenly worried him about himself. Pledging that very night to give up hard liquor, Barnum felt his worries dissipate. But his problems with alcohol were not yet over; they interfered increasingly with his work as well as his relationships. Lulled into a false security by the

Universalist minister Edwin Chapin's persuasive argument against drinking was key to the showman's final decision to take the pledge and by it take back control of his life.

Saratoga renunciation, and continuing to consume a full bottle or more of champagne each evening, by late 1847 he could no longer work after noon. And now not only his wife but her mother, Hannah, had begun to complain about Barnum's behavior while drinking. The criticisms infuriated him. At one point, he swore at them that he would go back to hard whiskey if they ever questioned him again. Terrified by such unpredictable anger, and perceiving him as "self-deluded," Charity kept increasingly silent.

And then, sometime in 1848, a breakthrough came. It arrived through the mediation of Universalist clergyman Edwin Chapin, later such a close friend to Barnum that the two would sign letters to each other as "Chang" and "Eng," after the Siamese Twins. Speaking on the subject of alcoholism to a Bridgeport audience which included Barnum, Dr. Chapin appealed to the so-called moderate drinker to quit alcohol entirely, if for nothing else than to set an example for others. Going strongly for the jugular, he added, "I warn you, in the light of all human experience, that you are in danger and should give it up for your own sake."

Barnum's conscience was convicted. He returned from the lecture that night so worried he could not sleep. "I had become fully conscious that I was pursuing a path of wrong-doing . . . fraught with imminent danger," he wrote soon afterward. And it was clear that the problem affected not just himself, but was destroying his marriage, his relationships, his work. Following "a wretched and sleepless night," Barnum later recorded, he arose from his bed, descended to his wine cellars along with his coachman, and proceeded to knock the heads off of 60 or 70 bottles of champagne and pour them out onto the ground. "I then called upon Mr. Chapin, asked for the teetotaler pledge, and signed it." It was the end of Barnum's drinking. When he went in to Charity to tell her what he had done, all the pent-up anxiety and pain she had been living with was finally unleashed, and she broke down before him in tears.

"The man who commences tippling is the last person in the world to discover his danger," Barnum later pondered. "If he has a wife, she probably is the first to know and shudder at his position." In the years ahead, there would be few personal causes Barnum would so passionately adopt as he did now the Temperance Movement. He had, at the same time, saved his marriage.

"I had gone so far in the miserable and ruinous habit of . . . 'liquoring up,'" wrote Barnum in later years, "that this unnatural appetite would soon have become stronger than resolution and I should have succumbed."

In an Oriental Mansion, Life Begins Anew

n November 14, 1848, following two years of ferocious building, the doors of an extraordinary sandstone mansion were thrown open to over 1,000 guests. Barnum had discovered the model for his ambitions while touring Brighton in 1845—the Royal Pavillion of King George IV of Wales, built in a Chinese- and Turkish-style opulence. Constructing his own version of it on a 17-acre seaside location in Fairfield, Connecticut, Barnum named it Iranistan. The finished home was like an ethereal dream. Three stories high, pillared and trellised, with its floors opening onto broad piazzas, the mansion was rimmed by satyrlike faces and surmounted by strange Turkish towers and minarets and a grand central dome soaring 90 feet into the sky. In its pure whimsy, wrote a guest, it seemed to be made up of "a little of Joice Heth, a sprinkling of Tom Thumb . . . the tail of the anaconda . . . and a monstrous slice of the two last giants."

The mansion's interior, if anything, was even more stunning than the outside. From its great central hall and drawing room, across from a fresco-walled Oriental library on the right of the building, mirrored doors led into a carpeted dining room capable of seating 40, which itself opened upon an octagonal greenhouse fitted with elaborate stained-glass windows. The family living quarters were at ground level; on the second floor, near the "Picture Room," was a series of guest bedrooms and chambers, each with its own bath containing hot and cold running water. Here too, in a room that would become increasingly important to him, was Barnum's private study, an orange-colored, satin-walled library and retreat which connected onto a modernistic bathing room equipped with full shower and tubs. On the top floor was the billiard room, serving also as a kind of music chamber and ballroom, and above it, linked by a spiral staircase, was the great central dome.

In the early 1850s, an eye-stopping addition appeared when Barnum put an elephant to work plowing his fields at Iranistan in full view of the railroad tracks running into the city. It was Barnum's hope that puzzled passengers would arrive in New York and head straight for his museum.

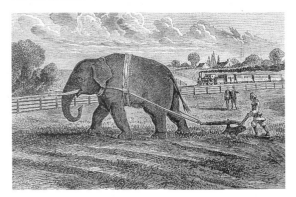

Heated by hot air, equipped with a full anti-burglary system and fire alarms, and lit by fuel from Barnum's own private gas works, Iranistan was the most unusual, most dreamlike home anywhere in the United States. Lacquered onto the doors of the special estate carriages was Barnum's newly created coat of arms, the motto of which seemed to sum up his life philosophy: "Love God, and Be Merry!" And by decade's end, he really was merry, and in a whole new way. Free from his drinking, newly appreciative of a wife who had stood by him in his problems, he could write, "I count these two years—1848 and 1849—among the happiest of my life." Calling his wife and children "dearer" to him "than all things in the wide world," and saying that "no place on earth was so attractive" to him as his own home, Barnum now settled down into a marriage that was finally solid, and which would remain so for the next quarter-century.

Work began on Iranistan during Barnum's final year abroad and continued during 1847–48, while Barnum and Thumb toured the U.S. and Cuba. His palace was to be constructed "regardless of cost," Barnum insisted, employing 500 local carpenters and laborers.

Barnum (far right) and
banquet friends of the 1850s.

Risking All on a Bold "Speculation"

Barnum designed elaborate stationery for his wealth of letters, unblushingly advertising his mansion, his museum, and later his circus. When Jenny Lind saw his Iranistan stationery, she took notice.

few months shy of 40 as the new decade commenced, P. T. Barnum seemed to have already accomplished everything he'd ever expected of himself. He was rich. He was famous. He had reared a family and built himself a showplace. He could easily retire now, on his laurels and his coffers. Instead, he was dreaming up an even more astonishing future, one that could help remake his image from humbug to serious promoter of the arts. What if, he was pondering, he could sponsor the greatest artistic performer in the world on an extended tour of the U.S.? And there she was for the taking—the great Jenny Lind, singer extraordinaire, the toast of Europe, Queen Victoria's favorite; they called her the "Swedish Nightingale" for the magic and magnificence of her Nordic voice. Like other readers of the New York *Atlas*, Barnum had learned of the Nightingale as early as June 1847, in a cover story with picture which emphasized a "Jenny Lind mania" already sweeping across Europe. "I had never heard her sing," Barnum later recalled. "Her reputation, however, was sufficient for me. I usually jump at conclusions, and almost invariably find that my first impressions are the most correct. It struck me, when I first thought of this speculation, that if properly managed it must prove immensely profitable, provided I could engage the 'Swedish Nightingale' on any terms within the range of reason. As it was a great undertaking, I considered the matter seriously for several days, and all my 'cipherings' and calculations gave me but one result—immense success."

As his representative to approach the 29-year-old diva, Barnum chose John Hall Wilton, a resourceful English horn-player who had recently brought a group of British musicians to New York. Wilton was shipped off across the Atlantic with instructions as to what he should offer and an understanding with Barnum that he would be paid on a sliding scale—the more Jenny received, the less he would get. Neither Wilton's Englishness nor his association with music was a sufficient lure: at first the Swedish singer refused to see the emissary. But perseverance and connections finally led to an exchange of letters, some initial conditions, and finally an audience in Lübeck, Germany. Yes, Wilton had engaged both Julius Benedict as music director and baritone Giovanni Belletti as accompanying singer for the proposed tour, just as Jenny had stipulated. Yes, servants, carriages, horses, a

This 1850 daguerreotype of Jenny Lind was taken by Mathew Brady and camera operator Luther Boswell in Brady's gallery across the avenue from Barnum's American Museum. Feeling that a true likeness of Lind might serve to hurt the cause, Barnum had tried to prohibit his songstress from going to Brady's, but an old schoolmate of Lind's had helped arrange for the sitting. No photograph, as it turned out, could ever catch Jenny's true spirit. "[N]ot even a daguerreotype," wrote Nathaniel Parker Willis, "was reasonably like our feeling of what a likeness should be." Lind's was a face, Willis insisted, "of singular beauty . . . and the pictures of her represent the plainest of commonplace girls."

Jenny Lind liked to be portrayed as an artistic heroine oblivious to the commercial world represented by Barnum. In reality she was a tough businesswoman, insisting early on that her contract with Barnum be altered in her own favor.

secretary, a companion, plus all expenses would be paid for by Barnum. Yes, all the money involved would be deposited in a London bank before her departure. Yes, the singer would have control over the number of times she would sing each week and over how many selections she would offer at each concert. Yes, during the tour Jenny could sing for charity whenever she chose. Well, what was the price? To ensure success, Wilton immediately made Barnum's top offer—$150,000 guarantee for 150 concerts. It was a staggering amount, many millions in today's money; no offer like it had ever been heard of before. Jenny later said that the reason she accepted was that the picture on Barnum's stationery showing his mansion with its gilded minarets and sparkling spires conveyed to her the manner of man he must be. To others she confessed that the money would allow her to free herself from performing in operas, which she detested, and accomplish her life's dream as well—to endow a music school "for poor, lost children" in her native country. To her best friend Jenny wrote, "I have decided to go to America. The offer from there was very brilliant, and everything was arranged so nicely, that I would have been wrong in declining it." Chevalier Wikoff, who had so successfully managed Fanny Elssler's American tour eight years earlier and had been trying to engineer a repeat performance with Lind, now scoffed at the singer when told of the signed contract. Barnum would "put you in a cage and exhibit you throughout the United States at twenty-five cents per head," he exploded.

On his return to America, Wilton wired Barnum at his recently opened Philadelphia museum using a predetermined code—"mission accomplished!" Soon it was time for Barnum to get the money up—$187,500 was the estimated obligation to Lind and company. It was one thing to be paying salaries and guarantees out of the proceeds as the concerts progressed; it was quite another to have to raise the entire amount before the fact, especially since American financiers took such a dim view of music investments. In large part, Barnum had to go it alone. He gathered together all his cash, sold real estate, mortgaged his mansion and the contents of his museum, and borrowed as much as he could, including $20,000 from the English bank that would be holding the money. Still he came up $5,000 short. But even while struggling with the financing, the confident showman was initiating a Jenny Lind blitz. "Perhaps I may not make any money by this enterprise," Barnum announced in the New York *Commercial Advertiser* on February 22, 1850, "but I assure you that if I knew I should not make a farthing profit, I would ratify the engagement, so anxious am I that the United States should be visited by a lady whose vocal powers have never been approached by any other human being, and whose character is charity, simplicity, and goodness personified." In those simple phrases Barnum had struck the keynote of the message he would hammer into the American psyche over the months to come—a message that moved an old minister friend to sit down and write Barnum a check for the whole $5,000 he still needed.

The cocky, confidant showman appears ready for anything in this 1851 daguerreotype, taken the very year of the Jenny Lind tour.

What Barnum Didn't Know About the Swedish Nightingale

This is how Jenny Lind looked in her early 20s, when she had already become the rage of Europe.

t wouldn't be easy, Barnum knew from the start. Jenny Lind was an unknown quantity in the United States; therefore, the manner in which she was brought before the American public would be all-important. Barnum mused on the potential pitfalls. "It was possible, I knew, that circumstances might occur which would make the enterprise disastrous. 'The public' is a very strange animal, and although a good knowledge of human nature will generally lead a caterer of amusement to hit the people right, they are fickle, and ofttimes perverse. A slight misstep in the management of a public entertainment, frequently wrecks the most promising enterprise."

Although Barnum didn't know it, Jenny Lind herself possessed a host of personal attributes which might easily lead to the wreckage of his enterprise. Her childhood had been devastating. Born in 1820 in Stockholm, Jenny was the illegitimate child of a bitter divorcée named Anna Marie Fallborg. To avoid public humiliation, she kept her pregnancy hidden, and Jenny was born in secrecy, out of town, and taken under cover to the home of distant cousins in the country. The child's aptitude for music was spotted early. Fiddling on a piano at four, she was able to duplicate the fanfare of a marching band she had heard. "I felt the music in my fingers," little Jenny said. Forced to reclaim her baby, Jenny's mother now answered the ad of a childless couple looking for a youngster to care for. At her new home the little piano-player was overheard singing to her cat by the maid of a professional dancer and forthwith "discovered." Admitted to the Royal Theater School, Jenny studied acting, languages, and dance along with piano and voice training. On March 7, 1838, at 17, the shy, unpretentious, straightforward, invariably honest, and unusually talented child "with little, piggy eyes and a big, broad nose," as Jenny described herself, starred in her first important opera and won a standing ovation.

No one alive had ever heard a voice like Jenny's before. Her crystal-clear, melodious soprano tones touched hearts and souls all over Europe, not only for their beauty but for the wistful quality they projected, like a lost bird. Jenny didn't merely sing parts, she lived them. There was something irresistible about her. Even her plain features, her "potato nose," her sallow skin, seemed transformed into sheer radiance as her quicksilver expressions drew now rapture, now pathos from her enchanted audiences.

Jenny was sensitive, spiritual, devout. She abhorred makeup and elaborate costumes, preferring to appear on stage in a simple white dress and without even a touch of rouge. She said she sang for Jesus, for God. Never could she forget the terrible seriousness of life, and thus she preferred sorrow to joy—"there is something exalted about it," she declared. Jenny's greatest attribute, after her voice, was her generosity. Feeling it her duty to use her God-given talent to help those less fortunate, she sang quantities of benefits and gave liberally out of her purses to innumerable charities. It was this unselfish, saintly quality of hers, fused with her peerless singing, that Barnum felt would captivate the American public. What matter if Jenny hated thanking people, disliked staying at a table after she had finished eating, cringed at too much attention, wished she were not a celebrity, was wracked with headaches and rheumatism, plugged her ears with wool stoppers at night "to shut out the noises of the world"? Barnum would come to know her quirks and learn how to deal with them. That was his business.

The great Danish children's-book author Hans Christian Andersen pursued his "Ugly Duckling" for years, but Jenny insisted on treating him like a brother.

Fifteen years Jenny's senior, the great Danish children's writer Hans Christian Andersen was madly in love with her. Jenny, curiously indifferent to him, would not take him seriously. He wrote stories about her and for her—"The Ugly Duckling," "The Emperor's Nightingale." She paid little attention. He traveled to see her one Christmas Eve; she left him alone and went out with others. In turn, her own attempts at love failed. Men she was drawn to inexplicably disappeared from the scene when things got serious. Almost manic in her moods, she believed herself to be the best, yet would never say so out loud. For years she had been frightened of appearing in England, and had almost fled the country before her first performance in London, attended by the Queen.

As she prepared to depart for America and for Barnum, Jenny was approached by Queen Victoria, who was by now her friend, and presented with a Pekingese lapdog. Not only at Liverpool, where she set sail, but all along the coast to the sea, hundreds of thousands bid the Swedish Nightingale goodbye. Snagging her was a great triumph for Barnum, but it might take a consummate student of human nature, a genius of tact and courtesy and generosity, to deal with this driven, fearful, complex artist who would ten days later take America by storm.

Months of Publicity and Preparation Begin to Pay Off

On September 1, 1850, the huge, new steamship *Atlantic*, completing its first crossing, slowed its paddles as it passed Castle Garden and approached the docking area at the foot of Canal Street, near the Hoboken Ferry Terminal. From her perch atop the forward cabin, Jenny Lind saw a forest of people, 30–40,000 of them, all awaiting her. Barnum had figured that if the ship was not delayed its arrival would come on a Sunday morning and, if his publicity campaign had worked, the whole city would turn out in its Sunday best. As usual, he was right. Every wharf, every window, every rooftop, every spar and mast, every stretch of rigging along the waterfront was crawling— "a landscape of humanity," one reporter described it—and the harbor was aswarm with small boats. In case the natural enthusiasm for the occasion turned out to be insufficient, Barnum had provided a small army of his men scattered through the crowd, each dressed in a black suit and carrying a bunch of red roses, their challenge being to keep the hysteria high. "Welcome Jenny Lind! Welcome to America!" claimed floral letters set above an evergreen arch. Once down the gangplank and headed for Barnum's carriage, Jenny was almost trampled in the crush. Over 200 bouquets were thrust through the carriage windows, drowning those inside with perfume and petals, as Barnum, at the driver's seat, himself guided his matched bays toward the Irving House, where he had reserved the most elegant quarters in the city. No one had to know that halfway across the ocean Jenny had got cold feet and begged to be taken home.

Twenty thousand took up vigil around the hotel. Afternoon turned to dusk, night descended, still the crowds increased, hoping to catch a glimpse of the Nightingale. At midnight, escorted by 300 firemen in red shirts, each with a torch held high, 200 singers of the Musical Fund Society serenaded Jenny, who now had appeared on her Bridal Suite balcony to listen to the strains of "Hail Columbia" and "Yankee Doodle" from below.

None of this had just happened on its own. Months of carefully conceived preparation on Barnum's part was coming to a head. Numerous newspapermen had been signed on to help tell the Jenny Lind story. Puffs had been planted and paid advertisements written and scheduled. Dignitaries had been visited to make sure the arrival would get special attention. Reviews from abroad had been pushed into print. In fact, at Barnum's request, Jenny had given a final recital in Liverpool just before sailing, and newsmen, hired by the showman's agents, had written glowing reports which had already arrived and made their way into the New York papers. Jenny's superlative voice was now almost taken for granted; it was her beauty of spirit that Barnum emphasized. "She would be adored," cried he, "if she had the voice of a crow." In order to engage the public, Barnum had initiated the Jenny Lind Prize Song Contest, with $200 to the winning ode, which would be set to music. A letter, supposedly from the tour's musical director but actually penned by Barnum, promised that at her opening recital Jenny would

Well before Jenny Lind arrived in New York, scores of publications about her began mysteriously blossoming in America. Most painted a blissful childhood, omitting the reasons why Jenny actively hated her mother even though she supported her and cried at her death.

Jenny had stipulated that Julius Benedict be her musical director or Barnum wouldn't get her. A pianist and composer as well as an accomplished conductor, and a calming influence, Benedict proved he was worth the $25,000 Barnum agreed to pay him for the tour.

sing the winning song. Seven hundred and fifty-three entries came in from all over the country as a news story each day recorded the progress of the judges. In the beginning of September 1850, there was only one subject to talk about in New York City and that was the Swedish Nightingale. Admiring his five-foot-five-inch treasure with the tiny waist and large heart, Barnum figured it would not be long before a new respect would be shown him by a public that had heretofore believed his capacities did not extend "beyond the power to exhibit a stuffed monkey-skin or a dead mermaid."

Under Jenny's Spell Even the Mighty Fall

John Genin, the hatter, was secretly urged by the showman to bid high in the Jenny Lind ticket auction. He did and became an instant celebrity. All over the country people soon were looking into their hats to see if by any chance they were lucky enough to be wearing "a Genin."

After the Lind tour, traffic on Broadway around Barnum's was so heavy a pedestrian bridge was erected. Known as "Genin's Bridge" after the now famous hatter, it brought customers safely to the east side of Broadway, to delight themselves inside the great museum or upgrade their chapeaux next door.

When, before, was a foreign singer the only theme among travelers and baggage porters, ladies and loafers, Irishmen and 'colored folks', rowdies and the respectable rich?" asked Nathaniel Parker Willis, one of the most perceptive recorders of the American scene. No one could stop talking about this rare princess from Sweden and speculating on what superlatives her first concert would provoke. To her hotel came a steady stream of merchants bearing gifts from their shops. Already, unauthorized Jenny Lind items were becoming the best sellers in the city—bonnets, gloves, shawls, dresses, handkerchiefs, earrings, cigars, snuffboxes, fishing flies, poker chips, a dahlia, a muskmelon, a gooseberry, paper dolls, a sewing machine, combs, mirrors, needles, chewing gum, cakes, a pudding, various meats, drinks, fabric, furniture, a bedstead, even a piano, a stove, and a buggy. Throngs gathered wherever she went, even though Jenny kept her face veiled in a vain attempt at anonymity. A single note had not yet been trilled, but nevertheless the people were dazzled by this jewel in their midst, unaware that much of her sparkle radiated from the deft work of Barnum, who, magnanimously, had already torn up his original contract with Jenny and offered to pay her not only $1,000 per performance, as promised but, after taking out $5,500 for expenses and his services, half of the profits as well. "No one can imagine the amount of head-work and hand-work I performed during the first four weeks," Barnum later wrote, "and little did the public see of the hand that indirectly pulled at their heart-strings, preparatory to a relaxation of their purse-strings." Planted stories were no longer necessary; the newspapers were wild for any scrap of Jenny news and had assigned special reporters to cover her every move.

Barnum still had work to do. First, a location had to be chosen for the opening concert. With Jenny's and her musical director's input obtained, Castle Garden was settled on, a gigantic auditorium set out in the water at the foot of the city and reached from Battery Park by a bridge. Next came the auctioning of tickets, a trick Barnum had learned in New Orleans almost a decade earlier from Fanny Elssler's manager, Henry Wikoff. Four thousand people turned out to pay a shilling apiece for the privilege of watching the bidding for the very first ticket, which was won by a hatter named John Genin whose store was situated a door away from Barnum's museum. At the showman's urging, Genin outbid his rivals, plunked down $225, and instantly became a national celebrity. That was small pickings compared with the $625 an obscure singer would put up in Boston (it made his career), the $650 paid out by a Providence businessman (he reaped his rewards without even bothering to attend the concert), or the $625 a Philadelphia daguerreotypist felt would improve his picture business (it did).

On the night of September 11, the first of six stunningly successful New York concerts was held. At the finish, Barnum himself was given three cheers and called to the stage, where he delivered a speech in which he put

A precious ticket to
a Jenny Lind concert.

After various halls around the city were visited and their acoustics tested, Castle Garden, a former fort that could hold 10,000, was chosen for the first Lind concerts. Here a stereo card shows the site in duplicate.

At the finish of opening night in Castle Garden (above), Barnum announced that Jenny's entire evening's take would be donated to charity. Just as he had planned, soon it was almost impossible to separate the angelic qualities of the Nightingale's voice from her generosity. Reviewers began dizzily writing of Jenny's warblings as things "which she spins out from her throat like the attenuated fiber from the silkworm, dying away so sweetly and so gradually, till it seems melting into the song of the seraphim and is lost in eternity."

forth his own new identity. "Ladies and Gentlemen," he began, "I have but one favor to ask of you—and that is, that in the presence of that angel (pointing to . . . Jenny Lind . . .) I may be allowed to sink . . . into utter insignificance. . . . Where is Barnum? . . . Barnum is nowhere!" And then he proceeded to announce that the star's entire earnings for the night—the unheard-of sum of $10,000, ten times what she would have made for a concert in Europe—would be donated to charity. And the top gift was to go to the working classes' favorite cause, the Fireman's Fund. It was a brilliant move, in a city in which working-class people and the elite were increasingly at odds. "The noble gratuity to the fireman," commented New York's aristocratic diarist and former mayor Philip Hone, "binds to her the support and affection of the red-shirted gentlemen. . . . New York is conquered; a hostile army or fleet could not effect a conquest so complete."

Requests and offers for Jenny to sing came in from all over the country, and a tour route was eventually put together. In a series of concerts stretching over the first nine months, it would take the Jenny Lind entourage north to Boston and Providence, south to Philadelphia, back to New York for 15 more performances in America's principal city, thence south again to Baltimore, Washington, and Richmond. A southern swing would include Charleston, Havana, and New Orleans, and, among other cities, St. Louis, Louisville, and Cincinnati would point the group back home. Competent advance men would stream out ahead of the party, secure the concert halls and hotel accommodations, oversee ticket sales, and make sure the local papers were bursting with Lind stories and the city was telegraphed Jenny's arrival time so there would always be huge crowds to greet the grand lady.

In the East, at least, men attending the concerts outnumbered women ten to one, for it was male plumage that was most acutely agitated by the Nightingale. Neither age nor reputation seemed a deterrent. Doddering old Henry Clay, and Daniel Webster himself, led a long line of admiring American leaders to her door.

The tour was a staggering triumph for Barnum. All along the way he was the consummate, controlled businessman, always generous, good-humored, and fair, as well as the perfect host, overlooking nothing to make his guest's journey enjoyable and less taxing. Sometimes Jenny was sweet and outgoing. At Christmas she showered the troupe with gifts. Once, much to his embarrassment, she made Barnum dance with her. They even tossed a ball back and forth together. But as the tour progressed, Jenny was growing increasingly distrustful of her mentor. Lawyers she hired to represent her hounded him. Her advisers kept telling her how much money he was making off her efforts and counseled her to break the contract and manage herself. "Humbug" was a word Jenny had come to use in America to describe anything false or overblown she disliked. And here, at her side and running the show, was the self-proclaimed Prince of Humbugs himself.

President Millard Fillmore called on Jenny at Willard's Hotel in Washington, found her out, and left his card.

General Winfield Scott had an extended visit with Jenny.

Henry Clay received three cheers at the theater before the grand old statesman stopped to see Jenny the next day.

Henry Wadsworth Longfellow attended a Boston concert and visited the star at the Revere House.

Daniel Webster (above) saw Jenny in Boston, New York, and Washington and was deeply affected (right).

Editor and poet Nathaniel Parker Willis kept a close eye on Daniel Webster during a Jenny Lind performance.

"We had listened with our eyes upon him. . . . The tone sped and lessened, and Webster's broad chest grew erect and expanded. Still on went the entrancing sound . . . and forward leaned the aroused statesman, with his hand clasped over the balustrade, his head raised to its fullest lift above his shoulders, and the luminous caverns of his eyes opened wide upon the still lips of the singer. The note died . . . but Webster sat motionless. The breathless stillness was broken by a tumult of applause, and the hand that was over the gallery moved up and down upon the cushion with unconscious assent, but the spell was yet on him. He slowly leaned back, with his eyes still fixed on the singer, and, suddenly observing that she had turned to him after curtsying to the audience, and was repeating her acknowledgments unmistakably to himself, he rose to his feet and bowed to her, with the grace and stateliness of the monarch that he is. It was not much to see, perhaps—neither does the culmination of a planet differ, very distinguishably, from the twinkle of a lamp—but we congratulated Jenny Lind, with our first thought, after it, at what is perhaps her best single triumph on this side the water, the sounding of America's deepest mind with her plummet of enchantment."

Washington Irving came all the way down from his Hudson Valley home to hear Jenny and was filled with admiration.

"I cannot say, however, how much of my admiration goes to her singing, how much to herself. As a singer, she appears to me of the first order; as a specimen of womankind, a little more. She is enough to counterbalance, of herself, all the evil that the world is threatened with by the great convention of women. So God save Jenny Lind!"

Holding Spellbound City After City

In Baltimore (left) 2,000 greeted Jenny on Canton Avenue, and when she accidentally dropped her shawl, it was whisked up and torn to shreds for souvenirs. On Sunday, at church, Barnum's 20-year-old daughter, Caroline, was mistaken for Jenny; strangely enough, although her voice was mediocre, Caroline's singing of the hymns that day was highly praised. The four concerts in Baltimore grossed $32,000, and when the mayor asked the songstress to entertain the children of the city, she arranged a free, fifth concert and held thousands of youngsters spellbound, then made them sing "The Star-Spangled Banner" in response.

The party sailed into Havana (left), but Cuba's was the only audience not won over before Jenny took the stage. At her appearance, though 300 clapped, six times that number hissed. Jenny summoned all her magic and by the end of the evening had won the Cubans over completely. Later, Barnum described the only truly emotional incident between the showman and his star on the entire tour. "When I witnessed her triumph, I could not restrain the tears of joy that rolled down my cheeks; and rushing through a private box, I reached the stage just as she was withdrawing after the fifth encore. 'God bless you, Jenny, you have settled them!' I exclaimed. 'Are you satisfied?' said she, throwing her arms around my neck. She, too, was crying with joy, and never before did she look so beautiful in my eyes as on that evening."

As he had so often during the long tour, in St. Louis (right) Barnum gave one of his enjoyable and persuasive temperance lectures and even managed to snag the famous comedian Sol Smith into signing the pledge. Five concerts in ten days were planned for spacious Wyman's Hall, but Jenny did not always have such imposing surroundings in which to sing in the West. In fact, the structure that would hold the most customers at the next stop, in Nashville, Tennessee, was a tobacco warehouse. This would never do, so the little Adelphi Theater was selected and work to enlarge it begun. Unfortunately, when Jenny took the stage, the work was not completed, and gaping holes in the walls let the wind whistle through. It was still far superior to the open-sided, pork-house shed that awaited the tour in Madison, Indiana.

For the touring company, March 1851 turned to April in Nashville (right), the site of two concerts and a flurry of Barnum's practical jokes to celebrate April Fool's Day. Having obtained a pile of blank telegraph forms and envelopes, Barnum sent messages to just about everybody in the company. Daughter Caroline was informed that her mother, who had declined the trip, was awaiting her at the next stop, along with Caroline's beloved aunt Minerva, Barnum's sister. Many clerks and musicians received lucrative job offers from banks and theaters back home. One expectant father got the unwelcome message that his wife had had twins. And, believe it or not, Barnum's chief agent and advance man heard from his "father" that the family village had burned down and his house was in ashes. It was a cruel practical joke reminiscent of Grandfather Phineas Taylor.

Disagreements and Intrigue Cut the Tour Short

As an offshoot of the Jenny Lind tour, female performers from all over began approaching Barnum in hopes he might engineer similar success for them. One artist he avoided, though, was the notorious European dancer Lola Montez, whose latest, well-publicized affair with the King of Bavaria was sure to make her box-office fireworks in America but at the same time stigmatize whoever promoted her. "Lola if rightly managed will draw immensely," Barnum wrote, "but I am not the man for her."

n Cincinnati, frustrated ticket seekers provoked a near riot and police had to fire over their heads to dispel them. The incident was upsetting to Jenny, whose nerves were always frayed by admission mix-ups and overblown prices. She had grown to despise the ticket auctions, believing Barnum was skinning the public in her name. After Cincinnati, it was on to Wheeling for a concert in a church, and then Pittsburgh, where drunken factory workers frightened Jenny and caused her to flee the city. Back in New York in early May 1851, a new series of 14 concerts met with enormous success, but the tour, only halfway through its schedule, had taken its toll on the principals. Barnum and Jenny were still painstakingly polite to one another, but oh so different. He was the eternal optimist, the genial, fast-talking, flagrant hawker. She was the pampered pet of Europe, publicly angelic but privately thin-skinned, quick-tempered, stubborn, and embarrassed by the very art she served. With her New York lawyer back in the picture and her secretary whipping up intrigue, even Barnum had begun to lose patience. Jenny now had a new accompanist, Otto Goldschmidt, whom she had summoned from Germany, and even though his solo numbers put audiences to sleep, she liked the 21-year-old and was determined to give him star billing and make audiences applaud him. Jenny's anxiety over being, as she saw it, wrapped in circus tinsel and exhibited like a trained seal was not helped when Barnum persuaded his singer to watch a procession of bandwagons, human curiosities, and wild animals—including ten elephants—come parading up Broadway. It was a celebration touching off Barnum's long-planned "Asiatic Caravan, Museum and Menagerie," a traveling version of his museum, which could have easily caused Jenny to envision herself right smack inside that rolling lion's cage. Prompted by her advisers, Jenny decided to terminate the partnership two-thirds of the way through her contract, after the 100th performance, even though she had to pay Barnum a penalty fee of $25,000. But an occurrence in Philadelphia made the parting of ways happen even sooner. Barnum had booked for Jenny a hall that had recently housed an equestrian show. Even though it had been thoroughly cleaned and transformed into a respectable-smelling opera house, the very idea offended the Lind camp. Fed up with criticism, Barnum decided to end it all right there and then, following the 95th concert. After all, he had grossed $712,000 in less than a year, and even after paying Jenny her share of more than $175,000 and covering all the expenses, he would be walking away with a fortune. During the year, Nathaniel Parker Willis had speculated in print on what a marvelous, dynamic, many-sided superman would be required when Jenny someday decided to marry. He was wrong. Early in 1852, in Boston, Jenny wedded an unassuming man almost ten years her junior—none other than Otto Goldschmidt, the prosaic German pianist she had recently tried to promote.

Long worshipped as a single woman, Jenny Lind possessed the allure of a virginal saint or some kind of unattainable wild bird. When she proceeded to marry her pianist, Otto Goldschmidt, however, her appeal quickly dissipated. "The Nightingale is mated," summed up one Boston newspaper. "The bird is caged; there is no Jenny Lind now—she's a goner!" Not for Barnum. Even though there were some unpleasant memories, to the end of his life he treasured Jenny's autograph, hung her picture in each of his homes, and kept a marble bust of her as one of his prize possessions; years later, he was still referring to her as "the divine Jenny."

By 1850, in order to greatly expand his lecture room and museum, Barnum had purchased the Chemical Bank building directly to his south, and raised its roofs to meet his own. He had hoped to push on farther all the way to Fulton Street, except that the savvy John Genin, who knew well the advantage of a proximity to Barnum's, had refused to sell his prosperous hat-company location. In this 1851 lithograph it can be seen how Barnum's activities were concentrated on his four upper floors, with his ground-level entrance flanked by stores selling cheap books and bank notes and clothing. Clearly visible, on Ann Street, is the little barber shop owned by J. M. Grant that Barnum dubbed "Philosopher's Hall" because of the group of friends who met there regularly to chat. Directly in front of Barnum's newly remodeled front entrance can be seen the tiny carriage and ponies belonging to Tom Thumb. And visible between Barnum's decorated windows are the oval medallions that helped turn the museum's exterior, Barnum thought, into a "great, pictorial magazine."

A New Emphasis on Theater Helps Modernize the Museum

If the Lind tour demonstrated Barnum's desire in the 1850s to be taken much more seriously, especially by the growing middle classes, so did his increasing emphasis upon legitimate theater at his museum. As usual, before he could make it all succeed, there was a battle to be fought.

For decades, under the influence of a puritanical clergy, American society had remained deeply suspicious of the theater. One early pamphlet claimed that the Richmond Theater fire of 1812, killing 70 persons and maiming hundreds more, was a judgment of God. "Who would be willing to close the career of mortality in the very act of displeasing his maker?" the harsh pamphleteer warned. "Who in a theater would be content to give up the ghost?" Henry Ward Beecher, following in his father's strict footsteps, called theater "an expiring evil," warning young men to avoid it like plague, along with card-playing, boxing, the circus, and female vocalists.

Old Knickerbocker New York had shown a love for the theater back in the early parts of the century, but by the 1840s obedient, churchgoing people were staying away from it in droves, leaving the theaters attended increasingly by ruffians, the high galleries frequented by prostitutes and their clients, and the lower floors, or "pits," filled with hooting, spitting, vulgar mobs. "The place was pervaded by evil smells," wrote one describer of New York's pre-eminent theater, the Park, situated almost adjacent to Barnum's. "[N]ot uncommonly in the midst of a performance, rats ran out of the holes in the floor and across into the orchestra." With ticket prices at all-time lows, theater managers depended upon sale of liquor at their refreshment stands to make up for lost profits. Prostitutes, who could lure customers to buy drinks at these bars, were provided their own special entrances to the top galleries, or "third tiers." Barnum's tremendous challenge, and ultimately his great contribution, was to reclaim the theater from both puritanism and vice, and to offer it up anew as a reputable, middle-class institution.

To accomplish this, he made sure first that his stage seemed nothing like any ordinary theater. Naming it his "Moral Lecture Room," and claiming that "not a word" would be uttered here "offensive to morals or religion," nor "a thought . . . breathed calculated to bring a blush upon the cheek of modesty," Barnum offered drama to the American public without their even knowing it. Theater lovers, like William Northall, considered Barnum hypocritical for pretending his lecture hall was not a theater. "If the stage be distasteful," Northall wrote in 1851, "why not eschew it altogether, not wheedle the public into his trap and oblige them to patch up their damaged consciences with the paltry excuse that it was the Museum and not the play they went to see?" Northall objected as well to what he called Barnum's "miserable trick" of calling his plays "moral affairs," as if "every well-written piece did not teach a moral lesson."

From the very beginning, Barnum worked hard to modernize his hall, punching open the third-floor ceiling of the museum in the early 1840s to pro-

An enlarged carte de visite of the innovative modernizer.

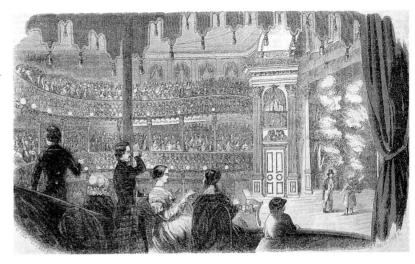

By the time this 1853 engraving was made, Barnum's "Moral Lecture Room" was one of New York City's largest and most modern theaters. Barnum kept a private box here and loaned it out when not using it himself. Above the stage, amid rich draperies, was soon erected the theater's official motto: "We study to please."

duce an open, two-story space with full balcony and box seating, and at the same time adding chandelier, gold-leaf moldings, and giant wall mirrors, all to create what he called a "sensation." Then, in 1847, he made further enlargements of the parquet, adding additional front seating and installing damask upholstery throughout. By 1850, with stage productions being stressed more and more, the newly ventilated theater could seat 3,000 and rose to three full stories. Beautifully wallpapered, with new embellishments to the proscenium and a novel drop curtain painted with scenes of the Capitol in Washington, it boasted a full orchestra, a $1,000 grand piano, and its own full-time staff, including a set designer, a machinist, and a costumer. From the beginning, Barnum worked hard to reach out beyond the typically all-male theater audiences of the day. Focusing on bringing in women and couples and families to his new stage, by the late 1840s he had invented the nation's first matinees. Determined to build on his growing good reputation, Barnum employed a staff of plainclothes detectives whose job was to turn out into the street "every person of either sex whose actions indicated loose habits." Furthering the decorum and family atmosphere, the teetotaling Barnum permitted no bar or intoxicating drinks anywhere in the house. "I would not even allow my visitors to go out to drink and return again without paying the second time," he bragged, pointing to the free ice water he made available by way of compensation on every floor of the museum. To inaugurate his refurbished lecture room in June 1850, Barnum opened with a play entitled *The Drunkard*, devised to both entertain and "at the same time minister to a refined and elevated popular taste." The play's hero was made up to resemble Barnum, and following performances Barnum himself would sometimes walk out and address the audience on the theme of temperance. And after each performance of *The Drunkard*, anyone wishing to was urged to go the box office and sign the teetotal pledge. When word got around, wives began bringing their wayward husbands to the show and practically dragging them back to the box office after the final curtain.

Francis Courtney Wemyss directed Barnum's new acting company at the opening of the 1850s.

Actor-playwright Harry Watkins assumed the management of the museum's theatrical enterprises in 1857.

The Museum Forms a Permanent Acting Troup

William B. Harrison first appeared on Barnum's stage in 1844. An improvisator and comic vocalist who accompanied himself on the violin, in 1850 he joined the newly formed lecture-room company under F. C. Wemyss.

George W. Thompson opened his own dramatic agency in New York after appearing on stage at Barnum's in the late 1850s.

Barnum had assembled for the first time his own permanent acting company, his resident ensemble. Under the direction of veteran English actor Francis Courtney Wemyss, the stock company included among its talented performers George H. Clarke, W. B. Harrison, F. H. Hadaway, and Sylvester Bleeker, with Corson W. Clarke signing up as stage manager in the spring of 1850. Immensely successful that first year, as well as cost-effective, this new ensemble led directly to Barnum's huge expansion of the lecture room in time for the 1850–51 season. Over the course of the decade, Barnum's troupe would serve as the backbone for a constantly shifting array of melodramas and comedies and farces that graced the museum stage, with new additions arriving to the team each year, including John Bridgeman and George Thompson and Mrs. J. J. Prior. By 1853, on top of a theater staff that included stage designers, property men, prompters, and musicians, Barnum's permanent acting company numbered 36—20 men and 16 women—making it one of the largest theater staffs in the city. Increasingly, Barnum began to lure to his stage some of the country's top actors, especially in the early phases of their careers, people like E. A. Sothern, Emily Mestayer, and Caroline Chapman. Museum ads spotlighted not only stars but entire casts as well, whole productions and crews. Actors and stagehands alike said they were paid better by Barnum than they were elsewhere, and this helped build up loyalty. His shows now ran twice daily. On holidays they were continuous (a Barnum innovation), with actors seen arriving at the museum at 7:00 a.m. carrying their own tin dinner pails, in order to stay all day. Setting the tone for all shows to come, Barnum's inaugural play, *The Drunkard*, became the first New York production ever to run over 100 successive performances. Other plays soon to follow included *Beauty and the Beast, Romeo and Juliet, Joseph and His Brethren, The Vicar of Wakefield, Blue Beard,* and, in 1853, *Uncle Tom's Cabin.* Just as Barnum was famous for excising unsavory passages out of Shakespeare, here, too, with Harriet Beecher Stowe's classic, the showman insisted on a "family-style," Barnumized adaptation. He found it in a watered-down, nonconfrontational script written by the playwright H. J. Conway and currently playing at the Boston Museum. Gone from it was any of Stowe's passionate attack upon the institution of slavery; black characters, such as Uncle Tom, were presented here as minstrel-like comics; even the novel's tragic finale had been transformed into a happy ending. When Stowe had attended a production of Conway's *Uncle Tom* in Boston, she had walked out in disgust; now, at Barnum's, the usually favorable New York *Tribune* condemned the play as "mere burlesque." To make up for the loss of Stowe's powerful prophetic energy, Barnum turned instead to brilliant stage effects and scenery. In Act Two he amazed audiences with a grand panoramic view of the Mississippi River under moonlight, and a steamboat moving across the stage belching real smoke. He called it "the sumptuous version of *Uncle Tom*"; competitors at the nearby National Theater called it "the hum-

Sylvester Bleeker broke in at Barnum's as a prompter before transforming into a versatile actor, a writer of farces, the museum's stage manager, and, finally, the showman's most trusted agent.

Corson W. Clarke was one of Barnum's finest actors, then stage manager, then, in 1852, director of amusements.

Thomas H. Hadaway began his career as a strolling actor in England, worked on the Philadelphia stage for years, and finally joined Barnum's in New York in 1849, to stay with him for over a decade.

By far Barnum's most prominent resident actor in the late 1850s, Mrs. James J. Prior opened as Amy in a March 1858 rendition of *Harvest Home.*

bug version." But despite all the controversy, Barnum's *Uncle Tom* drew immense crowds, proving he understood his middle-class, family audiences well, and knew how to offer them fare that satisfied. By 1853, Barnum's had become so admired for this nonelitist quality that *Putnam's Monthly Magazine* actually proposed him as manager of New York's Opera, because "he comprehends that . . . the opera need not necessarily be the luxury of the few but the recreation of the many." To the end, Barnum's theater remained strictly "popular," capable of excellence at times, but more regularly offering up melodrama and comedies for the middle classes. If he was ever tempted to run more serious dramas, friends like Horace Greeley would remind him that audiences came to his museum chiefly to laugh, and that Barnum's productions were "most successful when most ridiculous." "I myself relished a higher grade of amusements," Barnum apologized at one point to his readers, meaning he preferred opera and chamber music and lectures to melodrama. "But I," he reminded them, "worked for the million." Designating the nation's drudging work-ethic "the great defect of American civilization," Barnum saw, as almost his sacred calling, the nourishing of the whole spectrum of what he called the "needful and proper relaxations and enjoyments." Not the least of these lay in the pleasures of the theater.

A Never-Ending Search for Rare Beasts and Scary Serpents

Though his zoological exhibits and traveling animal acts were primitive by later standards, including his own, P. T. Barnum was a pioneer in the display of living natural history.

From its earliest years, the American Museum had been known for its collection of mounted zoological specimens, mostly of birds and small mammals. Inheriting his own resident taxidermist, Barnum soon began adding larger and larger animals to the collection—stuffed zebras, lions, grizzly bears, wolves, even huge preserved elephants. But from early on he wanted actual live animals as well. Snakes were an ideal starting place, and Barnum obtained numerous small ones right away. By the late 1840s, he was boasting of a 12-foot-long rattlesnake, "safely confined," he promised, "in a strong iron cage." And by the 1850s, he had discovered anacondas. "All other snakes shrink into mere worms in comparison," he trumpeted, calling attention to the two he now exhibited, one 18½ feet long, the other 35. "These snakes . . . are ravenous and dangerous," reported a newspaperman in 1853, parroting Barnum's press releases. Capable of eating "a good sized dog," the largest "had devoured a woman and a child before it was taken." Their cage placed at the rear of the main, second-floor gallery, Barnum's snakes became a terrific draw.

On the top floor, ever since the mid 1840s, was Barnum's caged "Happy Family," with its constantly changing array of strangely matched animals and birds. Here, too, was Barnum's zoo. In 1846, Barnum purchased, for $3,000, "the only living orang-outang in either England or North America." Calling her Mademoiselle Fanny, after the great ballerina Fanny Elssler, Barnum promoted the animal as a possible missing link. "Its actions, the sound of its voice while laughing and crying, approach as closely as possible to the human species," one paper reported. "Its hands, face and feet are pure white, and possess as soft a skin as any child living."

In 1850, unable to purchase elephants on the world market, Barnum commissioned an expedition to Ceylon under the leadership of Stebbins June and George Nutter. Presented with at least eight Indian elephants, Barnum put together the country's first colossal elephant parade and show, sending them out as a traveling exhibition under the title of "P. T. Barnum's Asiatic Caravan, Museum and Menagerie." With the largest elephant show prior to this being James Raymond's four-elephant team of the 1840s, Barnum's Caravan, with his elephants hitched to an unusual wagon he called the "Car of Juggernaut," was a harbinger of circus days to come.

Barnum's penchant for the "gigantic" and the "first of its kind" continued throughout the 1850s. By mid-October 1853, he had obtained two living giraffes, so unfamiliar to the American public they were known as "cameleopards." In the summer of 1854, he possessed a unique rhinoceros, a one-horned variety billed suggestively as a "Unicorn." And by mid-decade, his greatly expanded menagerie included a den of lions, a royal Bengal tiger, a llama, a leopard, and a large grizzly bear.

Late in the decade, at the beginning of the aquarium craze which struck England and then the U.S., Barnum constructed America's first public aquaria. He called them his "Ocean and River Gardens," and advertised them with colorful drawings, one of which is shown above. Amazed at finding a rainbow array of exotic tropical fish and plants, even such a Barnum adversary as the arrogant yet observant diarist George Templeton Strong had to admit it was all "very curious and beautiful."

In 1853, *Gleason's Pictorial* introduced a pair of Barnum giraffes, Colossus and Cleopatra, to its readers as "cameleopards." To the *Gleason's* writer, the cameleopard's tongue deserved more attention than its neck, being "long, rough, black and pointed," and the animal had the faculty "of forcing it a foot or more out of its mouth, thus to encircle branches that would be otherwise out of its reach." Leased out by Barnum to a traveling circus, one of these great animals later drowned while trying to disembark from a steamship off New Orleans.

Number 9 in Currier's Gallery of Barnum Wonders was "the only living Rhinoceros, or Unicorn, in America." That may have been true in the 1850s, but the very first rhino to grace American shores was exhibited at Peale's Museum in New York City when Barnum was only 16.

A Bearded Lady and a Family of Albinos

In March 1853, Barnum signed a generous contract to show the most heavily bearded woman ever presented before the public, Madame Josephine Cloffulia of Switzerland. Having once lifted the skirts of an English giantess to make sure she was authentic (she wasn't), Barnum submitted Cloffulia to a medical examination to ensure that he was hiring a woman (he was). With her beard left uncut since infancy, turned dark and "virile" since the age of 14, Cloffulia's brown whiskers could now be extended over five inches in length. The Currier & Ives lithograph above shows the 22-year-old bearded woman as she ap-

peared at Barnum's Museum in 1853. Not long afterwards, Josephine was photographed in St. Louis, Missouri, by Thomas M. Easterly. Showing her in the same stage dress and jewelry she had worn on Barnum's stage, Easterly's striking daguerreotype portrait also reveals the tiny brooch she wore containing the portrait of her bearded husband, Monsieur Fortune Cloffulia. Barnum garnered added publicity when Josephine's femininity was once again challenged during a well-publicized lawsuit, secretly instigated by the great showman himself.

Barnum obtained this family of albinos—the Lucasies—in Holland in 1857, while visiting Amsterdam, and brought them to America, where they became one of his most popular exhibits. Billed as of "black Madagascar lineage," the Lucasies had hair, skin, eyebrows, and eyelashes of pure white and it was advertised that their pink eyes stayed wide open when they were asleep. In a letter to his longtime employee Oscar Kohn, Barnum expressed a mounting distress over the albinos, writing that Rudolph Lucasie and family were acting more and more "disagreeable." Showing a firm, even harsh side that came out when he deemed it necessary, Barnum then added, "I will put them in jail if they don't behave." The Currier & Ives lithograph (above) is true in almost every detail to the Mathew Brady photograph on the left, except for the exaggeration of hair length, possibly requested by Barnum himself.

Tempting Contests for Poultry and People

ver since he had run lotteries in Connecticut as a young man, Barnum had known the huge popular appeal of contests. In the mid-1850s, now president of the Fairfield Agricultural Society, he began sponsoring a series of the country's first "national" competitions—flower shows, beauty pageants, dog shows, baby contests, and poultry exhibitions. His National Poultry Show, held first in the winter of 1853, was so successful it became an annual tradition.

In 1855 and 1856, with the help of assistants John Greenwood, Jr., and Henry D. Butler, Barnum introduced his first national beauty pageant, his "Gallery of American Beauty." A thousand contestants, "single or married," were to submit their photographic likenesses for display in the museum, where the visiting public was to do the actual selecting of winners (real names could be withheld). With a $1,000 first prize and more than $4,000 in additional prize money, 100 lucky winners were to have their likenesses painted in oil, and of these the top ten were to be included in an upcoming French publication to be entitled the *World's Book of Beauty*.

For women unable to submit their own pictures to his beauty contest, Barnum offered a list of 14 galleries that would photograph contestants free of charge, including R. Anson's small shop, shown here. Charles Frederick's large business, also seen here, offered a 30-percent discount for the same service.

The most popular of all Barnum's contests were undoubtedly his baby shows, the first one taking place, after months of public notice, on September 11, 1855. Calling it his "angelic display of juvenile humanity," Barnum offered "liberal" prizes (often merely a "diploma" or a cheap brass medal) for what was judged "the finest baby," "the handsomest twins," or, Barnum's favorite, "the fattest baby." During four days, more than 60,000 patrons packed the museum for this contest, streaming in not only from all parts of the city but from far-flung rural areas as well. The museum, for the occasion, was bedecked with a huge transparency studded with infants—babies in arms, babies on sofas, babies wrapped in the American flag. Charity Barnum helped judge this first contest, awarding the prize to one Charles Orlando Scott, and in the process alienating an Irish woman who felt she had been discriminated against because of her poverty. The Barnums soon learned to keep their distance from the "storm of indignation" that routinely broke out among the losers, making sure that all contests were henceforth judged not by themselves but by an impartial committee of women.

Barnum's baby contests (above) were so fraught with maternal emotion that the showman, to avoid criticism, disqualified himself as a judge. One of the winners of Barnum's "fattest baby" award may be pictured here (right). Such individuals were often kept on, to be displayed on stage along with the "freaks."

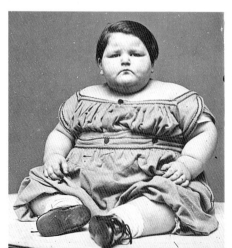

Barnum took his poultry contests seriously, pledging to one proud bird-owner that he would take "every care" with the man's "attractive specimens of the feathered tribe." In a note scratched off during the thick of one of his bird shows, however, with 8,000 chickens gathered on a single floor of the museum, Barnum gasped, "Gods! What a crowing!"

By Nagel and Lewis, this 1855 lithograph titled *Sleighing in New York* captures the sheer excitement of the city's focal point—Broadway at Barnum's. The same year the picture was made, a French actor named Léon Beauvallet visited New York, explored Broadway, and wrote this eyewitness account: "The city resembles nothing so much as a gigantic billboard for a traveling circus. Showmen, in fact, are perfectly at home here. Broadway is swarming with them. Quack doctors, tooth-pullers, trainers of performing dogs, exhibitors of bearded negresses, wild animal trainers . . . It is as if one were walking through an immense village fair. What a hurly-burly! What a din! Shouts and laughter; songs and oaths . . . the noise of carriages; the braying of the trumpets . . . the bells of the mules . . . the carts that collide, the horses that bolt, the people run over, the strollers being robbed, the drunks being knocked about"—all that and more, and then "you will have a very slight idea of the picture New York presents to the stupefied eye of the traveler."

Starting the City's First Pictorial Weekly

On January 1, 1853, New York newsstands carried the premier issue of a lavish pictorial weekly newspaper titled the *Illustrated News*. Owned and operated by P. T. Barnum in conjunction with Henry and Alfred Beach of the New York *Sun*, each a $20,000 investor, it was a bold venture and a fitting rival to *Gleason's Pictorial* of Boston. To oversee the all-important visual aspects of the paper, Barnum hired on a veteran engraver from the *Illustrated London News* and *Gleason's Pictorial* whom the showman had contracted in 1848 to produce an illustrated catalogue for the museum—Frank Leslie. "Our paper will be the only one in this country," Barnum boasted, "that publishes beautiful fresh cuts illustrating the times in which we live." And so the onetime editor of the *Herald of Freedom* re-entered journalism. Throwing out his net to a growing circle of contacts, including Horace Greeley and Charles Dana and William Thackeray, Barnum promised the most exciting, up-to-the-minute news journal in the United States, with "drawings and sketches of everything interesting." The paper's editor, Rufus Griswold, early on gave Barnum troubles, and was soon succeeded by the young writer Charles Godfrey Leland. "Of all the men whom I met in those days," Leland wrote later in one of the most important witnesses to Barnum's character and boyish charm, "Mr. Barnum . . . was by far the honestest and freest from guile or deceit. . . . [He was] kind-hearted and benevolent, and gifted with a sense of fun which was even stronger than his desire for dollars. . . . He was a genius like Rabelais, but one who employed business and humanity for material instead of literature. . . . I have said that I had no assistant; I forgot that I always had Mr. Barnum. . . . I think I see him now, coming smiling in like a harvest moon, big with some new joke, and then we sat down at the desk and 'edited'. How we would sit and . . . admiringly read to one another our beautiful 'good things', the world forgetting, by the world forgot!"

Costing 6 cents an issue, the *Illustrated News* carried engravings by staff member Frank Leslie and others and articles by famous writers on everything from President Pierce to Polish salt-mines, from Japanese art to Harriet Beecher Stowe. By April, Barnum had built up a list of more than 100,000 subscribers, twice that of the New York *Sun*. But when the partners began bickering over Frank Leslie's future position on the paper, Barnum found he could not keep it all going. "I have foolishly got so many thousand irons in the fire," Barnum wrote to a peevish Moses Kimball, "that I don't have time to write anybody." And so, after just 48 issues, the *Illustrated News* closed its presses for good, its engravings and subscription lists sold to *Gleason's Pictorial*, and New York City had to wait another two years for the arrival of a great pictorial weekly in the form of *Frank Leslie's Illustrated Newspaper*. "Many a fortune has slipped through a man's fingers because he was engaging in too many occupations at a time," Barnum later ruminated by way of advice to young entrepreneurs. "Engage in one kind of business only and stick to it faithfully until you succeed." For Barnum, who sometimes ignored his own advice, that "one business" meant show business, not publishing.

Charles Godfrey Leland was the second editor of Barnum's *Illustrated News*. He succeeded the irascible Dr. Rufus Griswold, whom Barnum fired after he demanded complete control of the editorial columns, "and that is what of course we who pay will give to no man," Barnum commented. Although the good-natured, scholarly giant who loved to eat and drink and write got along famously with the showman, Leland, too, was fired.

A co-owner of the New York *Sun*, Henry D. Beach, and his brother Alfred Ely Beach, were Barnum's partners in his second venture into journalism. Their conception of an editor for their publication was, in Barnum's words, "a good writer and compiler for about $1,000 or $1500 per year."

Like all editors of pictorial news, Barnum had to put up with the displeasure of important people who did not like the way their published pictures looked. To Edward Everett, who had recently been elected to the Senate, Barnum wrote, "I assure you I felt quite ashamed of your likeness as it appeared in our 'Illustrated.' We shall pretty soon make a good one & apologize for the other."

ILLUSTRATED NEWS.

No. 1. Vol. I.   NEW YORK, SATURDAY, JANUARY 1, 1853.   PRICE SIX CENTS.

BIRTH OF THE NEW YEAR.—A DESIGN BY THOMAS.

No. 1 Vol. I of the *Illustrated News*, published on January 1, 1853, featured this classical depiction of the "Old Year" signing out in the shadow of Father Time, as the "New Year" is borne in. To gather material for his pages, Barnum got in touch with many of the writers and newsmen he had met over the years. He asked Bayard Taylor, who three years earlier had won first prize in Barnum's Jenny Lind song contest, for "drawings of all important and interesting *things* and *events*, & especially when connected with the *Japan expedition*."

A Controversial Book About Himself, by Himself

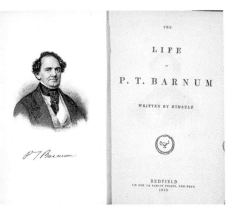

The showman's autobiography, *The Life of P. T. Barnum, Written by Himself*, was published in December 1854, but carried an 1855 imprint. Its frontispiece (above) reproduced an engraving of himself, plus his signature.

In early 1854, Barnum accepted the presidency of the already failing Crystal Palace Company, adding his influential name even to admission tickets, like the one here. There was nothing he could do, however, to save the ill-conceived uptown exhibition hall. After its collapse, he wrote his friend Moses Kimball, "I was an ass for having anything to do with the Crystal Palace."

In one sense, he had been preparing for this work for years, putting out sketches of his life in miniature inside most of his museum pamphlets and even printing them on the backs of Jenny Lind programs. Relying in part upon these biographies-in-outline, and upon such earlier writings as his 100 New York *Atlas* articles from the 1840s, in the summer of 1854 Barnum retreated to his orange-walled inner sanctum at Iranistan and began work on his memoirs. He began by writing to, among others, Moses Beach at the New York *Sun* for cutouts of his old Joice Heth ads, and to Moses Kimball in Boston for details of their Fejee Mermaid venture. With a reputed 57 publishers vying to bring out his *Life*, Barnum entered into an oral agreement with his old friend Julius Redfield, publisher of Edgar Allan Poe, promising the manuscript by November.

The book was completed in less than four months. Published in mid-December, in time for the holiday market, it became an instant best-seller, with 160,000 copies sold in the first year alone. With his contract specifying a price of $1.50 a book and an author's royalty of 30 percent, Barnum's profits for the year were close to $75,000. Never out of print, going into several new editions over the course of his life, and hawked by agents in his museum and later at special booths inside his circus, the book would eventually sell in excess of a million copies.

He claimed it possessed no real "literary merit." Later, he even said he had written it chiefly to help advertise the museum. But Barnum's *Life* was in fact one of the refreshingly original works of its time, marked by a down-to-earth conversational style, an almost shocking honesty, and an irrepressible spirit of fun. Mark Twain is said to have sat up nights to read the book by lamplight, so taken was he with it. And at least 1,000 favorable reviews appeared, all dutifully collected by Julius Redfield.

But, in shock at its open revelations of humbuggery, a massive negative press also emerged, nowhere more so than in England. "Its dullness, its conceited coarseness, and the disgusting way in which it glories in shameless frauds upon the public, have astonished us," wrote the austere *British Examiner*. "We have not read, for a long time, a more trashy or offensive book than this," blasted *Blackwood's Edinburgh Magazine*, simultaneously published in London and New York. "[It has] inspired us with nothing but sensations of disgust . . . and sincere pity for the wretched man who compiled it. . . ."

He had expected more appreciation. Stung by the *Blackwood's* review in particular, Barnum wrote a plaintive letter to a Universalist Church publication in March, pleading for "acknowledgment that there are some good streaks in me and in my book." Little did he know, worse surprises were yet to come.

Barnum chose this striking portrait by Mathew Brady to use as a calling card.

From Triumphs in Real Estate to Sudden Financial Ruin

A wealthy neighbor, William H. Noble (above in Civil War uniform), was Barnum's partner in a lavish scheme to develop the eastern extremity of Bridgeport into an ideal little manufacturing community. The two built a toll bridge which spanned the Pequonnock River and connected Bridgeport to the suburb of East Bridgeport (below).

Barnum's financial power in 1855 derived not only from his hugely successful book and museum, and from the immense profits of the earlier Tom Thumb and Jenny Lind tours, but increasingly from speculations in real estate. On October 31, 1851, he had entered into partnership with a Bridgeport neighbor, William H. Noble, to develop a thinly settled area just outside of town on the east side of the Pequonnock River. With an initial investment of $20,000, and then tens of thousands more poured into the construction of bridges and docks and factories and houses, by 1854 the two men's 174-acre property was worth more than $1 million, the value of the individual lots having skyrocketed tenfold. As part of his effort to persuade businesses to relocate to "East Bridgeport," Barnum now began making sizable loans to New Haven's huge Jerome Clock Company, whose move there would ensure permanent success to the development. Barnum placed almost reckless trust in this one company and its president, Chauncey Jerome.

By mid-January of 1856, the truth was out—the Jerome Clock Company was bankrupt and going under, its president claiming that Barnum had ruined him. In fact, Barnum, who had guaranteed over $450,000 in clock-company notes, was being sucked down alongside of Jerome. "My impulsiveness and confiding disposition in my fellow men have proved my ruin," Barnum lamented, as the full extent of his bankruptcy became evident. "It is the most sorry termination of my active life."

Leaving Iranistan forever and moving back to the city into a rented house on West 8th Street, Barnum found himself swept into a grueling court bankruptcy proceeding and a public humiliation. Men who had never liked Barnum, such as Thomas Carlyle and Ralph Waldo Emerson, rejoiced,

Emerson calling Barnum's ruin "the gods visible again." Many members of the press, delighting in the destruction of what they called his "ill-gotten gains," moved in like jackals, none more so than Barnum's old adversary James Gordon Bennett. "The author of that book glorifying himself as a millionaire . . . is completely crushed out," Bennett wrote with glee in an article titled "The Fall of Barnum." "All the profits of all his Fejee Mermaids, all his wooly horses, Greenland whales, Joice Heths, negroes turning white, Tom Thumbs, and monsters and impostors of all kinds, including the reported $70,000 received by the copyright of that book, are all swept away, Hindoo palace, elephants, and all, by the late invincible showman's remorseless assignees. It is a case eminently adapted to 'point a moral or adorn a tale.' "

Though Barnum had tried to safeguard at least some of his treasure, transferring real-estate holdings to his wife and his brother Philo, and selling the contents of his museum to John Greenwood and Henry Butler for $1.00, clearly he was in danger of serious ruin. "No man who has not passed through similar scenes can fully comprehend the misery which has been crowded into the last few months of my life," he wrote from the Long Island shore, where he had retreated with Charity, whose hypochondria was now acting up with a fury. Stung by the public criticism, castigating himself for a lifelong obsession with money, Barnum consoled himself that at least he had "never used money or position to oppress the poor" or to wrong his "fellow men," or to turn "empty away those whom . . . [he] had the power to assist." The irony was, Barnum pointed out, had he "robbed the widow and plundered the orphan like some of our Wall Street defaulters," he would not have been attacked by the press as viciously as he was being now for having dared not only to be a showman, and a good one, but to tell about it, too.

Whether guilty or not, clock-making tycoon Chauncey Jerome was blamed by Barnum for his sudden bankruptcy. Barnum had tried to assist Jerome's immense New Haven–based company, which in return was supposed to move to East Bridgeport. Undated bank notes for tens of thousands of dollars that Barnum signed to keep the company afloat did him in.

The waterfront of East Bridgeport some years later.

His Little Friend Comes Rushing to the Rescue

On his second trip to Europe, this time as a young man instead of a little boy, the General once again bamboozled the ladies with his antics and his Highland garb (above). To the left, the child with whom Charles Stratton poses with such affection might be his younger brother William Edward, born September 24, 1852. Otherwise— like the photographer, the location, and the precise date of this ambrotype portrait— Tom's companion is unknown.

Barnum still had good and true friends, and they came to his assistance now, literally in droves. Actors and lecturers and theater owners and performers seemed to come out of the woodwork eager to help—Laura Keen, William Niblo, John Gough, William Makepeace Thackeray, even Barnum's old friend Jenny Lind, now retired and living in England. One letter offering help and support was published in a New York paper with over 1,000 signatures, including that of Cornelius Vanderbilt. A Connecticut coalition, headed by the mayor of Bridgeport, offered him an outright cash gift of $50,000. All such offers of charity Barnum gratefully declined, saying he must "extricate" himself from debt by his own efforts or be "humiliated." Of all his old friends, however, no one offered aid more unreservedly or affectionately than did Tom Thumb. On May 12, 1856, writing from Jones' Hotel in Philadelphia, where he was on the start of his own Western tour, a teenaged Charles Stratton wrote the following words to his old colleague. "My Dear Mr. Barnum, I understand your friends, and that means 'all creation,' intend to get up some benefits for your family. Now, my dear sir, just be good enough to remember that I belong to that mighty crowd, and I must have a finger (or at least a 'thumb') in that pie. . . . I am ready to go to New York . . . and remain at Mr. Barnum's service as long as I, in my small way, can be useful. . . ." That summer the two friends fixed on a new European tour. And in late November 1856, having set up arrangements to pay off his debts over time, Barnum sailed forth with Thumb once again for England. Twelve years after Barnum and his "little brick" Tommy had taken the motherland by storm, they would now attempt to do it all over.

In the ambrotype portrait to the left, made by Cleveland photographer William C. North, most likely during Thumb's 1856 cross-country tour, the 18-year-old Charles Stratton poses as Robinson Crusoe. His elegant signature appears beneath it.

General Tom Thumb

GEN. TOM THUMB
In His different Characters.

CITIZEN.   COURT DRESS.   HIGHLAND.

NAPOLEON.   VILLIKINS.   OUR MARY ANN.

CAIN.   SAILOR.   ROMULUS.

Photographed by E. T. Whitney & Co., Norwalk, Conn.

Playing different dress-up roles, Thumb wore a skintight white suit and wielded a club to portray Cain, switched to a spear and a helmet for Romulus. He also dressed up in women's dress for two female roles and did Frederick the Great, Samson, an English fox-hunter, a sailor, and a "dandy." The Norwalk, Connecticut, photographer E. T. Whitney showed nine of the General's roles (above).

Repeating his victorious assault on England 12 years earlier, Tom was again commanded to perform before the Queen and along the way received a salute from a palace guard.

Chastened by Iranistan's Ashes

s determined as he was to look on the bright side of things, Barnum's financial collapse opened up the second great crisis of his life. The first, involving alcohol and pride and an endangered marriage, had led him into the arms of the Temperance Movement. Now, nearly crushed by anguish, he found his problems cried out for even deeper solutions. "I should have been tempted . . . to suicide," Barnum confessed in a candid moment, "if I supposed that my troubles were brought upon me by mere blind chance. I knew that I deserved what I received." Always a religious man, Barnum had intermittently doubted his motives as a showman, despising what he called his own "selfishness." Now his 20-year-long pursuit of wealth seemed like nothing but an empty and despicable waste, a "coining of his brain and blood into gold." But then, almost as if it had happened for the purpose of saving his soul, Barnum's prosperity had been suddenly stripped from him. It was a "chastening," he felt, "just the lesson" which he "most needed." Intended by God, Barnum believed, for his "ultimate benefit," the disaster had come to teach him that there was something "infinitely better than money or position or worldly prosperity." From this point on, Barnum saw the hand of Providence in every aspect of his life, both the good and the ill. It became the secret of his own overarching brand of cheerfulness, as well as a kind of armor against disaster and an anesthesia against heartbreak. "I think I never knew a more heartless man," wrote author J. B. Pond of Barnum in later years, after seeing him fail to react to the accidental death of a female performer. But Pond was wrong; Barnum was not heartless, he was simply numbed by a life philosophy that taught him that nothing evil can ever happen "except for an ultimate good purpose." And so how else could he react but stoically to the great tragedies that would sweep through his life with such regularity?

Leaving Tom Thumb in England in the summer of 1857 to continue his money-making efforts, Barnum returned to the United States to help prepare for the wedding of his daughter Helen. With Iranistan still boarded up and unsold, Helen's marriage to Samuel H. Hurd took place at her sister Caroline's house in Fairfield. Four weeks later, on the night of December 17, 1857, a workman's lighted pipe, accidentally left inside Iranistan's central dome, set fire to the mansion. Within two hours, the building was consumed. Barnum, who was staying at the Astor House in New York, was informed of the loss by his brother Philo, in a telegram. With the calm that would increasingly characterize him in moments of crisis, Barnum pointed out that the loss was not only to his own estate but to the public at large. Worth at least $150,000, but insured only to $28,000, the mansion had long been one of Connecticut's largest tourist attractions. Years later, it would still be remembered, "nearer a palace," wrote *Leslie's* in 1864, "than any building ever erected in this country." As late as 1874, Barnum's friend William H. Noble was still calling it "our showplace," because the people of Bridgeport considered it their own private pride and joy. "It was as original as our friend," recalled Noble; "seen by moonlight, Iranistan was like some delicate tracery of arch and pinnacles." In some ways, Barnum had known he could not keep it forever. He had once almost decided to sell the place and move to a Pennsylvania farm; and in October of 1852, at the time of Caroline's wedding, a fire had already once threatened the building. Now, with the mansion reduced to smoldering rubble, all that would live on was an engraved print of Iranistan that hung on the walls of his museum, a gold ring on which he had had an image of his big house beautifully embossed, and the fancy Iranistan stationery with which he had once lured Jenny Lind to America, and which he would continue to use, selectively, until as late as 1870. When the insurance settlement was finally added to the $50,000 that Barnum obtained from the sale of his grounds, all proceeds went immediately toward paying off his still-standing Jerome clock factory debts.

Since the bankruptcy proceedings, Iranistan had remained empty and boarded up. Now, with the financial picture clearing, there was the possibility for Barnum to move back in. But workmen ordered to spruce up the mansion accidentally burned it down instead. The palace that had symbolized Barnum's success now lay in ashes.

Barnum's Own Silver Tongue Helps Pull Him Through

Barnum spent the closing years of the decade trying to retire the last of his debts. Back in London by July 1858, he rejoined Thumb in his circuit of the provinces, but as the tour turned toward Germany, during the fall, it became clear that his supervision wasn't required, and so Barnum turned to a new idea for fund-raising: public lecturing. He had been an accomplished lecturer for some years now, ever since, in the flush of giving up alcohol in the late 1840s, he had thrown in his lot with the temperance platform, donating his speaker's fees always to the cause. Even while on the road with Jenny Lind, he had squeezed in an occasional lecture, taking over Jenny's stage on her off nights and addressing crowds from Baltimore to New Orleans. An engagingly funny, often powerful speaker—his legendary stamina once enabling him to deliver 40 talks in a single month—Barnum drew large crowds wherever he went, becoming one of the true stars of the anti-liquor movement. In the closing months of 1858, Barnum began expanding a portion of his autobiography into an address entitled "The Art of Money Getting." "I thought I was more competent to speak on 'The Art of Money Losing,'" Barnum jested to some friends, who then assured him that he "could not have lost money, if [he] had not previously possessed the faculty of making it."

His opening delivery of the new lecture took place on December 29 before an audience of 2,500 people gathered inside a packed St. James Hall, London. Though the cynical *Punch* called it a "sermon for snobs," the lecture in fact was an instantaneous success. Heavily advertised, repeated more than 60 times across England, it allowed Barnum to obtain the reception that had so eluded him with his book. He might be misinterpreted in print, but there was something about Barnum's actual presence that seemed to defuse most critics, winning over audiences even in the cynical university towns of Cambridge and Oxford. Accompanied by a Bavarian minstrel, Herr Knope, who offered musical interludes, and carrying around as a prop the actual Fejee Mermaid, loaned to him for the tour by Moses Kimball, Barnum devoted the largest chunk of his time to the subject of advertising. The lecture was broken up under key headings to which Barnum then added commentary: "Don't mistake your vocation," "Select the right location," "Persevere," "Don't get above your business," "Do not scatter your powers," "Be systematic," "Be charitable," "Preserve your integrity." As formulaic as some of these categories were, it was Barnum's treatment of them that was new, his peppering of his remarks with sharp and original business advice.

It took Barnum four years to extricate himself from the bulk of his Jerome Clock Company debts—all the way to the end of the decade, and beyond. But as the 1860s loomed, not only was Barnum a new and better man, he felt, but with the help of Tom Thumb and his own silver tongue he was now fiscally poised to enter a whole new epoch in his amazingly unpredictable life.

Barnum poses in England with his diminutive deliverer, who, typically, has a member of the fair sex by his side.

Barnum and dancer Ernestine de Faiber.

A New Mansion to Celebrate His Solvency

For nearly five years, the Barnums had been nomads. Living in a series of rented houses and apartments, the bankrupt showman had removed his family to West Hampton, Long Island, in the summer of 1856, in large measure to help soothe Charity's shattered nerves. "[I]n my poverty & seclusion at the sea-side with my family, I found more peace and contentment than Iranistan ever afforded," Barnum wrote, trying to look on the bright side, but clearly the situation was difficult. During his absences in England with Thumb in the late 1850s, the family seems to have stayed in the Fairfield home of daughter Caroline, in the house given to her by Barnum after her 1852 wedding to Bridgeport bookkeeper David W. Thompson. Now, in 1860, finally emerging from debt, Barnum announced plans for a new home, to be located adjacent to Caroline's, and within 1,000 yards from his old palace, Iranistan. Even more than the last time, this was to be a family enterprise. Charity, whose special love had always been flowers, would help design the gardens. Pauline, Barnum's teenage daughter, still living with her parents, would give ideas, as would the middle daughter, Helen, and the eldest, Caroline, who set to work searching out a proper name for the new mansion. Planning to remain at "Lindencroft" for the rest of his life, and surrounded by a family whom he adored, now once again Barnum had a home base from which to spring outward into new endeavors.

Shown here shortly after construction is Barnum's second home, Lindencroft, with its impressive outdoor statuary. Barnum did not name his house after Jenny Lind, as was widely reported, but tipped his hat to a fine stand of linden trees on the property instead; the brainstorm had come to him while he was drinking a bowl full of lindenberry tea.

A tired-looking Barnum appears with his family on the front porch of Lindencroft in a rare scene taken about 1862. Sitting next to him, looking relieved finally to have her own home again, is Charity Barnum. Her real-estate holdings in East Bridgeport helped Barnum weather his bankruptcy, and one of his favorite lines now became "Without Charity, I am nothing." Next to Mrs. Barnum is 16-year-old Pauline, still several years away from her marriage to Nathan Seeley. On the left is Helen Barnum Hurd, holding the youngest of her three children, Carrie. Seated in front are the two other Hurd girls, three-year-old Helen and two-year-old Julia. Missing from the family portrait are Barnum's oldest daughter, Caroline; her husband, David W. Thompson; and their daughter, Frances; as well as Helen's husband, Samuel H. Hurd.

The Museum Is His Again
and It Welcomes Him Home

As plans for the new home progressed in Connecticut, Barnum turned his attention to his first love, the American Museum. It had not done particularly well over the past four years under John Greenwood and Henry Butler, even with Barnum functioning quasi-officially as agent and consultant. But it had always been agreed that, whenever he wished, Barnum could resume ownership of the collection. Now he was "ready to return," Barnum wrote, "and to make, if possible, another fortune." In one respect, Barnum had an uphill climb before him. Over the course of the past decade, New York society had moved farther and farther uptown, largely abandoning the area around Barnum's Museum. "Nobody expected that money could ever be made [again] at the Museum—too far out of the way," wrote the lecture room's stage manager, Harry Watkins, in 1858, and by 1860 even Mathew Brady had abandoned his Fulton Street galleries for a fashionable new address at Broadway and 10th Street. What nobody who had given up on the old neighborhood had reckoned with, however, was the power unleashed by Barnum's return. Following an official repurchasing ceremony on March 17, posters and placards hammered up all over the city now declared, "Barnum's on his feet again." The great showman himself, it was added, would appear in person on the evening of March 24, to address the crowds from his museum stage.

"I lacked but four months of being fifty years of age," Barnum wrote of that memorable night, "but I felt all the vigor and ambition that fired me when I first took possession of the premises twenty years before." Even though the house was packed as he stepped onto the stage, he had never expected the outpouring of emotion that now took place. Cheers filled the huge theater, loud cries of support and a deafening applause shook the building. Barnum fought not to break down. Still, his voice faltered and tears welled up to think that after so much struggle he had finally come back into his own. "I have touched bottom at last," Barnum told his appreciative audience, "and here tonight I am happy to announce that I have waded ashore." Not yet ready to be "embalmed and put in a glass case in the museum as one of its millions of curiosities," Barnum was back before the public, ready to give "double or treble the amount of attraction ever before offered at the Museum."

In fact, that is precisely what Barnum went on to do over the course of this most extraordinary of decades. Not only did daily attendance immediately double at the museum following his return, but the whole place now seemed to explode into new life with exhibits and performers and sensational attractions. It was as if all the original drive that had fired Barnum and his museum in the 1840s, but which had withered in the late 1850s, was now back—and amplified. Toasting the reborn museum, the Boston *Saturday Evening Gazette* sang out, "The old salt hasn't lost its savor."

The image at right, previously attributed to Mathew Brady, is by an artist of the London Stereoscopic Company, probably William England, and is the finest of the few known photographs of Barnum's Museum. Taken in the summer or fall of 1858, approximately two years before the portrait above by A. A. Turner, the image shows how Barnum's name remained on the museum even during his bankruptcy. A large banner along Broadway depicts a scene from "Thiodon's Exhibition," a mechanical theater act Barnum had recently acquired in England. Leased to the museum on commission, it provided him with much-needed income. Clearly visible in the picture are the distinctive oval paintings Barnum had installed between each of the windows, as well as numerous details on the roof—flags, a large ventilation-shaft outlet, and several parapets, the highest of which housed the museum's famous Drummond Light. Set at the bustling intersection of Broadway and Park Row, an area affectionately known as "Barnum's Corner," by 1860 the museum was being called "Barnum's Circus" and "Big Show." "It was the tent of the village green enlarged," wrote *Harper's Weekly*, "built in brick instead of canvas."

A 100-Page Guidebook Describes an Infinity of Wonders

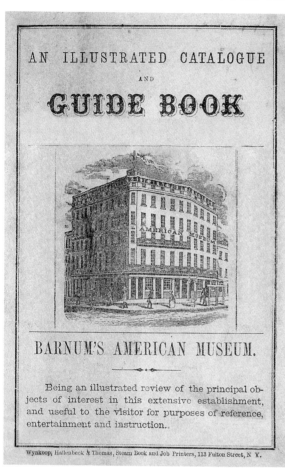

AN ILLUSTRATED CATALOGUE
AND
GUIDE BOOK

BARNUM'S AMERICAN MUSEUM.

Being an illustrated review of the principal objects of interest in this extensive establishment, and useful to the visitor for purposes of reference, entertainment and instruction.

Wynkoop, Hallenbeck & Thomas, Steam Book and Job Printers, 113 Fulton Street, N.Y.

Barnum's new *Guide Book* started out by sketching the meager early years of the American Museum and went on to extol the grand establishment it had become and the man responsible. "From a beginning so humble, and resources so limited, the American Museum has risen, under the care, energy, and enterprise of Mr. Barnum, to be the most extensive establishment of its kind in the world."

mall, twopenny tour pamphlets had always been on sale at Barnum's Museum, but in the early 1860s a special 112-page illustrated *Guide Book* was now published, as if to celebrate Barnum's return to solvency. Sold for a dime at the museum's front entrance, and available from vendors inside as well, the booklet was considered indispensable for negotiating the maze of exhibits within: "Every visitor should own one," the ads ran. Critics like *The Nation*, which considered Barnum's Museum a "man-trap" catering to "the worst and most corrupt classes" in the city and utterly lacking in "scientific arrangement," derided the so-called catalogue and what *The Nation* called Barnum's "heterogeneous heap of 'curiosities,' valuable and worthless, well mixed together." But as Barnum's new *Guide Book* showed, the mixing up of his exhibits was a deliberate attempt to create variety and surprise. It was Barnum's banishing of not just alcohol from his museum, but boredom.

Instead of devoting whole floors to minerals or shells or stuffed birds, as in other museums, Barnum sprinkled in unrelated and fascinating objects wherever possible—medieval armor, funny mirrors, an autograph collection, a piece of the trans-Atlantic cable, a collection of shoes, the arm of a pirate, a powerful magnet. It was the juxtaposition of the unexpected that made his museum so delectably entertaining, capable of being enjoyed by everyone from a foreign-speaking, working-class immigrant to the most educated member of New York's elite. "Who can forget, be he man or boy," agreed *The New York Times*, "the startling effect produced upon him when he first came upon The Three Men of Egypt, whose blackened skulls, and grinning, ghastly faces stuck offensively out from the top of the funeral wrappings?"

Promoting 850,000 "interesting curiosities," Barnum's *Guide Book* spelled out the contents of 883 numbered cases and exhibits, to be found on five floors and distributed throughout seven grand "saloons." It also hinted at the extraordinary infrastructure of the museum in 1860—its four entire buildings, now joined into one, its "workshops" and "laboratories" and "factories" and "offices," as well as Barnum's two off-site warehouses packed full of exhibits not currently in use. The enterprise now included not only its time-tested wax-figure department, striking off likenesses of the famous and the infamous, and its massive taxidermy operation, still under the

The museum was organized into seven saloons, the first incorporating the Cosmorama Department (above), where, behind glass and dramatically lighted, were realistic miniature scenes of foreign places and great moments in history—everything from "a public square in China" to Napoleon's funeral and the eruption of Mount Vesuvius in 1850.

direction of Emile Guillaudeu, but also a greatly enlarged aquarium, an expanded menagerie, and a modernized set-design department, capable of putting out elaborate stage effects such as an enormous, dramatic recreation of a New York iron foundry with machinery in full, pounding operation.

At least 50 full-time employees were attached to Barnum's Museum in the 1860s, not including his resident theater troupe. Four full-time errand boys were now on the staff, three scene shifters, three painters, two carpenters, two doorkeepers, two ticket sellers, a porter, an engineer, and a night watchman. There were assorted individuals in charge of house refreshments, the aquaria, flags and banners, the Happy Family, the "living curiosities," the shooting gallery, the taxidermy operation, and the menagerie. On top of this there were the permanent museum exhibitors—a sewing-machine demonstrator, an ivory carver, a postcard writer, a perfumist, and a team of glassblowers, the Woodroffes. Add to this growing army Barnum's permanent dancers and gymnasts, his property men, his dozen or more museum attachés, a ballet master, a prompter, a clown, a costumer, and a host of museum officials from treasurer to assistant managers, and it is easy to see why Barnum's payroll had more than doubled since the mid-1850s.

Seven Saloons Suggest the Seven Wonders of the World

A visiting family arriving at the front entrance of the American Museum filed into a gaslit, marble-floored vestibule, passed by animal murals and stained-glass-windowed offices on left and right, and then came to a ticket window across from a checkroom. Purchasing their 25-cent tickets, they then entered the first of Barnum's "Seven Grand Saloons," numbered thus to evoke the Seven Great Wonders of the World. Variously known as the "Cosmorama Saloon" or the "Cosmo-Panopticon Studio," this first chamber contained row upon row of face-sized windows, each opening onto an individual, lighted-up scene, perhaps of Italy or Egypt, Russia or Jerusalem, a kind of educational peep show with 194 original scenes to draw on. At the rear rose Barnum's huge central staircase, leading upward one flight to the museum's central and most important conglomeration of attractions. Here, on the only floor dedicated exclusively to exhibits, were Saloons Two, Three, and Four.

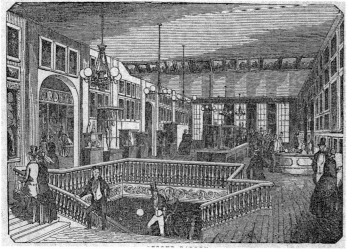

After buying a ticket and passing through the First Saloon on the ground floor, a visitor then proceeded up the grand staircase (above) to the Second Saloon, which was the main showroom of the museum and housed an ever-changing variety of exhibits.

Saloon Two, the main showroom, at the center, contained a true medley of exhibits— not only the huge Birds of North America Collection, but also the chief picture gallery, containing oil portraits and American landscape masterpieces hung high up on walls above tall standing glass cases. Here, too, was what Barnum claimed to be "Old Bet," the nation's second earliest elephant import, shot long ago by an irate New Englander. Here, often tucked away in dark corners for surprise effect, were many of Barnum's "living curiosities," his albinos and giants and dwarfs and others, offering their life-story pamphlets for sale and their 15-cent carte-de-visite photographs. Two saloons now boasted of "Wyberd's Patent Daylight Reflector," a new device which distributed light into dark places, just what was needed for Barnum's replica of the Koh-i-Noor diamond, billed as his remarkable "mountain of light." Separated from the main, central saloon by twin archways, the Third Saloon contained not only Barnum's tropical and exotic stuffed birds, but also his gem collection, his living anacondas, his Indian artifacts, his lung- and strength-testing machines, and a full, accurate model of a Russian fort. Here also, near the wax-figure department, the daguerreotype portrait gallery, the glassblowers' table, and a room for private consultations with Madame Dubois, the clairvoyant, were Barnum's own personal offices. On the opposite side of the floor, in the Fourth Saloon, was the new "Aquarial Department," its glass cases filled with tropical plants and with special tanks for reptiles, fish, and seals. Here lived Barnum's famous "Learned Seal," Ned, whose specialty was playing musical instruments.

On the museum's top three floors, sharing space beside Barnum's three-story Moral Lecture Room and Theater, were Saloons Five, Six, and Seven. Saloon Five was Emile Guillaudeu's chief concern, home to his prize stuffed animals—a constantly growing collection of lions and crocodiles, cougars and wild cats, leopards, rhinos, black bears, turtles, giraffes, and monkeys. Here also, in large glass cases, was an array of natural curiosities, ranging from sharks' teeth and butterflies to animal horns. Close by was Barnum's "rogues gallery," a collection of photographs of some of the world's great criminals. And in the midst of it all was the museum's refreshment stand, offering, among other delights, lemonade, oysters, and ice cream.

In Saloon Six was the mineral collection, more Indian curiosities, six cases displaying insects, the old sewing machine still operated by a dog, and the famous club that killed Captain Cook. And on the top floor, under open skylights, beside a bubbling, illuminated fountain, and beneath the rooftop aerial gardens, were the majority of Barnum's live animals, his menagerie. Included here was not only his famous Happy Family, with its full-time attendant, but also a "monster den of mammoth serpents, 30 in number," a pair of prairie dogs, and a full team of performing grizzly bears. One of Barnum's favorite exhibits topped off the house, his "Grand Skeleton Chamber," containing horses and hippopotami, a mastodon, and a man.

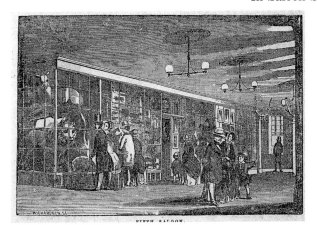

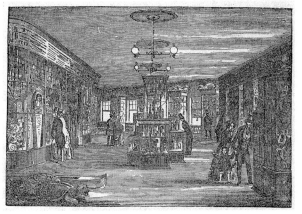

The Fifth Saloon (top) was largely devoted to stuffed animals and was a favorite with children because of its refreshment stand. The Sixth Saloon (above) displayed odd curiosities plus an extensive mineral collection.

It was truly a cornucopia of curiosities that filled this "haunt of all things wonderful," everything from the bill of a sawfish to a Chinaman's opium pipe, from a Turkish lady's boots to a hairball found in a sow's stomach. Here was a "gun for shooting whales," a dog sled from Kamchatka, a "cat o' nine tails" from Sing Sing Prison, and a sample of sea-worm–bored wood. But, most important and ingenious of all, here, throughout the museum, inside and out, was Barnum himself. Though the huge portrait of Barnum's face that had once hung on the building's exterior was gone, by April 1860 giant gaslit letters spelling out Barnum's name flooded across the entire front of the building. Pictures of him were displayed on almost every floor, and whole exhibits illustrated scenes out of his famous autobiography—clothing from Tom Thumb's tours, framed letters from Jenny Lind, wax figures of the Siamese Twins and Barnum's fat boys. There was even a full-sized wax statue of the smiling showman himself. Often on hand personally to greet his crowds, calling his theater audiences his "congregation," Barnum made sure that copies of his autobiography were always plentiful and available for sale from special museum agents. No proprietor of amusement had ever interjected his own personality so directly or powerfully into his presentations. Everywhere visitors went inside these halls, they were reminded that this was Barnum's Museum—that he, now of almost mythic proportions, was its chief curiosity.

An 18-Year-Old Prince Pays Barnum's a Visit

After dancing until four in the morning at the most gala ball New York had ever thrown, the Prince of Wales visited Brady's gallery the next morning, where 20 pictures were taken of Queen Victoria's "Bertie" and his 13-man traveling party. Four unmarried young ladies had danced with His Royal Highness the night before, and for weeks thereafter they were the envy of every maiden in America.

It was the first time British royalty had ever set foot on United States soil, and therefore the tour of America by the Prince of Wales in the fall of 1860 was a momentous event. The young man's entrance into New York City was tarnished by a much too long and elaborate parade in the lower wards, which left thousands farther uptown straining to make out the passing royal features as dusk settled. The bitterness that existed between the two powers still burned in some hearts, but it was believed that this royal visit could cement a lasting peace. Of the military welcome, the New York *Independent* commented, "[I]t was greeting, and not defiance, that the voice of the cannon carried forth. . . . [W]e are one in heart . . . with the empire from whose loins we sprang." After an enormous welcoming ball, the youth who would one day be King Edward VII called upon the famous Mathew Brady, asking him to shut down his 10th Street gallery and, without intruders, take pictures of His Royal Highness and his 13-man suite. The American Museum was high on the Prince's list as well, and on that same Saturday—October 13—the visit was made. Inexplicably, Barnum was in Connecticut at the time, and so John Greenwood, Jr., the museum manager, nervously showed Prince Albert Edward and his entourage through the building. Later, the showman wrote about the visit as if he'd been there. "Knowing that the name of the American Museum was familiar throughout Europe, I was quite confident of a call from the Prince, and from regard to his filial feelings I had, a day or two after his arrival in New York, ordered to be removed to a dark closet a frightful wax figure of his royal mother." The figure had been a mainstay of the museum for 19 years now, reaching back even further than Barnum's first visit to Queen Victoria with Tom Thumb, when the young showman had commented unkindly on her looks. No one quite knew what would be the reaction of his Royal Highness when he was finally led to the platform where many of the "living curiosities" were displayed. "The tall giant woman made her best bow," wrote Barnum; "the fat boy waddled out and kissed his hand; the dwarfs kicked up their heels, and like the clown in the ring, cried 'here we are again'; the living skeleton stalked out, reminding the Prince, perhaps, of the wish of Sidney Smith in a hot day that he could lay off his flesh and sit in his bones; . . . the 'What is it?' grinned; . . . and the Aztec children were shown and described as specimens of a remarkable and ancient race in Mexico and Central America. The Prince and his suite seemed pleased." What pleased Barnum even more than the Prince's pleasure was that the museum, as *Leslie's* later commented, was "the only place of amusement he visited during his American tour," and, upon hearing that Barnum himself was absent, the Prince had said that he had thus missed "the most extraordinary curiosity in the establishment."

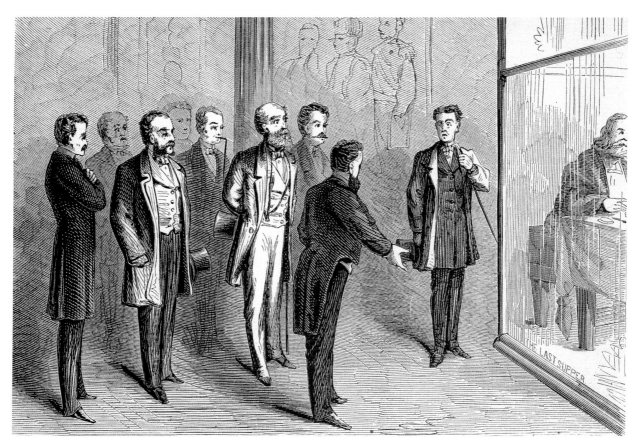

A sketch from an updated edition of Barnum's autobiography shows museum manager John Greenwood, Jr., pointing out to the Prince a waxwork exhibit of the Last Supper. To Greenwood's left is the most important member of the English group that traveled with the Prince through Canada and the U.S.—the Duke of Newcastle.

A Barnum ad in *Harper's Weekly* shows what curiosities were on exhibit at the time of the Prince's visit. Museum personnel were nervous their visitor would be put off by freaks—but he wasn't.

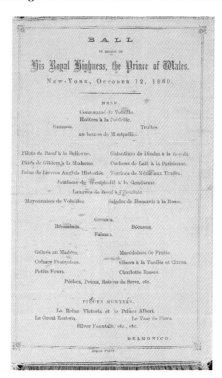

At the ball the night before, held at the Academy of Music and attended by 3,000, "supper" was served by Delmonico's, which printed the menu on silk. A portion of the dance floor collapsed during the evening from excessive weight, but no one was hurt and the Prince, a connoisseur of pretty young women, danced on.

The Favorite "Curiosity" of Just About Everybody

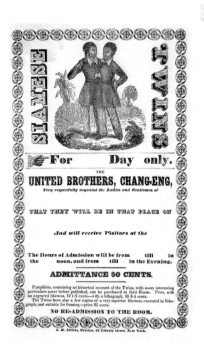

In the 1820s, a sea captain visiting Siam thought he saw a sea monster swimming in the river at Bangkok. When he discovered it was connected twin brothers, he took them to England, then to America. This is one of their early posters, before the Siamese twins had broken free from Captain Coffin to run their own tours. Showing them in Chinese garb and hairstyle, and referring to them as if to a single being named "Chang-Eng," the handbill advertised the "United Brothers" at 50 cents a look—date, time, and place to be filled in.

The difference between Chang and Eng, the original Siamese Twins, and almost every other "living curiosity" that Barnum ever employed was that, from the beginning, the self-made Chinese brothers never really needed Barnum at all. Perhaps the most successful Asian Americans of the mid-19th century, Chang and Eng had been born near Bangkok, Siam, in 1811, bound tightly stomach to stomach by an unforgiving, armlike tube. Asian doctors had recommended separation—one advised the use of a "red-hot wire"—but Chang and Eng's parents encouraged them instead to learn how to coexist. Working daily to stretch and stretch the thickening ligature, ultimately to three and a half inches in length, eventually the boys could stand side to side, dress separately, walk and run, and, in their own unusual way, even swim.

Their father's death in 1819 had cast the eight-year-old boys upon their own devices. Soon they were making and selling coconut oil, then peddling duck eggs to the big ships, as they sat side by side in their rowboat, each with his own oar. Increasingly renowned throughout Siam as "The Chinese Twins," visited by the King of Siam himself and his 700 wives, in 1829 Chang and Eng were "discovered" by an American ship's captain and whisked away to Europe and America to make their fortune.

World fame had come quickly, but at a price; by 1838, after seven years of exhibiting themselves in the U.S., the twins were exhausted. Sick of the roving show-life, and wealthy enough now to retire, they had adopted American citizenship and taken the name of Bunker, after a Boston acquaintance. Purchasing a plantation in the Blue Ridge Mountains of North Carolina, including slaves to go with it (eventually 33 of them), the brothers settled into an agrarian life that included marriage to unjoined sisters, and, very quickly, the fathering of numerous children. Excellent axmen, proficient carriage drivers and judges of horseflesh, the twins rarely spoke, but enjoyed games of chess together. Forced by their fleshy bond to sleep face to face, needing to cooperate in everything, they divided their time between two houses and two families, alternating three-day periods during which one or the other was in full charge of their whereabouts and activities.

No clear record exists of any Barnum contact with Chang and Eng prior to 1860, yet the showman was well aware of the pair, and for years he had been eager to participate in their profits. In the late 1840s, Barnum had had a wax figure of the twins crafted and installed in his museum, and in 1853 he had authored a hyped-up booklet on their life which seemed to imply a business encounter at the time. "The question naturally arises," Barnum had written, calling them "the deuce of hearts," "are they really

In the 1860s, Eng and Chang visited the gallery of Mathew B. Brady for an official portrait. Eng, always on his brother's right, was, at five feet two inches, a full inch taller than Chang. To make up the difference, Chang wore extra-thick soles on his boots.

This portrait shows Chang and Eng with their wives, the Yates sisters, and two of their many children. On the left is Sarah ("Sally"), next to her husband, Eng, and son Albert. On the right, with Chang, is Adelaide with their son Patrick Henry.

With approximately eight more years to live, the twins sit in the mid-1860s for a family portrait with their wives and 18 of their 22 children, 10 of them belonging to Chang and Adelaide, the rest to Eng and Sally. On the far right, holding a child, is Grace Gates—"Auntie Grace" to both Bunker families—a slave given to Sally and Eng as a wedding present in 1843.

two persons, or one man with a double allowance of legs, arms, heads, etc.? No one who has had opportunities of observing them closely will consider it impossible that one soul animates both bodies."

In 1860, Barnum's big chance finally came. Self-educated and literate, possessing a fine penmanship, Chang and Eng had decided to come out of retirement in order to raise money for the college tuitions of their now huge brood of children. In October, they arrived at Barnum's for a six-week engagement at the American Museum. Barnum, elated, turned to poetry. "The Twins of Siam—rarest of dualities—two ever separate, ne'er apart realities." But from the beginning, there were problems. "They never liked Barnum," explained Eng's son Patrick in a later interview. "He was too much a Yankee and wanted too much for his share of the money, and my father and uncle were close figurers themselves." Barnum didn't care much for the 49-year-old pair either. Unlike his cordial relationships with his personal favorites, his "creations," Barnum had no control over these independent-minded brothers, or their families. "The truth is," he wrote later in a note marked *private*, "the wives of the twins (who are sisters) fight like cats and dogs and they want their husbands separated." But it was not just the wives; increasingly, the heavy-drinking, irritable Chang was coming to dislike his quiet, teetotaler brother. "They had a sleeping room in Barnum's museum," recorded one little-known newspaper account, "as did the other curiosities; and one night a rumpus was heard in it. On breaking open the door, the twins were found fighting. Eng was on the floor, underneath Chang, who was choking him."

By November 12, 1860, the highly profitable but emotionally trying engagement was over. Turning down an offer to accompany Barnum on a whirlwind tour of the country, Chang and Eng orchestrated their own trip west, planning to sail from California to Siam for their first visit home in 30 years. On December 20, however, the Bunkers' neighboring state of South Carolina seceded from the Union. Scrapping their plans, the twins hurried home to their plantation and their slaves and their immense family just in time to be there for the eruption of the Civil War.

Their Confederate status would make them the brunt of much Northern humor and derision in the years after the Civil War. In 1865, their wealth demolished by the war, Chang and Eng came out of retirement once again to try out the lucrative Northern circuits. "As long as they go in for Union, they will do," wagged one Northern reporter; "the moment they attempt to separate they will perish as the Confederates perished. . . . United they stand; divided, the show is ended." In fact, separation was increasingly on the twins' minds. On August 31, 1868, Chang and Eng met again with Barnum, this time at George Wood's museum at Broadway and 30th Street. Soon afterward, Barnum announced his decision to send them on a tour of Great Britain and on a search for a surgeon who might finally separate them. The tour occurred, but their separation did not. Chang suffered a stroke in 1870 and from then on had to be partially carried by Eng. Just four years later, on January 17, 1874, to the horror of his brother, 62-year-old Chang died. Eng managed to live on for four fearful hours.

Visitors Wonder What the "What Is It?" Is

The believability of the "What is it?" was strengthened by an unwitting Barnum ally, the English scientist Charles Darwin, whose *Origin of Species* had sold out in one day just three months before Barnum introduced his new wonder.

In his posters Barnum depicted his "Man-Monkey" as a savage creature with the "anatomy" of an orangutan and the "countenance" of a human being—nothing less than the "missing link." "Is it a lower order of man?" Barnum asked. "Or is it a higher order of monkey? None can tell!"

In early 1860, Barnum introduced what would become known, along with Thumb and Jenny Lind, as one of his three all-time great human presentations. "A most singular animal," Barnum announced. "A creature which . . . for want of any name has been designated 'The What Is It?' or 'Man-Monkey!'" Just 12 years since the discovery of the African gorilla by science, and just months since the earth-shattering appearance of Darwin's *Origin of Species*, Barnum was playing into an international obsession with the search for the so-called missing link of evolution. And once again, as in the days of Joice Heth and the Fejee Mermaid, a fascinated public rushed in to see.

With his true identity kept deeply and permanently hidden, the "What Is It?" was in reality an 18-year-old microcephalic black dwarf named William Henry Johnson, discovered by Barnum in late 1859 or early 1860 and enlisted into a lifetime of coconspiracy. By February 1860, calling Johnson a "queer little crittur," and insisting on referring to him as an "it," Barnum had set up the newcomer in a little room in the museum along with two large snakes at the salary of $1.00 a day, and had begun the work of transforming a mildly retarded man into a singular mystery. Giving him a long staff to hold, as if the effort of standing alone on two legs were too great for him, and shaving his head to accentuate the long, sloping brow, Barnum taught Johnson to speak "jungle language," and how to smile continuously. He also threatened to dock Johnson's pay if he ever revealed his true identity.

And so William Henry Johnson was launched upon a career that would last over six decades, ultimately making him the most famous "freak" in the world. Audiences were soon fascinated by his "ant-eater-like nose," his "idiotic" smiling, his "fearfully Simian" anatomy, as George Templeton Strong put it. Laughed at, pelted with coins, called a "cross between a nigger and a baboon," and eventually renamed "Zip" after the archetypal Southern black figure Zip Coon, Johnson reportedly kept his silence for years, even though behind the scenes he was described as "noisy and irrepressible," swearing "like a pirate," and laughing scornfully at his own audiences.

Johnson's presence at Barnum's, like blackfaced minstrelsy and the often degrading display of nonwhite races, was evidence not only of humanity's cruelty but also of white America's deep prejudices. It was evidence, as well, of Barnum's own ongoing sense of race superiority, and of his willingness to parlay America's racism into profits. But as time went on, Barnum and Johnson became close personal allies. Given an ever-increasing salary and share in the profits, and impressed by Barnum's good humor and basic decency, William Henry Johnson maintained an abiding, lifelong affection for his inimitable proprietor.

William Henry Johnson in costume, shown here as he looked in the 1860s. Barnum introduced him as "a most curious human being, without a language and without a country."

"Pocket Editions" from a "Dwindled Race"

Among Barnum's assortment of human superlatives in 1860 was a pair of tiny individuals known as Maximo and Bartola, "The Aztec Children." Said to have been obtained in San Salvador, and having first appeared in America in 1849, the children had cone-shaped heads that were compared, in a published pamphlet, to portraits found in ancient Mayan inscriptions. They were declared representatives of a lost race, causing huge excitement all over the country. In 1853, the three-foot-tall Aztecs had obtained an audience with the Queen of England herself. And though Victoria was unimpressed, finding the pair so retarded they could barely speak and paling in comparison to her favorite dwarf, Tom Thumb, whose wit sparkled, nevertheless the Aztecs had gone on to successful visits with the royalty of France, Austria, Holland, Belgium, Prussia, and Denmark. Even the international scientific community was abuzz.

Barnum had scooped up the "children," now aged 13 and 20, fresh from their triumphant tour, and gone on to publish a 40-page booklet on them including endorsements from foreign scientists and notables. "They appear to offer a worthy study to those who seriously occupy themselves with types of human organization," attested the scientist Baron von Humboldt, ponderously. Though they were billed by Barnum as "the most remarkable and intensely interesting objects ever presented," in fact the origin and identity of the siblings remains in question. Maximo and Bartola may have hailed from San Salvador, as attested, but they also may have been, like William Johnson, American blacks suffering from microcephaly. Years later, during an official government tour, General Henry S. Taylor discovered what he claimed was the pair tucked away in the "idiotic department" of an Ohio insane asylum. Informed that they had been procured from this department in the first place, Taylor was told that the now middle-aged siblings, after years of working for Barnum, had been returned when they no longer were able to draw crowds. In a strange publicity stunt, they had even once been made to marry one another, and appeared for their wedding breakfast in London dressed in formal evening wear. Since brothers and sisters were permitted to marry in ancient Aztec culture, the ruse had helped extend the myth of their origins and had created a new furor of interest. It all raised disturbing questions about society's attitudes concerning the mentally retarded. Not only was Barnum, as well as other showmen, eager to exploit the retarded, but notable writers and newsmen such as Horace Greeley and Nathaniel P. Willis either were legitimately gullible or saw nothing wrong in such practices. Nor did the eminent doctors or clergy of the day. In an age of insensitivity, with Barnum generally following, not leading, in reforms, all that can be said is that he treated his retarded employees well, made a few of them rich, and offered at least one real alternative to the grim absence of opportunity that usually awaited them.

In 1853, the commentator Nathaniel P. Willis (above) came unannounced into a room where the Aztec Children were playing. "Two strange-looking little creatures jumped up from the floor and ran to shake hands with us," Willis reported. "If we had been suddenly dropped upon another planet . . . we should not have expected to see things more peculiar. . . . [T]hey were of an entirely new type . . . with physiognomies formed by descent through ages of thought and association of which we had no knowledge—moving, observing and gesticulating differently from all other children—and somehow, with an unexplainable look of authenticity and conscious priority, as if *they* were of the 'old family' of human nature, and we were the mushrooms of to-day."

"I hate monstrosities, however remarkable," said Horace Greeley (above), but the Aztec Children didn't fall into that category when the celebrated journalist visited them in 1852. "I did not expect to find ogres nor anything hideous, but, among all similar exhibitions, remembering with pleasure only Tom Thumb, I could not hope to find gratification in the sight of two dwarf Indians. But I was disappointed. These children are simply abridgments or pocket editions of Humanity—bright eyed, delicate featured, olive-complexioned little elves. . . . [T]hey are not Freaks of Nature, but specimens of a dwindled, minnikin race. . . . Idiotic they are not."

In their series of lithographs for Barnum, Currier & Ives made the Aztec Children seem playful and appealing, no threat to ordinary people (above). Supposedly, they had been discovered squatting on the altar of a temple as if they were idols in the lost city of Iximaya. In truth, Maximo and Bartola were dwarfish, retarded children, possibly of San Salvador peasants. Well after their heyday and no longer children, the pair was photographed in Aztec shirts (below).

In the first known photograph of Bridgeport, taken in the aftermath of an anti-secessionist raid on August 21, 1861, a group mingles among the debris tossed out of the smashed upper windows of the Bridgeport *Farmer* newspaper building. "The office has just been gutted," Barnum had wired to *The New York Times* at 8:30 the previous evening. "Type, job presses, ink, paper, books, all the paraphernalia of a printing establishment were thrown into the street," the *Times* then reported.

In a photograph taken from the second-story balcony of Barnum's Museum in 1861, a makeshift army barracks and recruiting station can be seen set up south of City Hall Park, across from the Astor House.

Sights and Sounds of Civil War

As the Civil War broke out, Barnum had already traveled far from his early views concerning slavery. Gone now was any lingering defense of the "evil institution"—the Lind tour through the South in the 1850s had opened his eyes, he wrote, giving him glimpses of "more than one 'Legree,' " so that he now "abhor[red] the curse from witnessing its fruits." If anything, his wife, Charity, had even stronger abolitionist views than he.

A longtime "Jackson Democrat," Barnum had begun to question his political party as early as 1854. Shaken by the massacres in "bleeding Kansas," and then by the mounting secession crisis all across the country, in 1860 he had thrown his support behind what he called the "active and exciting" candidacy of Republican Abraham Lincoln. Joining in with pro-Lincoln "Wide-Awakes," and illuminating the windows of Lindencroft on behalf of his candidate, Barnum participated in local rallies, celebrated Lincoln's election in November, and, as war broke out the following April, supplied four substitutes to fight in his place—at 52, he wrote, he was "too old to go to the field."

In the summer of 1861, however, from his home arena of Fairfield County, Connecticut, Barnum found a means for direct engagement. "There is probably no territory of equal extent, north of Mason and Dixon's line," wrote *The New York Times* in August 1861, "where so many secessionists can be found as in

On February 19, 1861, President-elect Abraham Lincoln had arrived in New York City on his way to Washington, D.C., and the inauguration. "President Lincoln has just assured me he will positively visit the Museum tomorrow," Barnum wrote a city newspaper that night after visiting Lincoln at the Astor House. "Don't forget, you're 'Honest Old Abe,' " Barnum wrote the next day; "I shall rely upon you, and I'll advertize you." But despite Lincoln's promise, he failed to attend on Wednesday, sending over instead his wife, Mary, and their boys Robert, Willie, and Tad.

the county of Fairfield." Headquartered at the offices of the Bridgeport *Farmer*, almost under Barnum's nose, Democrat subversives had made strong local secessionist inroads ever since the Union defeat at Bull Run. On August 21, attending a well-advertised "Peace Rally" led by secessionists in Stepney, Connecticut, ten miles from Bridgeport, Barnum spearheaded a raid on the speaker's stand and on its secessionist flag, letting himself be carried on the shoulders of his supporters up to the platform, amid threats to his life, to become the Unionists' chosen spokesman. Excited and inflamed by his words, the crowd then proceeded to Bridgeport, and here, despite Barnum's repeated pleas that it "refrain from acts of violence," the out-of-control group turned on the *Farmer* building. "Once within the walls, a scene of destruction occurred that almost passes description," reported *The New York Times*. Barnum, who found the mob action repugnant and later contributed his own funds toward the re-establishment of the *Farmer's* business, nevertheless agreed that it did help clean the state of secessionist leaders. "The events which have occurred in this vicinity," Barnum wrote proudly to President Abraham Lincoln, "have rendered secessionists so scarce, I cannot find one for exhibition in my museum."

The Museum Takes On a Distinctive Wartime Appearance

A popular automaton at the museum during the war was this soldier on crutches. The box he stands on contained machinery that made him talk in a squeaky fashion.

The uniformed midget above, Edward Newell, was introduced on Barnum's stage as General Ulysses S. Grant, Jr. Newell would later go on to marry into Tom Thumb's family.

Despite the country's growing gloom as war spread, Barnum continued to offer respite and entertainment within the walls of his fortresslike museum. If anything, the 1860s saw the museum's apogee, as crowds attended in record numbers to escape the terrible strain of wartime. "Barnum's American Museum is an institution that grows with the growth of New York," wrote one patriotic weekly. "[It] is the Elephant of Gotham." There were dog shows and high-wire acts, Samson the performing bear, and the magic of Professor Anderson, "Great Wizard of the World." There were Signor D'Olivera's 200 educated white rats, and the "operatic entertainments" of the Holman children, who had sung abroad in Barnum's behalf when he was in need in the late 1850s. There were actual working steam engines built out of glass so you could see their interiors, and daily at 2:00 p.m. at cage-side there was feeding time of the "monster serpents." There were pantomime shows and a ghost apparatus, a basement rifle range and a host of friendly "oddities"—four giants, each reputedly over eight feet tall, being advertised by mid-war. And for those who followed the careers of Hannah Perkins and John Battersby, Barnum's 700-pound fat woman and 45-pound "Living Skeleton," there was a well-publicized courtship and wedding that made them perhaps the most unusual couple on earth. (Barnum or his printer could never seem to get their name right, alternately billing them as "Battersby," "Battersly," and "Bettensby.")

To many it may have seemed like business as usual, but from the beginning Barnum threw everything he had into his own distinctive support of the Union. By May 1861, he had committed his lecture room and its stage to the Union cause, presenting the first in a series of original wartime dramas, *Anderson*, which dramatized the heroism of Fort Sumter's dashing and popular commanding officer. With house actor J. E. Nagle playing Robert Anderson, and with G. H. Clarke as Captain Abner Doubleday, who fired the first Union shot, the play built to an emotional finale involving the raising of the Stars and Stripes. Afterward, Barnum wrote General Anderson himself offering $100 for the loan of the actual flag that had flown over Sumter, claiming he hoped by exhibiting it to quell public concern that the flag had fallen into Confederate hands. But, as was true in many of his other requests for official state property, including a later attempt to procure the alleged petticoats of Jefferson Davis, Barnum received back a resounding "no."

By June 1861, Barnum had begun to present "patriotic dramas" twice daily in his theater, along with a constantly changing array of specialty acts on war-related themes, such as Addie LeBrun singing "Viva l'America" and Dora Dawson, whose stage costume was an American flag. Even tried-and-true acts now had to be presented with a war "twist"; for the 1862 appearance of Barnum's "Fairy Amazons," the female performers were to be under the direction of a "Drill Master of the 71st Regiment." And then, of course, there was Barnum's world-famous general, Tom Thumb, active at the museum off and on throughout the 1860s. But since Thumb had so long been associated with his role as Napoleon, now Barnum introduced two brand new, very "American" midgets, each with his own proper military title. They were General Grant, Jr., representing the army, and Commodore Nutt, in charge of the navies.

On top of Barnum's live acts, a steady stream of war-related exhibits poured into the museum: "relics" from Fort Sumter; slave shackles and cutlasses from the confiscated Southern ship *Savannah*; a secession flag, possibly the one Barnum himself had had torn down in Stepney, Connecticut. There was Barnum's automaton Union soldier, who could march in place, an actual Seventh District draft wheel, a regularly updated supply of new wax figures depicting important war heroes, and a so-called Confederate "Drill," formerly belonging to General P. T. Beauregard (whose initials, one paper commented, were, strangely, the same as P. T. Barnum's). "A month can be agreeably spent at the corner of Ann Street and Broadway," wrote *Leslie's Weekly*, proclaiming Barnum's "a great institution of the Republic."

Turning down opportunities to travel overseas during these years, Barnum claimed he couldn't bear to leave his "own country while she is in peril." To him the war was the "damnedest, [most] barbarous, mean and causeless rebellion ever known," and though history would eventually "set the matter right," now it was his job to do all in his power "to assist in making history." By this, Barnum meant not only his museum-based patriotism, but his free lectures for the wounded, his behind-the-scenes fact gathering for old friend Gideon Welles, now secretary of the navy, and his well-appreciated White House entertainments for President Lincoln. He also meant his own total personal commitment to the Union cause. "If needs be I am willing to be reduced to the last shirt and the last dollar," he wrote in an 1862 letter to Englishman Thomas Brettell, "yes, to the very last drop of blood . . . [if] that will help to preserve this nation as one and inseparable."

And as war dragged on, in his own unique way Barnum became a kind of symbol for Northern resolve. Though its proximity to well-guarded City Hall helped keep Barnum's Museum safe during the 1863 draft riots, not long afterward his buildings began to become targets of pro-Southern conspiracies. In mid-war, his museum was hit by a Confederate arsonist. And in Connecticut, at Lindencroft, soldiers soon had to be posted round the clock. Barnum—himself now a member of a home-front vigilante organization called the "Prudential Committee"—was provided with rockets to shoot off from his rooftops if he was ever attacked.

Even though Harriet Beecher Stowe was disturbed by Barnum's version of *Uncle Tom's Cabin*, her anti-slavery classic was a staple at his museum.

Actresses in theaters all over New York enfolded themselves in the American flag and added to the ongoing patriotic fervor. Here Mrs. Harry Watkins, wife of a former Barnum stage manager, wears the Stars and Stripes.

In Barnum's inspiring production on the start of the Civil War, actor J. E. Nagle played the part of Robert Anderson, the Union hero of Fort Sumter.

On Barnum's Wartime Stage, a Procession of Union Heroes

Before the War our patriotism was a fire-work, a salute, a serenade for holidays and summer evenings," wrote Ralph Waldo Emerson in 1864. "Now the deaths of thousands and the determination of millions of men and women show that it is real." To capture this new patriotism and with it stir his customers, Barnum hired men, women, and children who had tasted war and could convey on his stage adventure, heroism, and self-sacrifice. How better to put lumps in the throats of audiences than to present the brave little face of Robert H. Hendershot, the "gallant Drummer Boy," who was only 11 years old when he joined the Eighth Michigan Infantry and distinguished himself by his bravery at the Battle of Fredericksburg? How better to excite than by introducing Major Pauline Cushman, the actress turned federal scout and spy, and hear her tell of her double-agent exploits behind Rebel lines to help save the Union? It was a Union that had been created by the Revolution—and now to Barnum's stage came a dignified ancient who had actually been there at the nation's origins, had fought under General Washington; 102 years old now, he was Samuel Downing, so admired by Barnum that he had Downing's photograph personally copyrighted. The old man had voted for both Washington and Lincoln and now he wanted to see Jeff Davis hanged. "How would Washington treat traitors if he caught them?" Downing had been asked, and he answered like a shot, "Hang 'em to the first tree!"

In early 1863, 12-year-old Robert Henry Hendershot did his drumming on Barnum's stage instead of the battle-fields of Fredericksburg, where, when his drum was shattered by a shell, the boy had grabbed a musket and taken a Confederate captive. Not until 1864 did Congress pass an act making enlistment under the age of 16 unlawful.

Pauline Cushman, the actress turned federal spy, appeared at Barnum's Museum in June 1864, causing intense excitement. Americans streamed in by the thousands to hear about "her arrest on Hardin Turnpike; attempted escape; re-arrest within four miles of Franklin, illness, recapture . . . [and] good-bye [to the] Confederates," as Barnum ads promised they would hear.

In 1865, along with two 21-foot alligators and a one-legged dancer, Barnum presented Samuel Downing, a 102-year-old veteran of the Revolution.

Wartime Spectacle of Monumental Mammals

If Barnum had astonished the public a decade earlier with his ten elephants and his white rhino and his twin giraffes, in the 1860s he outdid even his own mammalian record. Using international dealers and the help of foreign consulships, he imported a steady stream of unusual and rarely seen animals to his museum, among them zebras, polar bears, camels, sea lions, and kangaroos. But nothing could compete with Barnum's top two imports of the decade—his hippopotamus and his white whales.

Because they required a special watery environment for transport, no living hippopotamus had ever been seen in America. Determined to be the first to exhibit one, in August 1861 Barnum finally obtained from Egypt a full-grown animal. "The Greatest Wonder of the Animal Kingdom," his large pictorial ads exclaimed. "The Behemoth of the Scriptures . . . Should be seen by every man, woman and child." Barnum set up the animal in its own special habitat inside the museum, its "artificial ocean or river," and touted the creature's exotic, "oriental" mystique, enhanced by the presence of an Arabian keeper, Salaama, billed as "the only man who can control or exhibit his hippopotamuship."

Herr Jacob Driesbach was hired by Barnum in 1861 to take charge of a dancing-bear act located on the top floor of the museum. Following in the footsteps of Barnum's earlier specialist, John "Grizzly" Adams, the 53-year-old lion tamer was known nationwide for his thrilling wrestling matches with big cats, and for having survived an all-out tiger attack in the ring.

In the midst of the hippo excitement, Barnum learned that a group of Canadian fishermen had captured a white whale near the mouth of the St. Lawrence River. Deciding he had to have one, Barnum proceeded to devise a method for transporting the huge mammals by rail inside a seaweed-lined box, the necessary salt water to be delivered to its mouth and blowhole by means of attendants with sponges. In the depths of the museum basement, amid the fumes of gas lamps, Barnum prepared a 40-by-18-foot brick-and-cement holding tank. He himself then traveled to Canada in order to supervise a capture of his own, followed by a five-day trip back to New York. By summer, not one but two beluga whales were in place in their new home, drawing thousands into the museum. Within days, however, tragedy struck. Barnum had filled the whales' tank with uncirculating fresh water instead of salt water, and this, along with high temperatures, incorrect diet, and what Barnum admitted was "bad air in the basement," hastened their death. Determined to master the art of keeping captive whales alive, Barnum paid off local aldermen for the right to pipe salt water into his museum from New York Harbor. Then, after building a $4,000, 24-foot square tank on the museum's second floor—this time with a base of slate, and sides made of imported, one-inch-thick glass—Barnum proceeded to obtain two more white wonders. Following a short but profitable run, however, each of these also expired. By December 1861, a third pair, caught off the coast of Labrador, finally adapted successfully to the museum environment. Upstaged, Barnum's hippopotamus seems to have been relegated to the old cement tank in the basement.

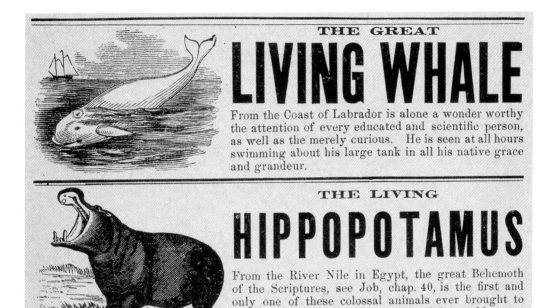

Barnum's "Holiday" ad for year-end 1864 featured his two big new imports as well as continuous performances on Christmas and New Year's.

The image Barnum used for his hippo posters and ads was copied almost exactly from an English painting by Joseph Wolf.

Stars of Barnum's Stage During the Years of War

On the cover of a September 1862 issue of *Vanity Fair*, Barnum is shown at his museum blowing his own horn.

Throughout most of the war, John Denier starred on the tightrope (above) and, like his high-wire brother, Tony, was an excellent comic pantomimist as well.

A few highfalutin critics found Barnum's seemingly irrational conglomeration of exhibits, relics, animals, "freaks," and entertainments vulgar and offensive, and his blatant promotions a perverse influence on the American scene. But most customers had only fond memories of the Broadway emporium, especially if their first encounters had occurred at a tender age. Here they had seen their first specimens of a veritable garden of animals—some alive, others stuffed; had encountered objects of historical wonder relegated before to the dry pages of their history books; had watched down-to-earth drama that would have been forbidden them under another roof; had gaped and gulped at out-of-the-ordinary people for the first time; had tried out the shooting gallery firsthand, or the balloon ride from the rooftop, or had a cold lemonade at the refreshment stand. After they left Barnum's portals wide-eyed, a whole new world had opened up, and, for many thus exposed, life would never be quite the same again. Typical of the recollections of the museum around the time of the war were those of Edward P. Mitchell, who became the editor-in-chief of the New York *Sun*.

"For one, I thank and bless across the years the proprietor of the Fount of Eternal Youth at the corner of Ann Street and Broadway. To have read his book when almost a baby 'way down in Maine and now to be in his living presence, to have him come out of the little room behind the ticket-office and in person actually shake hands and advise me not to miss the wax figure of fat Daniel Lambert in the left-hand case on the second floor, was an experience beyond the dreams of ambition. Miss it? Miss anything from the Happy Family down to the white whale in the basement tank? It was Mr. Barnum's humorous way of suggesting the impossible. I knew the Museum by heart and could have recited it to him backward. I knew the different talents of the Bohemian Glass Blowers, sitting in a row behind a counter and producing fragile miracles which Murano never surpassed. I had studied mathematics under the professorship of Hutchin[g]s, the Lightning Calculator. Grizzly Adams, with the silver plate in his skull, was scarcely more familiar than I was with the idiosyncrasies of his several bruins. . . .

"The Lecture Room was the small theater thus designated by Barnum to accommodate the prejudices of patrons to whom the naked truth might be repulsive. On this stage were produced plays ingeniously alternating the scriptural and the mildly sensational. . . . Between acts Barnum himself walked majestically before the advertising drop-curtain, leading his procession of dwarfs, giants, and living skeletons, and imparted to the audience ideas of an ethical propriety to which no bigot could object."

Clog dancer Tim Hayes clogged away at Barnum's in early 1865.

Billed as one of Barnum's "Living Skeletons," 54-pound Alexander Montarg (right) measured four inches through the chest and had arms just a hair more than one inch in diameter.

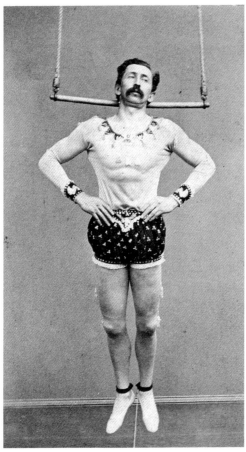

A gymnast who performed at the museum in 1861, H. W. Penny could hang from a trapeze by the back of his neck.

Performances by the captivating Walby Sisters—Augusta, Lizzie, and Louisa—were featured in 1863.

When a Second Thumb Appears, Barnum Orders, "Nail Him!"

Two very self-assured showmen, Barnum and his new prize, Commodore Nutt.

With the development of glass negatives, multi-lensed cameras could produce a number of similar images on a single sheet of glass, thereby speeding up the printing of cartes de visite. The three pictures of Commodore Nutt shown above were meant to be cut apart, mounted side by side on a clear strip of glass, and then contact-printed in unison, turning out for mounting a trio of the little pictures so popular in the 1860s. One such carte appears below, with a book making Nutt look even smaller than he was.

COMMODORE NUTT

Barnum watched his wealthy Bridgeport neighbor Charlie Stratton (alias Tom Thumb) sail his yacht and drive his thoroughbreds and smoke his imported cigars, and grow steadily taller and fatter. The times when they had made so much money together he could only dream about. Then, one day, the past offered itself up again, as Barnum learned of the existence of a tiny man even shorter than Thumb was in his prime. From a New Hampshire farming family, 29-inch-tall George Washington Morrison Nutt was the spitting image of Tom a decade earlier—"looks like him, talks like him, and acts like him," Barnum excitedly declared. Already a minor celebrity being exhibited by a showman named John H. Lillie, Nutt, if "put in training by the right man" and "properly educated," Barnum wrote a friend, could become "a genteel accomplished and attractive little man." Commissioning his old friend and former employee Fordyce Hitchcock to take the first train to Manchester, New Hampshire, to "secure if possible the dwarf," Barnum authorized $30,000 to be offered for the "privilege of exhibiting [Nutt for] three years," all expenses to be paid as well. "I hear that several showmen are after him," Barnum added. "Nail him, and don't let them get ahead of you." They nailed him, all right, and after briefly presenting him as a Union drummer boy, Barnum bestowed upon Nutt the rank of commodore. On October 17, 1862, Barnum and his new prize paid a call at the White House, and President Lincoln interrupted a special Cabinet meeting to greet them. As Barnum told it, Lincoln "bent down his long, lank body, and taking Nutt by the hand, he said: 'Commodore, permit me to give you a parting word of advice. When you are in command of your fleet, if you find yourself in danger of being taken prisoner, I advise you to wade ashore'. The Commodore found the laughter against him, but placing himself at the side of the President, and gradually raising his eyes up the whole length of Mr. Lincoln's very long legs, he replied, 'I guess Mr. President, you could do that better than I could.' " In his new "Prince of the Lilliputs" Barnum had found a duplicate of the young Tom in quick wit as well as appearance.

Tom Thumb Asks the "Queen of Beauty" for Her Hand

Huldah Pierce Bump, Lavinia's mother and the wife of James S. Bump of Middleborough, Massachusetts, bore eight children, two of whom were dwarfs. "My father was nearly six feet tall and my mother was termed 'a large woman,'" wrote Lavinia in later years. "Their lives were proverbial for a high standard of integrity, morality and charity."

A perfectly proportioned 20-year-old woman, 32-inch-high Lavinia Warren Bump was named the "Queen of Beauty" by Barnum. He also convinced her to drop the "Bump."

Lavinia had four full-sized brothers and two full-sized older sisters, one of whom is shown here.

n 1862 I heard of an extraordinary dwarf girl," wrote Barnum in the 1869 edition of his autobiography. Fate had somehow played into his hands again, this time to concoct the makings of a love match not even the showman could have topped. Mercy Lavinia Warren Bump was a 21-year-old beauty from Middleborough, Massachusetts, who was only 32 inches tall. In her childhood, Lavinia's father had built a pair of portable steps which his tiny daughter could shove around the kitchen so that she could reach the top shelves. At school, her size allowed her to run around beneath the desks and pinch unsuspecting fellow pupils, good practice for a short-lived job as a schoolteacher. First displayed to the public by a cousin in a flat-bottom, floating theater on the Mississippi, Lavinia was subsequently signed by Barnum for $10 a week plus expenses. The New York *Commercial Advertiser* commented, "She has dark, rich, waving hair, large, brilliant, intelligent eyes and an exquisitely modeled neck and shoulders. Her bust would be a study for a sculptor." No wonder Generals Grant, McClellan, Burnside, and Scott had clamored to call upon her and Stephen A. Douglas had once tried to kiss her, saying, after being rebuffed, that he would not eat her, "although," Lavinia recalled the Little Giant adding, "you almost tempt me to do so." Tom Thumb took one look at the museum's dainty addition and fell head over heels in love. So had Nutt, but Barnum refused to arbitrate. One night, all three were invited to the showman's Bridgeport mansion, and, before the Commodore arrived, Tom made his move. According to Barnum, two "mischievous" young-lady houseguests overheard the proposal that ensued.

"So you are going to Europe soon?" asked Tom. "Yes," replied Lavinia, "Mr. Barnum intends to take me over in a couple of months." "I wish I was going over, for I know all about the different countries, and could explain them all to you," remarked Tom. "That would be very nice," said Lavinia. "Would you really like to have me go?" asked the General, quietly insinuating his arm around her waist. "Of course I would," was the reply. "Don't you think it would be pleasanter if we went as man and wife?" The little fairy quickly disengaged his arm, and remarked that the General was a funny fellow to joke in that way. "I'm not joking at all," said the General. Tom now gave Lavinia a kiss. Lavinia hesitated. "I have always said I would never marry without my mother's consent." "Oh!" said Tom. "I'll ask your mother. May I do that, pet?" The kisses that followed, the eavesdroppers reported, sounded like the popping of corks from beer bottles. The General's petition to Lavinia's parents was short and sweet. "Ever since I met your daughter . . . I have felt that kind heaven designed her for my partner in life. . . . I assure you that if she becomes my wife, I shall always do all in my power to make her happy."

After the hotheaded Nutt had cooled down, an alternate romance between the Commodore and Lavinia's even shorter younger sister, Minnie, was cooked up by Barnum. Nutt's on-the-knee proposal, pictured here in Brady's gallery, a few weeks before the Thumb wedding, was a sham. Although the two performed together for years along with Tom and Lavinia, no liaison ever developed.

Tom Thumb poses holding his yachtsman's hat a couple of years after his marriage. Even though his self-indulgent lifestyle was catching up with him, his kindly personality still shone through.

The Nuptials of the Lilliputians Is by Invitation Only

In the days before the big event, Barnum created wedding fever. It was "NOW OR NEVER" to see the "fully matured and developed woman" who was to become Tom Thumb's wife.

Barnum thought of everything. Lavinia's bridal gown was even on display in the window of a Fifth Avenue store for several weeks before the ceremony.

Barnum footed the bill for the wedding, and well he might have, for, as the Lilliputian nuptials approached and excitement mounted, the museum was taking in over $3,000 a day, and even the showman admitted that "Lavinia's levees . . . were crowded to suffocation." To keep the bonanza going, Barnum dangled $15,000 in front of the lovers if they would postpone their wedding a month in order to continue their exhibitions. "Not for fifty thousand dollars," said the General; Lavinia thought he ought to have made it $100,000. Barnum had no doubt that he could pick up a cool $25,000 if he were to "let the ceremony take place in the Academy of Music" and "charge a big price for admission." But the showman had promised to give the couple a genteel and graceful wedding, and he kept his word. Grace Episcopal Church was picked as the site, and Bishop Henry Codman Potter was asked to perform the ceremony. Even though the bishop first accepted, and then, under pressure from the more "squeamish" members of his clergy, withdrew, the lesser clerics enrolled did nothing to diminish the most lustrous social event of the season. With cordons of police holding back the huge crowd outside the church, at a few minutes before noon on February 10, 1863, the parents of the bride and groom took their places along with the Barnums in the front pews, signaling the start of "the Fairy wedding." Next, as *Leslie's Weekly* reported, best man Nutt and maid of honor Minnie began their march down the church's center aisle to "voluptuous" organ strains. And then came Charles Stratton and Lavinia Warren, he in full evening dress, she in a bridal gown of rich white satin with a diamond necklace and a lace veil matching her star-shaped bouquet. The specially invited congregation, consisting of the rich and powerful of the city, all dressed to the teeth, now "swayed over towards the common centre, as the tops of tall trees are bent by the force of the storm." Approaching the altar, the bride and groom climbed six little steps to a tapestried platform so that all could see. Lavinia's pastor from Massachusetts gave the bride away, and the minister who had baptized Charlie in Bridgeport assisted the Reverend Dr. Thomas H. Taylor, rector of Grace Church. The ceremony was conducted with the "utmost gravity and decorum," up until the question "Is there any reason why this man and this woman should not be joined in the holy bonds of matrimony?" At the inquiry, registered *Leslie's*, "an irrepressible titter ran from pew to pew." After the ceremony, a reception was held at the Metropolitan Hotel, where, standing on a grand piano, the bride and groom received 2,000 guests. Among the gifts on display, many locked under glass, were a pair of slippers from Edwin Booth, a set of Chinese fire screens from Mrs. Lincoln, a locket and chain from Mrs. August Belmont, a piece of diamond jewelry from Mrs. John Jacob Astor, and a singing bird-automaton from Barnum.

Those lucky enough to be invited by Barnum to the wedding at Grace Church stood on their pew pillows to glimpse the scene.

Where the Wedding Pictures Were Really Taken

Mr & Mrs "General Tom Thumb" in their wedding costume.

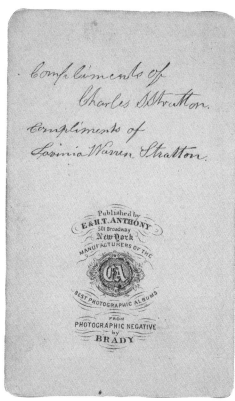

Compliments of Charles S Stratton.
Compliments of Lavinia Warren Stratton.

Published by E & H. T. ANTHONY 501 Broadway New York MANUFACTURERS OF THE BEST PHOTOGRAPHIC ALBUMS FROM PHOTOGRAPHIC NEGATIVE by BRADY

On the far left is an example of a carte de visite of the Thumb wedding turned out by the thousands. On the back of the card (left) appears a facsimile of the participants' signatures. The real McCoys were harder to obtain. "You have the autographs of the four smallest and most fascinating adults in the world, I think," Barnum once scribbled as he sent along a set of asked-for signatures. "They do not reply (nor do I) to 1/10th of the applications made for their autographs and I could not have the heart to ask them to write more than their names."

The obvious choice to take the wedding photographs was Mathew Brady. He hated having to make little carte-de-visite prints, so he turned that job over to the Anthony brothers.

Even though the setting looked distinctly churchlike, the photographs of the Thumb wedding scene were taken with the help of a deceiving backdrop in Mathew Brady's gallery well before the ceremony. For almost 20 years, the eminent photographer's business had prospered largely because of the patronage funneled through Barnum and Tammany Hall. In the early days, it had been a simple task for Barnum to get a new curiosity or performer photographed; all the subject had to do was wander across Broadway and climb up to the top floor of Brady's to the camera rooms, which were lit by the sun through a honeycomb of skylights. By 1860, Brady had moved his operation several times, always farther uptown, and was now at Broadway and 10th Street, the most fashionable location in the city. In the 1840s and '50s, when a duplicate of a picture was ordered, Brady technicians had to go through the slow process of making a daguerreotype of a daguerreotype, but now, with glass negatives and paper prints, any number of copies could be produced. Thank goodness, for before her wedding Lavinia Warren had been selling her Brady cartes de visite at the remarkable rate of 1,200 a day. No scenes had ever been photographed more thoroughly than the official wedding poses; dozens of negatives would be needed to handle the expected avalanche of orders. The photographic printing and supply house of E. & H. T. Anthony would mass-produce the prints and have them ready for sale at 25 cents apiece on the very day of the wedding.

Barnum himself sat for one of Brady's multi-lens cameras. Since the lenses were separated by about the distance between human eyes, prints of any two adjacent negatives appear three-dimensional when viewed in a stereopticon.

An appropriate visitor to the "set" of this all-important sitting was Edward Anthony, one of the most lustrous figures in early American photography, posing here with the little bridegroom. Anthony, along with his brother, Henry, had developed the biggest chemical-and-printing house for U.S. photography, which already did the carte-de-visite printing for Brady's branch in the nation's capital.

The Newlyweds Are Received at the White House

Abraham Lincoln,
President

Edwin M. Stanton,
Secretary of War

John P. Usher,
Secretary of the
Interior

Benjamin F. Butler,
General

Salmon P. Chase,
Secretary of
the Treasury

After spending their wedding night at the National Hotel, the Thumbs took a honeymoon trip to Philadelphia, Baltimore, and Washington. Stopping at Willard's in the capital, they received an invitation to be guests of honor at a White House reception. Practically every important person in Washington, including those shown here, turned out to meet the famous couple. The author Grace Greenwood described the scene. "The pigmy 'General' . . . wore his elegant wedding suit and his wife . . . her wedding dress. . . . I well remember the 'pigeon-like stateliness' with which they advanced, almost to the feet of the President. . . . It was pleasant to see their tall host bend, and bend, to take their little hands in his great palm, holding Madame's with a special chariness, as though it were a robin's egg, and he were fearful of breaking it."

After 20 years on stage, Tom Thumb was no longer the cute little mite that had captivated millions. Not only had he grown and put on weight, his mustache made his face look older than his 25 years. But his marriage would revive his career, and Barnum used the fortunate union in masterful fashion. The year following the wedding, under the deft management of Barnum's trusted Sylvester Bleeker, the couple was off to England and Europe for three years of high success.

In 1869, Barnum had another Thumb brainstorm. "What do you think of a tour of the World, including a visit to Australia?" he wrote Bleeker. "Talk it over with the little people. Decide quickly." In June, the General Tom Thumb Company, which included Commodore Nutt and Lavinia's sister Minnie, headed west. Three years and 55,487 miles later, after 1,471 entertainments in 587 different cities and towns around the world, the troupe was finally home. It was then that Barnum showed himself to be a man of conscience and sentiment. "Although I am part owner," he told Bleeker, Lavinia later recalled, "you have been the captain of the ship so long . . . that I feel as if I had no right to my share of the profit from the voyages. I therefore resign my interest, which you may take and divide between [the] General, Lavinia and yourself. . . . But don't thank me; you could easily have thrown the old man overboard long ago as thousands would have done, but I honor you for your friendship and fidelity to me. God bless you for it." Lavinia remembered, too, that as Barnum took their hands "tears stood in his eyes."

The perceptive writer Grace Greenwood attended the Lincolns' reception for the Thumbs. "There was nothing to reveal to that shrewd little pair," Greenwood observed, "[Lincoln's] keen sense of the incongruity of the scene."

Tom's mustache was cut thin as a pencil for the wedding, even though Lavinia's mother objected to it in any form. During Tom's proposal, in order to get the mother's consent, Tom had promised Lavinia to cut the mustache off, "and my ears also, if that will induce you to answer my question in the affirmative."

John J. Crittendon,
Kentucky
Congressman

Gideon Welles,
Secretary of the
Navy

Montgomery Blair,
Postmaster General

Important Members of Barnum's Staff During the War

Barnum himself was so famous and charismatic, and his leading performers were so well known and admired, that little attention was ever given to the scores of individuals behind the scenes at his museum who made it all work. Some were indispensable, such as John Greenwood, Barnum's manager, and Emile Guillaudeu, who continued on as house naturalist after more than 50 years at the American Museum. By 1864, Barnum had included two sons-in-law, Samuel Hurd and David Thompson, in top staff positions, even though Hurd's marriage to Helen was already tottering and Thompson's copperhead, secessionist views were abhorrent to his father-in-law. Other family members got privileges as well, such as the sewing-machine exhibition granted to Barnum relatives 1. W. and D. Barnum. But loyal nonrelative staff members found promotions, too, such as C. K. Fox, the great clown, now stage manager; E. F. Taylor, Barnum actor turned producer and arranger; and Sylvester Bleeker, once a prompter and bit-part actor for Barnum, now superintendent of the museum. Special among Barnum's employees were those who worked with his "living curiosities," and who were often moved from task to task. Dr. Oscar Kohn, for example, who originally managed the Lucasie Albino Family, was later shifted to the aquaria department, and then to the care of Barnum's hippos.

For more than 20 years, John Greenwood, Jr., was Barnum's right-hand man at the American Museum. Of English birth, but raised in Barnum's hometown of Bethel, Connecticut, Greenwood was trained as a hatter. Eight years Barnum's junior, he joined the museum staff in 1846 and, following Fordyce Hitchcock's emotional breakdown, took over as Barnum's business manager. Serving variously as treasurer, assistant manager, interim owner, confidential agent, and finally manager of the American Museum, Greenwood endeared himself to many and impressed Barnum by his tact and intelligence. "I always found him trustworthy and perfectly precise in his accounts and dealings with me," wrote Barnum toward the end of their long association. "[He was] honest to a penny."

Charles Kemble Fox was first a pantomimist for Barnum, and then later, in the 1860s, stage manager.

Barnum's orchestra director in the mid-1860s was W. J. Peterschen.

Posing with Mrs. Tom Thumb's sister Minnie is Mrs. Sylvester Bleeker, a part-time staff member of the American Museum. Wife of Barnum's museum superintendent, Mrs. Bleeker later served as wardrobe mistress for Tom Thumb and Company's round-the-world tour.

Shown here with Commodore Nutt and General and Mrs. Tom Thumb is Barnum employee William B. Harrison. Starting out with Barnum as a comic singer and violinist, Harrison became one of the showman's most trusted assistants, as well as a close personal friend of Mrs. Thumb.

Barnum liked to add the title of "Professor" to many of his employees' names. Over the years, in addition to Professor Cromwell, shown here at right with the Lilliputian King and John Drummond, he had Professors Todd and Stanzrood, both accordionists; Professor McCormick, the upside-down walker; Professor Brunswick with his statuary; Professor Smith of the seven-octave piano; Professor Livingston, a Barnum actor turned phrenologist; Professor Cosporess, a magician; and, most famous of all, Professor Hutchings, Barnum's "Lightning Calculator."

An Easygoing Giantess
and Two Temperamental Giants

Colonel Routh Goshen, the Arabian Giant, insisted he was from Palestine, but others claimed he was an American black.

Barnum was especially proud of his giantess, Anna Swan. "I first heard of her through a Quaker," he wrote, "who came into my office one day and told me of a wonderful girl, seventeen years of age, who resided near him at Pictou, Nova Scotia, and who was probably the tallest girl in the world." Anna's father had emigrated from Scotland and was only five feet four inches tall. Her mother stood at an even five feet. Anna, the third of 13 children, weighed 18 pounds at birth, was as tall as her mother at six, and at 15 was seven feet and still growing. "I at once sent an agent," Barnum wrote, "who in due time came back with Anna Swan." Attractive, friendly, and intelligent, she lived in the museum, was tutored there, posed in tableaux, and was usually exhibited with Barnum's smallest midgets, whom she could easily pick up in one hand. As Barnum described her, Anna was "an extraordinary specimen of magnified humanity." She became an expert on giants and lectured on them. Fortunately, Anna had two male examples right there in the museum who gave her plenty of lecture material. Colonel Routh Goshen, the Arabian Giant, and Monsieur E. Bihin, the French or Belgian Giant, were Barnum's two reigning behemoths. Each loved to act—especially in comedy routines, playing straight man for the midgets. Tom Thumb would run right between their legs, and, pretending to be befuddled, they would look every which way for him. Monsieur Bihin had worked at Barnum's as early as 1847 and by the 1860s was a regular, appearing in plays like *Jack and the Beanstalk*, and *Hop o' My Thumb*. Goshen claimed to be a Polish Jew from Palestine, but one story had it that he was an overgrown black youth loafing around the Bowery in the late 1850s and had run into Barnum by accident; Barnum had paid him $40 a week, and Goshen appeared wearing a wig of long, fine locks covering his Afro-American hair. The rotund Goshen and the slim Bihin soon became good friends, although jealous of each other's fame. One day they quarreled, and, as Barnum told it, "a lively interchange of compliments ensued, the Arabian calling the Frenchman a 'Shanghai,' and receiving in return the epithet of 'Nigger.'" Enraged, one seized a club, the other a huge sword. "Hearing the disturbance, I ran from my private office to the dueling ground, and said 'Look Here! This is all right; if you want to fight each other . . . that is your affair; but . . . if this duel is to come off, I and the public have a right to participate. It must be duly advertised, and must take place on the stage of the Lecture Room. No performance of yours would be a greater attraction, and if you kill each other, our engagement can end with your duel.' This proposition, made in apparent earnest, so delighted the giants that they at once burst into a laugh, shook hands, and quarreled no more."

Eventually married to Kentucky giant Martin van Buren Bates, the Nova Scotia giantess Anna Swan went on to give birth to the biggest baby ever recorded up until then, bigger than the Lilliputian King, whom she holds in this picture.

Billed as seven feet eight inches high, and weighing 320 pounds, Monsieur E. Bihin, called alternately the Belgian and the French Giant, could easily lift a full-grown man, at arm's length, over his head.

"Ferocious" American Indians Are a Barnum Staple

Despite Barnum's broad intercultural perspective, he maintained a low opinion of Native Americans. Calling them "lazy devils" who didn't want to work, he hid Indian performers away from the public in his back workshops between shows, or put them to work paddling canoes in the Hudson River to stir up interest in the museum. Though Barnum in later years would finally begin to appreciate Native American culture, in 1863 even a visit from the greatest chiefs in the West failed to modify his prejudices.

From his earliest days at the museum, Barnum had been tapping into a widespread fascination with American Indians. Reaching westward to less disturbed tribes, in 1843 he had brought east a delegation of fifteen Sac, Fox, and Iowa war chiefs and squaws, including the niece of the great Chief Black Hawk himself. But, although their war dances and scalping demonstrations sent chills down audience spines and beefed up Barnum's revenues, they, like all Indians on his stage, remained among Barnum's least favorite performers. "They are a lazy, shiftless set of brutes," he wrote at one point to Moses Kimball, then added quickly, "though they will *draw*." During the 1850s, Indian acts seemed to wane at the museum, though a delegation of Crow Indians from Wisconsin spent nearly a week there in 1850 and even accompanied Barnum to Castle Garden to hear Jenny Lind sing.

In March of 1863, a month after the Thumb wedding, Barnum learned that a group of prominent chiefs from the far West was paying a visit to Abraham Lincoln. "By a pretty liberal outlay of money," Barnum recorded, "I succeeded in inducing their interpreter to bring them to New York and to pass some days at my museum." Among the group were some of the most powerful chiefs in the West, including War Bonnet and Lean Bear of the Cheyennes, and Lone Wolf and White Bull, nephew of Sitting Bull, of the Kiowas. "You can only keep them just so long as they suppose all your patrons come to pay them visits of honor," warned the delegation's agent, Samuel G. Colley. "If they suspected that your museum was a place where people paid for entertaining, you could not keep them a moment after the discovery." After seating the dozen or so men and women on his stage, and dismissing their interpreter, Barnum proceeded to introduce the Indians as honored guests. In the group there was one man Barnum particularly despised—Yellow Buffalo, an alleged murderer of white pioneers whom Barnum later remembered as "Yellow Bear." Whenever he came to this man's introduction, Barnum would pretend to compliment him, while in fact he insulted. " 'This little Indian, ladies and gentlemen . . . has killed no doubt scores of white persons, and is probably the meanest, [most] black-hearted rascal that lives in the far West.' Here I patted him on the head, and he, supposing I was sounding his praises, would smile, fawn upon me, and stroke my arm, while I continued. . . . 'He is a lying, thieving, treacherous, murderous monster. He has tortured to death poor, unprotected women, murdered their husbands, brained their helpless little ones, and he would gladly do the same to me!' " And so it went, an unsavory ruse, with Barnum's audiences lapping it all up, until eventually the Indians grew wise to his tricks and with "wild, flashing eyes" refused to remain a single day longer. "I hardly felt safe in their presence," Barnum admitted after this, and he was only too happy when the chiefs were finally gone.

These nine Native American visitors to Barnum's stage were photographed by Mathew Brady.

Though precise identification remains elusive, here are four of the Native American chiefs who spent eleven days with Barnum in early April 1863, following their official visitation to President Lincoln. Third from left is almost certainly the Kiowa chief Little Heart, wearing his distinctive crucifix. Shoeless on the far left appears to be his Kiowa colleague, Chief Yellow

Buffalo, brunt of Barnum's worst dislike. Second and fourth from the left
are Chiefs War Bonnet and Standing in the Water of the Cheyenne tribe of
Colorado, probably, though not certainly, in that order. Both these men
would be among those slain by white soldiers at the Sand Creek Massacre,
just eighteen months after departing Barnum's.

Exotic Beauties Rescued
from a Sultan's Harem

In April 1864, Barnum sent his assistant museum manager, John Greenwood, Jr., on an expedition abroad. Charged with collecting "relics" from the Holy Land, Greenwood was also to look into claims that on the island of Cyprus lived a horned woman. In mid-May, Barnum sent further instructions to Greenwood by mail, telling him that if he got the "woman with horns," Greenwood was to get the word out that he'd outbid a flock of eager European showmen. But the main thrust of the letter was Barnum's desire for "a beautiful Circassian girl," to be found in the mountains near the Black Sea. According to well-known racial theories, Circassians were the "purest" example of the Caucasian race. Circassian "stock," the myth ran, supposedly produced the most beautiful white women in the world, and was in demand for the harems of Turkish sultans. Barnum now wanted "one or two of the most beautiful girls you can find, even if they cost $4000 or $5000 in gold." Although Greenwood was to "buy" these women at auction, Barnum wrote, he must make it look, especially while passing through Paris or London, as if they were free women.

For Greenwood, all this was merely business as usual. He knew Barnum intimately, having been the son of a Bethel minister at the time Barnum acquired his museum and having managed it for the showman for years. When the Cyprus horns turned out to be nothing more than wens or tumors, Greenwood sailed for Constantinople to search for beauty. "To carry out his purpose of getting access to the very interior of the slave-marts," Barnum wrote later, "he dressed himself in full Turkish costume. . . . In this manner, he saw a large number of Circassian girls and women, some of them the most beautiful beings he had ever seen." But Barnum failed to describe the purchase of one, even though, within a short period after Greenwood's return, the museum's first Circassian Beauty was put on display. According to publicity materials, she was the daughter of a prince, rescued by Greenwood and Barnum from certain slavery. But according to another account, Greenwood had returned to America empty-handed and Barnum, not to be denied, had gone out and hired a pretty young local woman who was after a job and happened to have frizzy hair, fitting her out with Turkish attire and giving her the name of Zalumma Agra, "Star of the East." With the proper commentary—a mixture of bogus science, graphic slave-auction detail, and erotic suggestion of harem life—the Circassian Beauty was an instant success at the museum, and was soon followed by other Barnum "imports": Zuruby Hannum, Azela Pacha, Zribeda, Zoledod, and others, the mysterious letter "Z" figuring in all of their names. Almost certainly, all of them were dressed-up local women who were taught to wash their hair in beer, then tease it, for the frizzy look of Circassian exotica.

Zalumma Agra, "Star of the East," Barnum's original Circassian Beauty, became the prototype for a whole new category of museum and sideshow presentation. The absence of a language barrier, explained a Barnum pamphlet, "would puzzle the most cunning linguist."

Circassian Beauty Zuruby Hannum often hobnobbed with other Barnum performers, such as giantess Anna Swan, shown here.

The amply endowed Circassian Beauty Zobeide Luti wore low-cut dresses to enhance the stories of her "harem-life past."

The Showman's Most Provocative Photograph

Barnum usually kept his distance from pretty women. He could be puritanical about sex, never learned to dance, claimed that before his marriage to Charity he had never even kissed a girl. Although he was away from his wife for months, even years at a time, and was often thrown into show-business or social situations that could easily have been compromising, he claimed to have complete mastery of his emotions and, even in the face of temptation, could exercise total self-control. There is no evidence this was not true. But through the years, biographers have made much over the implications of a certain photograph, shown opposite. This pretty, 22-year-old dancer named Ernestine de Faiber was in Barnum's employ for the spring and summer of 1864. As in his use of mysterious gypsy fortune-tellers and scantily clothed Circassian beauties, it was Barnum's custom to leaven the moral dramas performed on his stage with intermittent pirouettings by pretty young things—certainly not chorus girls but, rather, "danseuses"—

During the photography session at Brady's, Ernestine struck a pose in front of a prop representing a stage box. Below is Barnum's "Ernestine Souvenir."

"nothing to offend the most fastidious," he advertised, "but everything to gratify healthy curiosity and refined taste." Ernestine was a solo performer, listed with Wood's Minstrels as a "wench dancer" and as a ballet performer in many of the country's leading theaters. It was perfectly normal for her, probably at Barnum's request, to go to Brady's for a sitting. There was nothing extraordinary about the little stage box that was set up in the gallery. In fact, in her posing that day, one of Brady's many exposures caught Ernestine beside the small, empty box. Then, in another shot, a leering Barnum suddenly appeared between the little curtains, creating for all to see an intimation, at least, of salacious intimacy. In all probability, it was simply a red-blooded appreciation of feminine beauty and an uninhibited love of fun. But 20 years later, when Barnum was asked if the photograph could be used in a new edition of his autobiography, his answer was no—"it would not be a proper picture" for such use; he could not even remember the name of the girl who had worked for him, as much, he thought, as 40 or 45 years earlier. The picture was probably an "advertising dodge," he said, meant to excite the public long before his museum days. And she wasn't, in his recollection, much of a dancer anyway. Who knows whether the 74-year-old showman protested too much or was just befuddled. In any case, mystery or no, it is certainly the single most provocative photograph of him.

Ernestine Souvenir

Years later, Barnum tried to dismiss the picture at right as a long-forgotten publicity stunt inflicted on him by others.

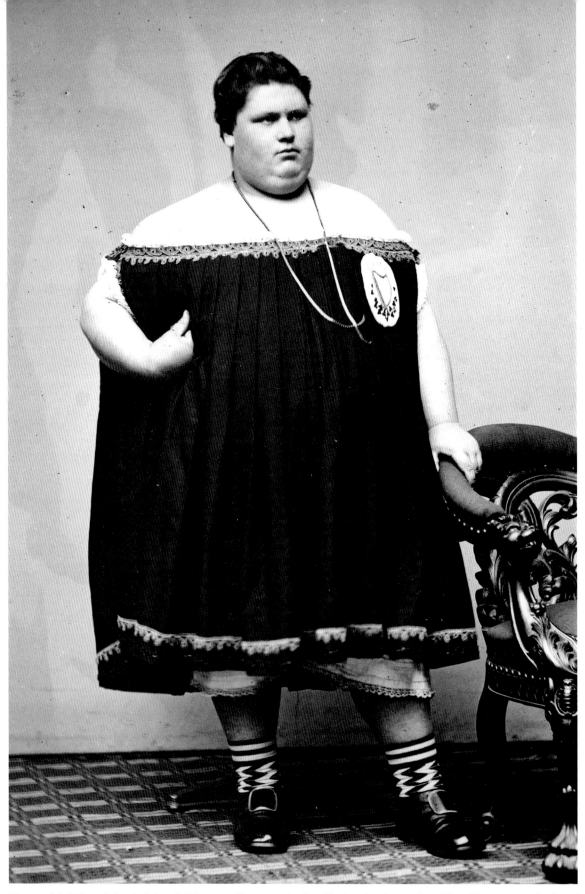

Along with tall and short, fat and thin were Barnum staples. Six-hundred-pounders like this were easily found.

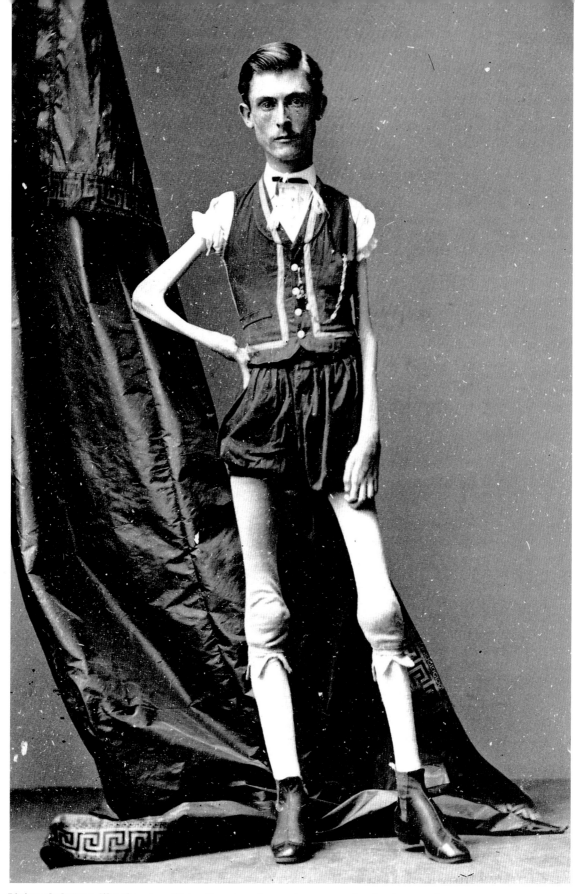

Living skeletons, like the young Isaac Sprague shown above, were harder to come by.

BARNUM'S MUSEUM

TWO DAYS ONLY

OF THE

ROMANTIC AND THRILLING DRAMA

AZUCENA.

WEDNESDAY AND THURSDAY,

APRIL 12 and 13th,

Afternoon at 3, - - Evening at 7 1-2,

The Romantic Drama, with Appropriate Scenery, Dresses, Banners, and Appointments, founded on the Grand Opera of
IL TROVATORE, Music selected
from the most POPULAR
AIRS, by VERDI,
entitled,

AZUCENA;

OR,

THE GIPSY'S VENGEANCE.

Overture on Airs from Il Trovatore arranged by F. W. Peterschen.

Count Di Luna......Mr. W. L. Jamison	Diego...................Mr. Hunter
Ferrando—his Esquire..Mr. J. Bridgman	Manuel...................Mr. Stevens
Manrico—the Trouba-	Soldiers, Attendants, by Auxiliaries.
dour................Mr. Milnes Levick	Abbess of Merida....Miss Jennie Cleaver
Maccaroni—a Servitor	Leonora—betrothed of Man-
...............Mr. L. J. Mestayer	rico ....Mrs. J. J. Prior
Fatalio.................Mr. Hadaway	Inez—her Lady of Hon-
Pablo..................Mr. Anderson	or............Mrs. CARRIE Jamison

Ladies of the Court, Nuns, &c.   Corps de Ballet.

GITANI, OR GIPSY TRIBE.

Allidorio............Mr. B. Porter	Azucena—the Gipsy Pro-
Fabio.................Mr. Haviland	phetess...............Mrs. France
Ru'z............Mr. Cunningham	Ugliana...........Miss Nannie Cook
Scipio—a Boy.......Addie Le Brun	Carina...........Miss Laura Graham

Zingari Girls, &c.

Programme of Scenery and Incidents.

ACT I.

Vestibule and Garden of the Palace of the Count di Luna.   The Count.   The Troubadour.   The Combat.

TABLEAU.
ACT 2.

Ruin and Gipsy Encampment in the Mountains of Biscay.   Gitani Dance and Chorus.   Azucena's Story of Wrong and Vengeance.   Church and Convent of Merida.   The Novice.   The Sacrilege.   The Rescue.

TABLEAU.
ACT 3.

Camp of Di Luna's Army and Fortress of Castellar.   The Prophetess.   The Recognition.   The Curse.   Castle of Aliaferia.   Prison of Manrico.   The Condemned.   The "Miserere."   The Victim.   Dungeon beneath the Castle.   Azucena and Manrico Doomed.   The Brothers.   The Signet.   The Gipsy's Vengeance.

TABLEAU.

Previous to Play,

Great Dancing Giraffe, - - - Tony Denier.

GRAND NATIONAL POULTRY, PIGEON and RABBIT SHOW, APRIL 24. $500 PREMIUMS.   Circulars may be obtained at the Museum office, No. 8 Ann St.

Thomas Mellroy, Steam Job Printer, 10 Spruce Street, N. Y.

Museum flyers just before Lincoln's assassination advertised attractions that continued to be presented even in the days of mourning that followed.

Six months after Lincoln's death, Barnum was in Washington, hoping to add to a collection of hats worn by notable people. For a hat to represent Lincoln, he may have been after this one, worn by Lincoln on April 14 to Ford's Theater. Barnum would have been pleased to know that since early on Lincoln had been very much aware of him. In a speech in 1856, Lincoln had joked that, to keep slavery out of the West, he would "go for the woolly horse itself . . . with which . . . Barnum humbugged the public."

Was Barnum Strangely Oblivious to a National Tragedy?

As different as they were, P. T. Barnum and Abraham Lincoln had many things in common. Exact contemporaries, each had been born of a poor working family, each had been put to farmwork early on but soon graduated to keeping store, each vastly preferred headwork to manual labor, and each had risen through his own efforts to extraordinary national prominence. On top of this, each was a loner, a humorist, a storyteller, and an original user of words. Whereas Barnum employed "business and humanity" as his chief arenas, observed journalist Charles Godfrey Leland, "Lincoln, who was a brother of the same band, employed patriotism and politics." Each expressed "vast problems, financial, intellectual, or natural, by the brief arithmetic of a joke." "Who will not embrace the opportunity to look upon The Nation's Head, The Nation's Deliverer, The People's Favorite and Friend?" Barnum advertised in 1861 when Lincoln was in New York, and it seemed to sum up the showman's admiration.

After the assassination, fully aware that the President had been murdered while watching a play, New York theaters hurried to drape themselves in black. But Barnum's Museum remained strangely oblivious to the tragedy. Its ads offering a normal fare of rabbit shows and turtle dances, just days after Lincoln's death Barnum's declared "a Grand Gala Week!" In contrast, New York City theaters had voted to remain closed for two weeks, centering around the April 20 city-wide observance of Lincoln's funeral. "We were shocked and surprised," commented *The New York Times* on April 21, "to find that notwithstanding [the] arrangement . . . Barnum ventured yesterday to open his Museum. Whilst the city was humbled in prayer on one side of the street, Mr. Barnum's players were mouthing it on the other. The various managers view the preceding with disgust and the public will look upon Mr. Barnum's greedy haste with the contempt it merits."

In fairness to Barnum, though his nonobservance and silence are puzzling, he may not have been present in the city during any of this controversy. Following great effort, he had finally won a coveted seat in the Connecticut Legislature, and by mid-April he seems to have removed to a new base of operations, leaving the museum in the hands of John Greenwood. Barnum never wrote a single word about Lincoln's death in any of his books or articles or known letters. It is almost as if his personal theology, his perpetual optimism, was ignorant of how to cope with such darkness and such sorrow. But in the months ahead, instead of trying to profit by the assassination and duplicate the room in which the President had died, as some urged him to do for an exhibit, he unveiled in his museum a symbol of life, not death—an exact replica of one of Lincoln's own log cabins.

When it was suggested that Barnum purchase the relics from the room where Lincoln died (above), the showman responded, "It won't do! Such a spectacle, for the purpose of making money out of it, would be in bad taste and against the public sentiment of our people."

Instead of assassination relics, Barnum's exhibited a replica of the log cabin Lincoln had built in 1830 in Macon County, Illinois (above).

"Is It Real?" Asks an Astonished Visitor

At the war's end, essayist John E. Hilary Skinner visited Barnum's museum and, wandering through the maze of exhibits, felt the same confused excitement so many had for so long. "I paid my thirty-five cents and entered amongst a crowd of returned veterans. . . . We may watch Houdin's automaton letter-writer, or the glass steam engine, at work. Then there is a case full of historic relics; from the first American flag hoisted over New York to the playbill of Ford's Theater picked up in President Lincoln's box on April 14th. Those who prefer living curiosities may linger round Ned, 'the performing seal'. . . . A pair of white porpoises are to be seen in their tank on the second floor. Barnum's is something unique. A child would enjoy, as thousands of children are enjoying, the waxworks, the giantess, and the seal, whilst a profound zoologist might spend hours before the neglected illustrations of natural history which have drifted into this museum. 'Is it real, or is it humbug?' asks an astonished visitor, and Mr. Barnum replies with a smile, " 'That's just the question; persons who pay their money at the door have a right to form their own opinions after they have got up stairs.' "

Eleven-year-old Young Nicolo, known professionally as The Great Child Wonder, amazed Barnum's museum audiences in 1865. Using three trapezes that he called "cloud swings," Nicolo would soar across a 100-foot space above the theater, turn somersaults on a high central swing, and, as a finale, fall 40 feet onto a special crimson-colored bed perched on the museum stage. The following year the child wonder of the flying trapeze was lost at sea.

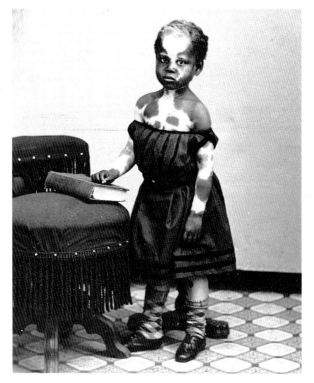

At the same time that the "Leopard Child" (above) was being exhibited at the Museum, Barnum was advertising a miraculous weed, the juice of which was supposedly capable of turning black skins white.

Two of Barnum's albino children smile angelically for the camera.

His Empire of Amusement Is Wiped Out by Sudden Fire

Addie LeBrun appeared as a "child vocalist" at Barnum's in the 1860s, and was part of the resident theater company in 1865, at the time of the fire.

Milnes Levick, a regular at the American Museum for almost a decade, was one of the last actors to adorn Barnum's stage before it burned.

For some time now, Barnum had known the name of his museum's worst enemy: fire. Not only had he seen it claim his beloved home Iranistan, but, one after another, with sickening regularity, it seemed to consume New York's most prominent theaters and entertainment houses. With the city still lacking a municipal fire department, without a single horse-drawn truck yet in use, and with no building codes or fireproofing statutes yet in place, emergency services remained in the hands of neighborhood volunteer groups. Barnum, taking safety matters into his own hands, installed a large water tank on the museum's top floor, specifically for fire emergencies, erected fireproof shielding around his basement boilers, and put in his own water-pump system and a hefty supply of hosing. "If it should be burned or injured here," Barnum wrote to a would-be loaner of a fine painting, it would "cause trouble, and I prefer therefore not to have it."

In one sense, it is amazing that his building did not succumb to fire earlier than it did. Built out of marble, it was supposed to have been lightning-proof, but everyone knew that the crowded wooden interiors and the dusty exhibits were like a pile of old rags just waiting to ignite. The whole place had almost gone up in late 1864, when it became one of 12 New York City landmarks to be targeted in a Confederate incendiary plot. Masterminded by former Buchanan Cabinet member Jacob Thompson, the Canada-based saboteurs' Greek Fire had sputtered out, and Barnum had gone on to display proudly a wax figure of the very man who had attempted to burn the place down. But as late as July 1865, at least one group of men had been overheard discussing details of a new plan to destroy Barnum's museum by fire.

On Thursday, July 13, 1865, at 12:00 noon, smoke was discovered billowing up through the floorboards near the stuffed elephant on the museum's second floor. "The fire probably originated in the engine room," Barnum later wrote, "where steam was constantly kept up to pump fresh air into the water of the aquaria and to propel the immense fans for cooling the atmosphere of the halls." But Barnum was not present at the time, and his son-in-law Samuel Hurd, in charge of the museum and on the scene, learned specifically that the engine room was not on fire. Instead, Hurd attested, the fire had originated "in a small room which had been formed by an enlargement of the Ann Street staircase." And according to the house treasurer, H. O. Tiffany, fire broke out simultaneously in three separate locations in the building, suggesting arson.

The museum's morning performances had finished just minutes earlier, and the house crowds were already thinning. Hurd estimated that 400 customers remained in the building, many of them already in the process of exiting. Taking charge of their retreat, Hurd ordered the great water pumps to be started and the museum hoses to be readied for flooding the Grand Saloon. As dense smoke filled the air now, museum personnel began

This contemporary painting by C. P. Cranch shows the losing battle waged by firemen on the blazing museum.

to act furiously. Tiffany, having raced to the top floor to throw open the valve of the emergency water tank, was suddenly trapped there by flames. Thinking quickly, he ripped down one of the draperies and managed to lower himself out the window and down to the third-floor balcony, from where he could jump to the lower balcony and then the ground. House actor William B. Harrison fought frantically through the smoke in search of his dressing room, determined to rescue his character wigs and his cash box, which contained $100. Samuel Hurd, having helped the last guests out, raced back to the second-floor offices and removed thousands of dollars in bank bills from Barnum's desk, locking them safely in a fireproof chest.

Out on the street, pandemonium reigned. Thousands of spectators had by now gathered in front of St. Paul's Church and the Astor House and on Park Row to watch the growing inferno. Firemen, setting up ladders to the Ann Street balconies, were breaking open windows and beginning to spray in water from their hand-drawn fire trucks below. With the steam engines letting out erratic, blisteringly loud screams, at one point the crowd panicked and stampeded.

One by one the last occupants of the building emerged—one of Barnum's fat women, assisted by Officer Dodge of the Broadway Fire Squad; the "Living Skeleton," who had remained for as long as he could by

Sketched by A. R. Waud for *Harper's Weekly*, the ruins of the museum still smoke the morning after the fire.

the side of the giant girl, Anna Swan, who was unable to fit through any available exit; and then, finally, Anna Swan herself, ingeniously rescued by her own museum colleagues. "The employees . . . procured a loft derrick," reported the New York *Tribune*. "A portion of the wall was then broken off on each side of the window, the strong tackle was got in readiness, [and] the tall woman was . . . swung over the heads of the people in the street . . . and lowered from the third story, amid enthusiastic applause." By 1:00 p.m., the entire building was a mass of flames. Now all attention turned to the hideous screams of the animals still caught inside. Of all the dozens of large animals and the hundreds of small ones, only a handful were ever to escape. The birds were the luckiest, set free at first alarm, parrots and hummingbirds and vultures and eagles all flying away into the New York skies. Then Ned, the Learned Seal, was saved by a Brooklyn fireman, "dragged out by his flukes," reported the New York *Clipper*, "placed in a champagne basket and conveyed on a cart to Fulton Street where a . . . fish tank was found." A *Tribune* reporter at a third-story window across Ann Street became an eyewitness to the fate of the unlucky animals still inside. "The monkeys were perched around the windows, shivering with dread and afraid to jump out. The snakes were writhing about, crippled and blistered by the heat. . . . [T]he alligators dashed fiercely about endeavoring to escape, opening and closing their great jaws in ferocious torture; but the poor whale . . . with great ulcers bursting from its blubbery sides, could only feebly swim about. . . ." Though a number of large snakes now managed to escape from the building into the crowds, most of them were quickly trampled to death or killed with sticks. All the other animals— lions and polar bears and monkeys and kangaroos, even the two beautiful recently arrived beluga whales—were either burned or boiled alive.

With 18 adjacent buildings now in flames as well, at 2:30 p.m. the museum's outer walls fell. Nothing left to do, Samuel Hurd wired Barnum in Hartford, where he was addressing the Connecticut Legislature on the subject of railroad schemes. The telegram announcing the museum's doom was handed to him literally in the midst of his address, and Barnum later recorded his reaction: "I glanced over the dispatch, folded it, laid it on my desk, and calmly continued my speech as if nothing had happened." Then Barnum, who had come to believe nothing ever happens without the express will of the Creator, drew his lecture to a close, drove home to Fairfield, and proceeded to get a good night's sleep. Only the next morning did he make the trip in to New York City to inspect firsthand the scene of the disaster.

In one terrible day, he had lost "an assemblage of rarities which a half million dollars could not restore," he estimated, "and a quarter of a century could not collect." *Leslie's Weekly*, which did not know Barnum's insurance covered just $40,000, estimated the loss at $2 million. *Harper's* simply called it "a funeral pyre." But on that first morning after the fire, Barnum was gathering with friends at the Astor House, where he was already talking about building a new and better museum, "three times the size of my late establishment."

Barnum's favorite newspaper, the New York Tribune, *like many of the city papers, ran a sympathetic editorial on the day after the fire.*

"The destruction of no building in this city could have caused so . . . much regret as that of Barnum's Museum. . . . Pleasant memories clustered about the place, which for so many years has been the chief resort for amusement to the common people who cannot often afford to treat themselves to a night at the more expensive theatres, while to the children of the city, Barnum's has been a fountain of delight, ever offering new attractions as captivating and as implicitly believed in as the Arabian Nights Entertainments; Theatre, Menagerie and Museum, it amused, instructed, and astonished. . . . It was a source of unfailing interest to all country visitors, and New York to many of them was only the place that held Barnum's Museum. It was the first thing—often the only thing—they visited when they came among us. . . . We mourn its loss, but not as without consolation. Barnum's Museum is gone but Barnum himself, happily, did not share the fate of his rattlesnakes and his, at [last], most un-"happy Family." There are fishes in the seas and beasts in the forest; birds still fly in the air and strange creatures still roam in the deserts; giants and pigmies still wander up and down the earth; the oldest man, the fattest woman, and the smallest baby are still living, and Barnum will find them."

Only Eight Weeks Later, His New Museum Opens

Within days of the fire, Barnum had leased the Winter Garden and opened a temporary museum show, its featured performers listed in his July 28 flyer (above).

Six weeks after the fire, Barnum's new museum was ready for opening. Its advertisement of September 16 (above) shows that many of the old faithfuls had turned out and Barnum was already claiming 100,000 new curiosities.

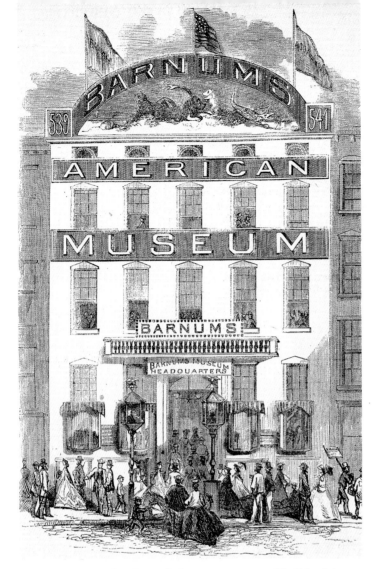

Leslie's Illustrated **welcomed the new museum with this picture and praise for the proprietor. "Long ere the ruins of his old Museum were cold, he had dispatched agents to Europe to gather up, without any regards to cost, every article of purchaseable curiosity they could find."**

The entrancing Kate Pennoyer performed at Barnum's new museum as both "danseuse" and pantomimist.

Born without arms, new addition Anna Eliza Leak could perform wonders with her feet and toes.

Barnum's first inclination was to retire. "Accept this fire as a notice to quit, and go a-fishing," his old friend Horace Greeley told him. But, as Barnum wrote a few years later, two other considerations weighed heavily upon him—the fact that 150 employees were suddenly out of work, and the real need of a large city like New York for a good museum. A benefit was held for his employees at the Academy of Music, and at it he announced his decision. He had engaged the Winter Garden Theater for a few weeks, would start performances there immediately, and hoped to complete a new museum in the fall. Incredibly, in September, the new museum opened. Barnum's choice for the site was not random. It certainly had to be on Broadway, and it had to be farther uptown, above Canal Street, where the center of the city now lay. Back in 1850—in his Oriental phase, which had helped give rise to Iranistan—he had bought the contents of the prestigious new Chinese Museum and leased its building at 539 Broadway. Coinciding with the Jenny Lind tour, it had been part of a concerted attempt to upgrade his public image. After a year, however, Barnum gave up his lease on the building and moved the immense collection of Chinese objects and figurines down to Ann Street, and later into storage. After Barnum left it, 539 Broadway had fallen into a downward spiral; first it was a ballroom with apartments, next a minstrel stage, next a saloon advertising "pretty waiter girls," and then a notorious dance hall and pickup joint which was shut down on morals charges. In 1863, the building had been taken over by the world-renowned animal-trainer Isaac Van Amburgh, and it was from him that Barnum now leased the three-story granite building as a home for his new museum.

The establishment shaped up quickly. Barnum constructed five long saloons and filled them with new curiosities. Importing a London collection once owned by the famous lion-slayer Gordon Cummings, Barnum put up displays of the skins, tusks, heads and skeletons of nearly every large African animal. And when Van Amburgh finished his summer tour, Barnum invited him on as a partner, making room for his live animals in the adjoining building, number 537. Once again, visitors to Barnum's Museum could see a host of rare animals—Tipoo Saib, a huge African elephant; America's only living giraffe; and famous Ned, the Learned Seal, the only animal to have been saved from the fire on Ann Street. But also here were Van Amburgh's lions and tigers, his zebras and camels, llamas, kangaroos, hyenas, ibexes, and polar bears. Expanding the museum backward as well and putting in a second entrance on Mercer Street at the rear of the building, Barnum opened a brand-new lecture room and theater that could seat 2,500 spectators.

It had long been Barnum's dream to open a free museum next door to his paying one, and to this end he now got President Andrew Johnson to request that all U.S. ministers, consuls, and commercial agents assist in the collection of rare objects and oddities all over the world. He would store them, he promised, until the free museum existed. And so Barnum was back in business. The new museum quickly became as popular as the old. Barnum had an art gallery, a rooftop rifle range, a glassblowers' exhibit, and an in-house photography studio, where customers could have their portraits taken while they waited. And on the top floor of the building, with its own apartments and living room and common kitchen, was space enough for Barnum's "living curiosities." Here they all were, the old faithfuls—Anna Swan, Zobeide Luti, Routh Goshen, tiny General Grant, Jr. Soon, downstairs, new bearded ladies took the stage, fresh beauties batted their brand-new Circassian eyes, Noah Orr the Ohio giant gazed down at the customers from the stratosphere, Adelaide Powers and Adah Briggs displayed their mountains of fat. For the most part, only the names had changed.

He was back in business for sure, but Barnum was not quite the enthusiast he had been at his original museum.

Barnum added much-needed zest to his new museum by going into partnership with Isaac Van Amburgh, the country's foremost lion-tamer and menagerie-owner. In his most celebrated act in the cage, Van Amburgh actually convinced a lion and a lamb to lie down side by side.

By 1866, Barnum's new American Museum, now in conjunction with Van Amburgh's Menagerie Company, had spread into the adjacent building on Broadway, almost doubling its size. In this idealized drawing from Barnum and Van Amburgh's letterhead, the museum's large new plate-glass window is visible; this allowed people to look in from the street upon the wild animals.

George L. Fox joined Barnum at the new museum in its first year, and his artistry helped make it a success. The changes in expression of his mobile face and the subtle use of simple props made Fox the most hilarious yet poignant clown of his day.

197

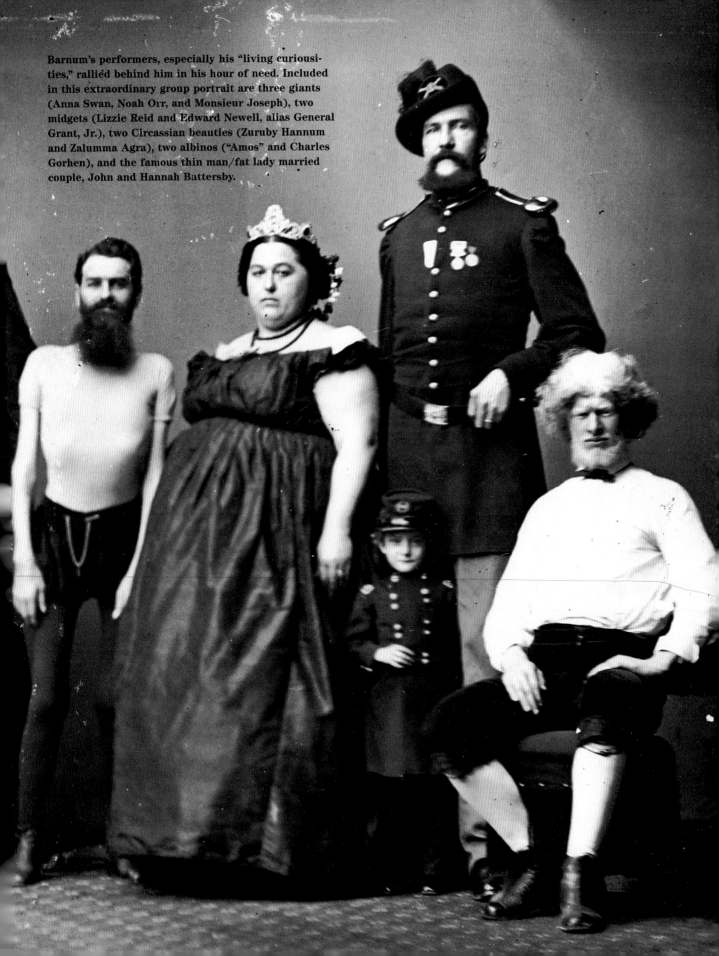

Barnum's performers, especially his "living curiousities," rallied behind him in his hour of need. Included in this extraordinary group portrait are three giants (Anna Swan, Noah Orr, and Monsieur Joseph), two midgets (Lizzie Reid and Edward Newell, alias General Grant, Jr.), two Circassian beauties (Zuruby Hannum and Zalumma Agra), two albinos ("Amos" and Charles Gorhen), and the famous thin man/fat lady married couple, John and Hannah Battersby.

"Reluctantly," He Finally Runs for Office

It always seems to me," observed Barnum in the 1860s, "that a man who 'takes no interest in politics' is unfit to live in a land where the government rests in the hand of the people." Claiming that he found politics personally "distasteful," Barnum had in fact long hungered for elected office, even flirting in the 1850s with a run for governor. In 1865, Barnum allowed his name to be put forward for the Connecticut Legislature. "I did this because I felt that it would be an honor . . . to vote for the then proposed amendment to the Constitution of the United States to abolish slavery forever from the land," Barnum wrote, and this was clearly his primary motive. It was also the case that Barnum, after three decades in show business, wanted to do something to prove his public-spiritedness. Nominated on March 24 as the Republican representative for Fairfield, he was elected to the State House on April 3 by a majority of 187 votes.

In 1864, *Leslie's* captured Barnum's immense vitality in this engraving of the soon-to-be candidate at his desk, with a portrait of Jenny Lind on the wall over his shoulder. "In person Barnum is about 5 feet 10 inches and weighs about 170 lb.," the paper stated. "He is always quick and energetic in his movements, and his sharp gray eyes see more at a glance than can be performed in a month. His complexion is light, and about his face there is a perpetual smile."

As a state representative, Barnum fought the railroad price-fixing tactics of Cornelius Vanderbilt. Looking like a dapper gentleman in this Brady portrait, Vanderbilt was actually a ruthless, coarse, yet dynamic financial infighter, amassing a fortune of over $100 million through steamboat and railroad ventures. "Is it possible you are Barnum?" he once roared at the showman. "Why, I expected to see a monster!"

Joseph R. Hawley, the Republican candidate for governor of Connecticut, thought his party's only blunder was nominating Barnum for Congress. Still, he admired the showman-politician.

On May 2, Barnum arrived in Hartford to begin his new work. Appointed to the chairmanship of the State Agricultural Committee, his chief struggle over the next two years would be with Commodore Cornelius Vanderbilt and his price-fixing monopoly over Connecticut's commuter rail lines. Barnum's high-water mark in politics came not in the railroad controversies, however, but in an address delivered before the state legislature on May 26, 1865. With Connecticut's ratification of the 13th Amendment needed to ban slavery officially and open up suffrage to black Americans, Barnum gathered up all of his eloquence and his power and his "heart of hearts" in behalf of the great cause that Lincoln had died for. Guided by deeply held Universalist beliefs, and standing before a huge crowd, Barnum became suddenly oracular. "A human soul is not to be trifled with," he proclaimed. "It may inhabit the body of a Chinaman, a Turk, an Arab or a Hotentot—it is still an immortal spirit!"

Following two successful terms in the legislature, Barnum became the Republican candidate for U.S. Congress in 1867. Opposing him was a distant relative, William H. Barnum, but from the beginning the showman had a host of other troubles as well. With a national spotlight now focusing in on him, suddenly all the old puritanical prejudices against showmen were resurfacing. "He is the personification . . . of . . . a certain low kind of humbug," blasted *The Nation*, "which, funny as it often appears, eats out the heart of religion." Speaking of Barnum's "intense and concentrated vulgarity," his "rottenness and uncleanness," and his "twenty or thirty year-long . . . depraving and demoralizing influence," *The Nation* concluded that Connecticut should be ashamed for finding "no fitter representative of its ideas than the proprietor of the whooly horse and the bearded woman."

"Let them show me as I am," Barnum had pleaded when he first entered politics; "God knows that is bad enough!" But with "half the Christian Community" now believing he wore "horns and hoofs," and even the humorist Mark Twain ridiculing his candidacy in print, the humbug image, Barnum found, was almost impossible to shake.

By the April 1 vote, the verdict was in, and even Joseph R. Hawley's surefire gubernatorial candidacy had been swept under by the Democrat flood. "Our platform is the best that we ever had," wrote Hawley on April 2 to Charles Dana, "and the party is cleaner and purer, save for the great blunder . . . in nominating Barnum." But if Barnum had hurt the Republicans, continued Hawley, he was "a better man than many out of State suppose. He is one of those fellows who have double characters, one professional and scoundrelly, the other private, church-going, decorous, and utterly abstinent from pocket-picking." Disgusted by the whole situation, Barnum wrote that he was tired of trying to be "all things to all men" and having to "shake hands with those whom I despised" and "to kiss the dirty babies of those whose votes are courted"; that he was tired of all the "filth and scandal, the slander and vindictiveness, the plottings and fawnings." Wanting nothing more to do with the life of the "oily politician," Barnum claimed he was not at all disappointed to have lost the election.

His Private World Includes an Inner Circle of Intellect

Barnum thought his friend Phoebe Cary, with whom he liked to drive around Central Park and match minds, was the "wittiest woman in America."

Tender and tactful Alice Cary was the counterpart of the less reserved, quick-witted Phoebe. In their home the poet sisters ran an informal salon for the city's best and brightest, with Barnum a big part of it.

Despite his deep love for Connecticut, where his rural homes afforded him, he wrote, "the highest pleasures" of his life, in many ways Barnum was a true city boy. With his museums offering him a base of operations in New York, he had long kept apartments for extended stays in the city. Now, in the summer of 1867, deciding to spend seven months a year in New York, Barnum bought an elegant mansion on the corner of 39th Street and Fifth Avenue, near the site where the old Crystal Palace had once stood. New York in 1867 was a different city from what it had been in the mid-1850s, when Barnum had last lived there; much larger, its center had crept gradually northward to encompass Murray Hill and beyond. "I am convinced that the city is the most congenial residence during the cooler season of the year," Barnum wrote soon after his move. "There is a sense of satisfaction even in the well-cleaned sidewalks after a snowstorm, and an almost selfish happiness in looking out upon a storm from a well-warmed library or parlor window. . . . The city is the center of attractions in the way of operas, concerts, picture galleries, libraries, the best music, the best preaching, the best of everything in aesthetical enjoyment." The new house was well situated, close to everything Barnum wanted to be part of.

And so Barnum settled into his enjoyable routines, waking up daily to a pot of "delicious coffee," and loving to find the morning paper "fresh from the press, lying on the breakfast table," something impossible in the country. By now Barnum was famous worldwide, with letters from faraway places, like New Zealand, reaching him addressed simply "Mr. Barnum, America." After attending to correspondence and visitors at home during the morning, Barnum would head out to his offices for meetings with agents and assistants. Guests at Barnum's table discovered him to be an "incorrigible humorist," "ready to gush at any time," observed writer Joel Benton, and "seeming to have no power to keep jokes back when knife and fork were at play." Dinner was served at 6:00 p.m. sharp, for Charity's benefit. She then retired early after dinner each night, leaving Barnum alone in the evenings. Ever since the Jerome Clock fiasco, she had been a kind of invalid. And yet relatives spoke of her many kindnesses, how she was always ready to help far-flung cousins and nieces when they were sick or in financial difficulty. And she continued to enjoy friends, too, at times rallying herself to join in the fun. "I do not recollect an instance in which she started a joke," wrote clergyman George Emerson, but she often sent "back a gibe with good interest! 'Well,' [Barnum] would say to me when we reached the library, 'Charity gave me a stinger that time, didn't she?' " Inviting Emerson into her home once in the late 1860s, Charity whispered, "[M]y husband needs your company so much," proof of her ongoing concern for Barnum during her nightly absences. But it was not only to Emerson that Barnum turned to help fill his evenings. Increasingly, it was to a pair of unusual and fascinating women, the poets Phoebe and Alice Cary. On

Whitelaw Reid, top editor of the *Tribune* and later Minister to France and Ambassador to England, was one of the distinguished newsmen in the Cary inner circle. Reid volunteered to help Barnum with a rewrite of his autobiography.

The writer Bayard Taylor usually came to the Cary tea table with his bright and talented wife. Back in 1850, it had been Taylor who was given first prize in the Ode Contest to welcome Jenny Lind.

Ole Bull, the great violinist from Norway, who had first delighted American audiences back in the 1840s, was a frequent visitor to the house on 20th Street.

Sometimes present at the Sunday-evening receptions was the gentle poet John Greenleaf Whittier, dressed in his simple Quaker uniform. Whittier wrote a poem for Alice Cary upon her death—"And bird and flowers are lost to her/ Who was their best interpreter."

Of all the eminent women reformers who dropped in on the Carys' reception, none
was more outspoken and iron-willed than Susan B. Anthony.

Sunday evenings, as he had done from time to time earlier, Barnum now slipped out after dinner regularly and walked over to a house on 20th Street belonging to the Cary sisters. Here, over the course of 15 years, had evolved the most distinguished, eclectic, and strangely tender literary circle anywhere in New York, what John Greenleaf Whittier came to call a "trysting place of Liberty." Here, as if drawn to a beacon, were Horace Greeley and John G. Whittier, Bayard Taylor and the brilliant young editor Theodore Tilton, as well as Whitelaw Reid and the great musician Ole Bull. Here, too, came some of the leading women of the age, Elizabeth Cady Stanton and Susan B. Anthony, Anna Dickinson and Kate Field and the vivacious author and editor Mary Louise Booth. Known as "the Cary Salon," it was a place where anyone thoughtful was welcome, "where everybody thinks," wrote one contemporary, "but nobody is tabooed for *what* he thinks." One wag dubbed it, because of its diversity, an "ecclesiastical and political 'Happy Family,'" showing how Barnumisms were creeping into daily parlance. On the surface, P. T. Barnum might have seemed like an unlikely guest among such literary and spiritual refinement. But he was an equal among equals here, a man "with great brains," wrote the Carys' pastor, Charles Deems, "which would have made him notable in any department." Members of the salon were drawn to his storytelling genius, his penetrating grasp of human character, his plain good nature. Plus, Barnum and the Cary sisters simply hit it off. "On one of those pleasant Sunday evenings on 20th Street," Barnum wrote once in a letter, "I tried to leave the house early, without attracting attention, and was just selecting my hat and coat from the hat stand when Phoebe and her niece came out to remonstrate. 'Now why do you follow me out,' I said laughingly, 'I am not going to carry anything away.' 'We wish you would,' she quickly replied, throwing back her arms as if she was ready to be 'carried out.'"

Growing closer and closer to Phoebe, Barnum took her carriage riding in Central Park, shared hours of "rollicking laughter" with her, had her to his home often, and gave her tours of his museum as well. On one such visit, escorted by Barnum past his tank filled with large serpents, Phoebe let out a loud scream, jumped backward, tripping, and fell into Barnum's outstretched arms. As he held her for a moment, she looked up at him and then, with her typical lightning wit, quipped, "Well, I am not the first woman who has fallen through the wiles of the serpent!"

Another Cary habitué was Elizabeth Cady Stanton, who worked closely with Susan B. Anthony in the battle for women's suffrage. When she married Mr. Stanton in 1840, Miss Cady had the word "obey" stricken from the ceremony.

Kate Field, the graphic journalist and lecturer, was among the dozens of fascinating women in the Cary circle. To the group Field brought a combination of earnestness and eccentricity.

A Friend and a Foe in the Newspaper World

Jovial, outgoing, fun to be with, Barnum prided himself on his wide circle of friends. None was closer than the New York *Tribune*'s Horace Greeley, who offered the showman stimulating companionship and helped open his way to high intellectual circles.

After paying too much for the old museum land, New York *Herald* editor James Gordon Bennett asked for his money back. Barnum's icy reply was, "I don't make child's bargains."

O f all the eminent guests at the Cary Salon, none was a more important ally and friend to Barnum than Horace Greeley. The two country transplants had practically grown up together in New York City; opening up shop in the early 1840s and then flourishing, they burned with the same kind of energy. Greeley's *Tribune* was quickly the most influential paper in the city, if not the country, and from the beginning had a decidedly pro-Barnum tone. By the early 1850s, the two men were fast friends. Accepting hospitality at Iranistan, Greeley wrote articles there in the great Chinese Library. He was a regular visitor to the museum as well, advising his showman friend to stick to comedy on stage, for did not museum audiences "come to laugh"? By 1867, Greeley had become a regular guest at 538 Fifth Avenue, sometimes moving into Barnum's new townhouse for weeks at a time. As in Bridgeport, where Barnum had a special "Greeley" bedroom, in New York the absentminded newspaperman was supplied with house slippers and a dressing gown and issued his own key to Barnum's front door.

The magnitude of Greeley's friendship was equaled by the intensity of hostility felt for Barnum by another newsman, James Gordon Bennett. Editor and owner of the New York *Herald*, Bennett had been out to get Barnum ever since the young showman had gleefully hoodwinked him with the not-so-aged Joice Heth, back in 1835. Later, Barnum complained that the *Herald* was giving bad notices to Jenny Lind, when actually Bennett's articles focused not on the singer but upon her manager and what the paper thought were Barnum's questionable tactics to promote his import and to sell tickets. Infuriated, Barnum sent Bennett a sworn affidavit claiming innocence. Back and forth they sparred. Bennett described the American Museum as grubby, not "worthy of the city." Barnum led the theaters of New York in a boycott of the paper. Once, Barnum had even written the owners of a competing paper, the New York *Sun*, that Bennett's wife was really the power behind the *Herald* throne, that she was a heavy drinker and social climber and claimed to edit her husband's paper herself. "Please make what use you can of these facts," Barnum concluded, "and keep my name secret." At another point in their long feud, Barnum sent the newsman a letter which he called "a Flag of Truce." Even though he claimed to like any kind of newspaper mention, no matter how critical, back in 1854 Barnum was already exhibiting remarkably thin skin and trying to bury the hatchet. "I doubt whether you really entertain any enmity against me. . . . But having been in the habit of making me a kind of target for the last 18 years, this habit has become a kind of 'second nature' to you. . . . Don't you think it is time to let me drop?" Bennett didn't, and the back-and-forth bashing continued.

Horace Greeley could be found at the Cary home Sunday evenings drinking "his two cups of sweetened milk," a nightly ritual, and joining lively debates about women's suffrage.

Fresh Curiosities Enhance the New Museum

As a mere child Annie Jones was billed as "the infant Esau" (above) when she first displayed her fuzz at Barnum's new museum for a healthy salary. Annie's mother (below) stuck by her as she grew to become the famous "Bearded Girl" (right). As an adult, Annie would become the country's top bearded lady and spokesperson for Barnum's "freaks," a word she tried to abolish from the business.

Millie-Christine, Barnum's "Two-Headed Girl" (left and far left), actually was two girls, joined at the buttocks, with part of their spine in common. Born in the South to slave parents, they were sold as infants to a "Southern gentleman" exhibitor for $30,000.

According to their official booklet, Hoomio and Iola, the "Wild Australian Children," were spotted by explorers who first thought they were kangaroos. With the help of lassos and meat for bait, these "long, sharp-toothed cannibals" were brought to bay and were now thought, so said their cruel pamphlet, to be the "link" between the orang-utan and man.

The "curiosity" platform at the new museum outdid its predecessor—if that was possible. Barnum billed little Annie Jones as "the Child Esau" and described her as unique. "Never . . . has there been known an instance of a mere child, and a female at that, who . . . supported such a marvellous development of mustache and side whiskers." Annie went on to educate herself, become an accomplished musician, marry twice, and retire rich. That was more than Millie-Christine could claim. Single all their lives, yet joined together for life, they danced on stage, skipped rope, and, billed as "the Two Headed Nightingale," they harmonized, Millie the alto, Christine the soprano. After singing, they turned around and their point of joining was shown to the audience "without any infringement of modesty." An announcer explained that the girls were able to sleep at separate times but felt hunger simultaneously. In their pamphlet, which was for sale, Professor Pancoast stated that "physically there is no objection to the marriage of her, or them, but morally a most decided one." The treatise closed with an attempt at humor: "One man courted her successfully, but before popping the question, kissed one face first and could never get the consent of the other head. She is now waiting till a two-headed man comes along and is gay with hope."

Nearby on the platform were the Wild Australian Children. Publicity pamphlets had them belonging to "a distinct race hitherto unknown to civilization." Their small, "strangely shaped" heads were adapted "for creeping through the tall rank grass of their native plains, and springing upon the sleeping game or unsuspecting foe." The secret that only showmen back then knew was that, in truth, the Wild Australian Children were severely retarded microcephalic siblings from Circleville, Ohio.

Another Inferno Ends the Museum Days Forever

During the bitter winter of 1867–68, it had snowed more than 30 times, and on the morning of Tuesday, March 3, the Northeast was frozen solid and encased in snow. In his New York mansion, while taking breakfast with Charity and a friend, Barnum was leisurely reading aloud from the morning newspaper when he came upon a familiar headline. He recorded his reaction not long afterward. " 'Hallo!' I said. 'Barnum's Museum is burned.' 'Yes,' said my wife, with an incredulous smile. 'I suspect it is.' 'It is a fact,' said I, 'just listen; "Barnum's Museum totally destroyed by fire." ' This was read so coolly, and I showed so little excitement, that both of the ladies supposed I was joking." Barnum was not joking in the slightest. A son-in-law later that day remarked to his wife, "Your father won't care half so much about it as he would if his pocket had been picked of fifty dollars. That would have vexed him, but he will take this heavier loss as simply the fortune of war."

Harper's Weekly captured the terrible plight of Barnum's animals at the height of the second fire (above). "Hundreds of beasts of every description," reported *The New York Times*, "[were heard] giving vent to feelings of mortal agony and fear." A bear managed to stay alive and lived for the next two days in the ruins of the smoldering building.

Yes, it had happened all over again. A defective flue at 539 Broadway had been the immediate cause, and shortly after midnight on March 3, fire had swept through the building. The animals were the first to get wind of trouble, their moans and howls waking the "curiosities" sleeping on the top floor of the building, who then put in the call of "Fire" before fleeing the museum for an all-night tavern across the street. A major delay now occurred. Firemen were off on another call and the streets were so filled with snow that their horses could only proceed slowly on their way to Barnum's. By the time they finally arrived, it was 1:00 a.m. and the fire, now almost an hour in progress, had spread into the other half of Barnum's Museum and into the large theater at the rear of the building. "A more bedraggled and bemoaning set of sufferers never were seen," Barnum later described the scene secondhand—"half-drenched, half-frozen, half-clothed, the women clad in cheap calico, with old shawls, or blankets." But it was the animals Barnum mourned most, "burned to death in their cages." Crowds encircled the flaming building and fire engines played their hoses upon it—but to no avail. "The water froze almost as soon as it left the hose," Barnum wrote, "and when at last everything was destroyed, except the front granite wall of the Museum building, that and the ladder, and lamp-posts in front, were covered in a gorgeous frame-work of transparent ice." For days following, thousands of persons congregated in the streets, Barnum concluded, "in order to get a view of the magnificent ruins."

This time it really was over. Barnum never had the heart to start up his museum again.

The day after the fire, only the ice-encased granite front of the new museum remained standing. *Harper's* reported that "at night, when the moon shone down upon the ruins, the scene from Broadway was one of exquisite beauty."

In Mansion Number Three, Guests Are a Priority

Charity continued to deteriorate. No one quite knew what her ailments were, apart from having to cope with a frenetic, indefatigable jokester of a life partner. But they kept Barnum's nervous wife from traveling with her husband or sharing much of his full life.

Mansions came easily to Barnum; each one he built satisfied some deep need in the part of his life he was then leading. First feeling the millionaire flush in the late 1840s, he had constructed the closest thing in the U.S. to an actual palace. Iranistan was an exotic showplace, a symbol of grandeur rather than hearth and home, and when fire consumed it in 1857, he waited until he was firmly back on his financial feet and then constructed Lindencroft. Much less ostentatious, highly elegant, yet eminently useful, it was a place to live in, he thought then, for the rest of his life. But seven years later, with Charity's health deteriorating and her doctor urging her to live closer to the sea, Barnum acted in his usual precipitous manner, selling Lindencroft and moving into a small "interim" farmhouse near the seashore. In March 1868, just two weeks after the burning of the American Museum, Barnum learned of the death of his 83-year-old mother, Irena. Unlike her high-living son, Barnum's mother had stayed on in her small Bethel home with few of life's luxuries to help smooth her way. In 1866, her son had surprised her with a gift of a real bathroom, her first, a replacement for the free-standing privy she had made do for so many years. Now, after taking charge of her funeral, and the auctioning of her house and its meager belongings, Barnum began dreaming up a new mansion for himself, this time not in Fairfield but in Bridgeport. This one was to be an elaborate summer manor overlooking the water, envisioned by the increasingly gregarious showman as a giant guest-house, "with dressing rooms and baths to every chamber," he described it, and "two beautiful cottages" on the property. His plan was to live in this immense gingerbread confection of comfort during the hot summer months and reside at his city mansion, amid "metropolitan excitement," in the fall, winter, and spring. Barnum liked to ask his intellectual friends to help him name his new dwellings. Witty Phoebe Cary, playing with the petrel's second name of "Mrs. Carey's chicken," wrote him, "If the house were my own, being one of Mother Cary's chickens, I could call it 'The Petrel's Nest' but do not see how I can get your name in euphoniously unless I name it 'The Cove of Finny-as!' Is that too scaly—or does it sound of-fish-all?" Bayard Taylor was asked how he liked "Waldameer" "as signifying (in German) 'woods near the sea.' " The spelling was changed and "Waldemere" the estate became. Barnum was to live here for 20 years among the treasures he had gathered over a lifetime. Some of those treasures were human. One of the cottages on the grounds, named "Wavewood," was occupied by his daughter Caroline and her family. The other cottage, for visitors, was actually called the "Petrel's Nest," maybe in hopes that Phoebe Cary would leave the city for a short stay. Mark Twain came to visit. Horace Greeley stopped in so often he had a room named after him. And Charity was happy there, by the sea.

When Barnum decided on something, he wanted the result fast. Waldemere, with its forest of transplanted trees and its own gas generating plant to supply light, was built in eight months' time by, as Barnum put it, "a regiment of faithful laborers."

A stereoscopic card shows Waldemere's driveway as it looked from Barnum's elegant, pillared front porch.

This is the cluttered main sitting room in Waldemere. Barnum lived here longer than in any of his other houses.

Out-Hoaxing a Hoax with a Hoax of His Own

In the "spirit" photograph Barnum had made of himself, the specter of Abraham Lincoln loomed as it does in this double image.

The original foundling to play the part of Lavinia Thumb's baby was a boy who in a few years had become bigger than his "mother." Lavinia remembered taking the problem to Barnum. "He agreed with us," she told an interviewer. "He thought our baby should not grow. Thus we exhibited English babies in England, French babies in France, and German babies in Germany."

As usual, hoaxes and humbugs came in all guises, and as the catastrophic decade of the 1860s reeled to a close, there came a burst of them. A few years earlier, P. T. Barnum had been the author of a new and telling book, *Humbugs of the World*. In it he tried to differentiate between harmless hoaxes that actually gave people pleasure and criminal misrepresentations "daily practiced on the ignorant and superstitious." Spirit photography was one of the cruel hoaxes he singled out—unprincipled photographers taking advantage of the bereaved by creating trick pictures of them which, when the emulsion dried, also contained the hazy likenesses of the deceased so missed. In April of 1869, Barnum offered to testify in the trial of a notorious spirit photographer named William Mumler. To prepare himself, Barnum told the court he had the day before visited the gallery of the celebrated photographer Abraham Bogardus, "and asked him if he could take a spirit photograph, telling him that I did not want any humbug about it; he said he could do it; I examined the glass and discovered nothing in it. . . . When done, it had my likeness and the shadow of Abraham Lincoln." It was by just such methods that Mumler was preying on his innocent victims! Under cross-examination, Barnum went on to defend his own "dabblings in humbuggery" throughout his career. "I have never been in any humbug business," he claimed, "where I did not give value for the money." Lavinia Thumb's "baby" was in that category. For several years now, Lavinia had been increasing the public interest in her and Tom by exhibiting a tiny child as her own. In fact, it was an orphan acquired by Barnum. After the child outgrew its "parents," Lavinia and Tom rented native babies to perform with them in each country they visited. Another value-laden hoax occurred in August of 1869, when a huge "petrified giant" was dug up on a little farm in Cardiff, New York. Before long, the colossus was housed beneath a tent, and money was pouring in from ticket sales. The Cardiff Giant's fame caught Barnum's fancy, and after trying his hardest to buy it, he fashioned an exact replica and put it on display in New York. This hoax of a hoax was soon outdrawing the real thing, and it made little difference to public enthusiasm when the truth came out— that a stonecutter had fashioned the original giant out of a block of gypsum, after which it had been aged by the use of darning needles, water, and a sulfuric acid bath, and then buried for its subsequent "discovery."

More important than humbugs to Barnum in 1869 was the publication of a new, updated version of his autobiography. He had worked hard and long on it, and not only had the events of the 15 years since its first publication doubled the size of the original book, but also it was clear that a different man was now writing, one who had survived enormous adversity and grown. The title alone conveyed this message. *The Life of P. T. Barnum* had now become *Struggles and Triumphs*.

The original Cardiff Giant is exhumed from the New York farm where he was "discovered" in 1869.

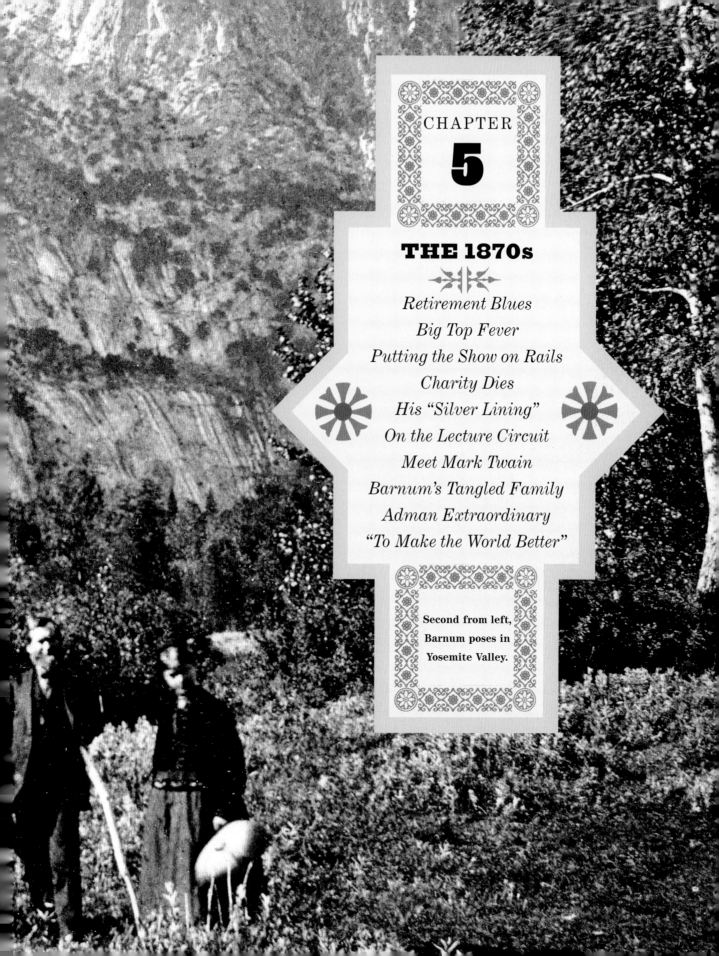

CHAPTER

5

THE 1870s

Retirement Blues
Big Top Fever
Putting the Show on Rails
Charity Dies
His "Silver Lining"
On the Lecture Circuit
Meet Mark Twain
Barnum's Tangled Family
Adman Extraordinary
"To Make the World Better"

**Second from left,
Barnum poses in
Yosemite Valley.**

Fighting Retirement Blues, Barnum Goes Exploring

Under the management of Sylvester Bleeker (above), the Thumbs and Minnie Warren were already off on their world tour as the decade opened. "Mr. Bleeker, if we tell this to the folks back home, they will not believe us," Tom was to exclaim in Japan after viewing mixed bathing. "But it is so! Men and women bathing together with not a rag upon them, and they don't mind it a bit. Write and let P. T. know what we have seen. If he had that place . . . in the United States, it would be the biggest show he ever had."

s the decade of the 1870s opened, Barnum was bored. It had been nearly two years since the destruction of his second museum, at which time the showman considered his career ended. "I have done work enough," he told himself then, "and shall play the rest of my life." Even so, in 1869, Barnum had silently entered into a couple of schemes that would keep him attached to the world he so loved—his replica of the Cardiff Giant was displayed in the New York City museum of George Wood, who was now paying him 3 percent of gross receipts for permission to advertise as "Barnum's successor"; he had dreamed up and helped finance a three-year world tour for the Tom Thumb Company; and he had masterminded European schedules for Anna Swan, a Circassian beauty, and the Siamese Twins, the latter trip well publicized as a search for the Old World surgeon most skillful in the art of separating connected people. It was a ruse that worked, for the gullible Brits crowded in for a last look at the aging partners, convinced that soon Chang and Eng would either be just plain brothers—or dead. But Barnum wanted more than sub-rosa success, and he was learning the hard way "how utterly fruitless it is to attempt to chain down energies which are peculiar to my nature." He was therefore doubly pleased when his English friend John Fish finally accepted his invitation to visit and be shown the wonders of the United States. Fish was a cotton-mill proprietor from Bury, England, who had literally forged his way from mill hand to successful company owner by studying Barnum's autobiography and learning by heart its lessons on how to make money. Flattered, Barnum had been trying to get Fish to visit him for years, but never more urgently than now, as he found himself "like the truant schoolboy . . . [with] no playmate." Now he had two, for Fish had brought with him a daughter in her 20s, his eldest, Jane Ann. With nervous, aging Charity safely tucked away in the New York town house, her rambunctious husband set off to show his friends America. First he guided the Fishes to Niagara Falls; then, in late January of 1870, the three headed for Cuba, where, watching a beautiful scenic view, Barnum was deeply moved to see "tears of joy and gratitude roll down the cheeks of the young English lady." It was on this trip, which took the trio on to New Orleans and up the Mississippi, that Barnum was allowed to read Fish's letters from his 20-year-old younger daughter, Nancy, back in England, and was so entranced he began writing her, too.

Once home, Barnum straightaway began planning an even more ambitious trip—"a small congenial party of ladies and gentlemen" who would traverse the entire country, "if," Barnum wrote a friend, "my poor nervous wife is well enough to spare me." Fish and his daughter were to be the guests of honor, and the goal would be the west coast, "to see the elephant," a common way to describe taking in California wonders. Traveling luxuriously in Pullman Palace Cars, the party stopped off at Salt Lake City, where the showman was confronted by Brigham Young. "Barnum, what

Restless from self-imposed retirement, Barnum left Charity at home while he and his friends explored Canada, Cuba, and the American West. This portrait of the couple was handed down in the Barnum family for a century.

"In Utah all girls marry young—Brigham Young," Barnum once joked. In fact, despite the polygamy, Barnum liked his friendly Utah host.

General George Custer helped ease "the restless spirit of an energetic man of leisure" with a buffalo hunt during which the showman "brought down two and . . . half killed another."

will you give to exhibit me in New York and the Eastern cities?" the Mormon leader asked. Quickly figuring in Young's almost two dozen wives, Barnum estimated such an exhibit would be worth half the receipts against a $200,000 guarantee, "for I consider you the best show in America," he told the dignified polygamist.

In San Francisco a new case of "show fever" started to get the best of him. Thinking he might "fence in a bit of the East River" and give exhibitions, Barnum offered $50,000 for ten large sea lions, which were to be captured off the coast and delivered alive to the East. Then, when a German named Gabriel Kahn offered up his little son, Leopold, Barnum could not resist. "He is a dwarf more diminutive in stature than General Tom Thumb was when I first found him," Barnum wrote, and commenced to sign up this "valuable nugget" and name him Admiral Dot, the El Dorado Elf. The trip continued to Yosemite Valley, which Barnum found "wonderful, wonderful, sublime, indescribable, incomprehensible; I never saw anything so truly and appallingly grand; it pays me a hundred times over for visiting California."

Back home at Waldemere, Barnum got the travel itch again almost immediately and, this time abandoning Charity in Bridgeport, headed north to Canada with the Fishes and a few other friends. Then, in September of 1870, selecting Fish and eight other male friends, Barnum swept west for a grand buffalo hunt in Kansas. "General Custer, commandant at Fort Hayes, was apprised in advance of our anticipated visit," wrote Barnum, "and he received us like princes. He fitted out a company of fifty cavalry, furnishing us with horses, arms and ammunition. We were taken to an immense herd of buffaloes, quietly browsing on the open plain. We charged on them, and during an exciting chase of a couple of hours, we slew twenty immense bull buffaloes. We might have killed as many more had we not considered it wanton butchery."

Barnum had treated himself to the "sensation" of a big-time hunt, "but 'sensations' cannot be made to order every day," he rightly figured. Therefore, he now decided that he had better have some permanent bracing pastime. As luck would have it, in the fall of 1870, just such an enterprise awaited him.

Unable to refrain from show business, in San Francisco Barnum signed up Admiral Dot, shown here with his mother.

Dating from the period of his restless retirement, most likely after the all-male
buffalo hunt in the West, this is the only known photograph of Barnum sporting a beard.
The baby in his arms appears to be one of the Seeley grandchildren, probably Jessie.

Embarking on His First Major Circus Venture

Barnum's early circus partners were half his age. William Cameron Coup had been lured away from his Indiana home at 16 by a traveling "mud-show." In his later, ghostwritten account, Coup claimed that it was he, not Barnum, who proposed the partnership.

Dan Castello had a show of his own which most recently was playing the lumber camps along Lake Michigan. Coup had been helping him out and so it was natural that both of them enter the Barnum partnership.

In early fall of 1870, Barnum was approached by a 33-year-old Midwestern-based circus manager by the name of William Cameron Coup. Barnum already knew of the man—he had given him his start almost two decades earlier, as a roustabout in the Asiatic Caravan, Museum and Menagerie, then one of the largest traveling shows in America. Having worked his way up through a series of circuses, in 1869 Coup had become part-owner of the Dan Castello Show, and now Coup and Castello hoped to create a special new circus in which the great Barnum himself might be persuaded to join. Their timing could not have been better. Barnum had returned from his trip west burning for new excitement. "I thought I had finished the show business," he wrote to his old friend Moses Kimball, but now "just for a flyer I go it once more." In Barnum's account, it was he who chose Coup to participate in the new enterprise, selecting the young man as "manager" because of his "good judgment, integrity and excellent executive ability." Whoever it was who originated the proposal, on October 8, 1870, Barnum wrote Coup from Bridgeport and, despite protests from family and friends, committed himself to a partnership. Promising to finance the entire venture, Barnum was to have two-thirds of all profits, the other third to be divided equally between Coup and Castello. Barnum was hardly just leasing his name; he bristled with ideas—a Cardiff Giant display, a huge assembly of automatons, his new "find" Admiral Dot, and a return of the Siamese Twins. "We can make a stunning museum department," he wrote excitedly, the old juices moving in him once again.

And so "P. T. Barnum's Grand Traveling Museum, Menagerie, Caravan and Circus" was born, the largest circus ever attempted in America, but with the word "circus" strategically last in its title. From the beginning, in Barnum's mind it was not so much a circus as a resurrection of his beloved museum, this time on wheels. All his old friends of the museum days were to be invited on board—Anna Swan, the "What Is It?," Colonel Goshen, Annie Jones—as well as a host of new acts and surprises. As the big show shaped up over the course of the winter, its scale was astonishing—100 wagons were to be needed, 20 for the museum collection alone and at least ten for wild animals. Seventy-five full-time employees were hired on for the wagon train, as well as 60 stars and secondary performers. "[It will be] the largest group of wonders ever known," Barnum exclaimed. "My great desire is . . . to totally eclipse all other exhibitions in the world." Over the course of the winter, Coup claimed Barnum was spending money "like water," terrifying his partners that the show would be too big, too expensive. "We ought to have a big show," Barnum responded, "the public expects it, and will appreciate it." "It is big," wrote one journalist, but "better still it is clean." In the first year of operation, Barnum's big, clean show grossed $400,000.

Barnum's first big circus venture, advertised in the poster above, was an extension of his old museum, a unique combination of curiosities, menagerie, and live performances, taking place under the extravagance of three tents (see lower-left portion of poster).

To insert some more "Barnum" into the partnership, Samuel H. Hurd, the showman's son-in-law (left), was persuaded to "sell out his business, take stock in the show, and become its treasurer and assistant manager," Barnum wrote. "Hurd is clear-headed, but he moves cautiously and 'looks before he leaps.' " The rare image to the right is the earliest view existing of a Barnum circus. Showing Barnum's magnificent revolving "Juno Wagon" in the foreground, it was taken on August 4, 1871, as the traveling show paraded its way through Watkins Glen, New York.

Beneath Five Acres of Canvas, a Vast Arena of Talent

Some of the secret of Barnum's great success lay in the scale and efficiency of his operation. By the second year, his "magic city" could be found springing up literally overnight in each new town, its tents covering up to five acres and able to accommodate 10,000 or more seated customers at a time. Set up in a long row to accentuate their cumulative size, the tents funneled customers in past scores of lesser acts on the way toward the Big Top. Barnum's unique six-tent arrangement included centers for his museum, his menagerie, and his hippodrome. There were also dressing-room tents for "ladies" and "gents," and, close by, files of smaller tents for stables and sleeping. Like almost all circuses, the Barnum show started out traveling by horse and wagon. Off the well-worn highways, this could prove difficult, with many roads literally impassable during rainstorms. When swollen streams blocked the roadways, elephants doubled as wagon pushers, but sometimes even they could not move all that canvas through the mud.

"Colossal tents" housed a "magic city" of entertainment which, trumpeted Barnum ads, "at a challenge of $100,000, is ten times larger than any other show ever seen on Earth." As this newspaper ad shows, Barnum was already in 1872 using the distinctive phrase "The Greatest Show on Earth!"

Starring in 1873 was the Matthews Family of gymnasts, known for their triple somersaults and a spine-tingling act entitled "The Ladder Perileuse."

By 1872, Barnum had added the most accomplished equestrian family in America, the Melvilles. Serving later as Barnum's trainer of horses and elephants, Frank Melville would also become a writer of vivid circus-advertising copy.

Barnum himself had discovered this "bright young Digger Indian," as he called him, while visiting Yosemite Valley in 1870. One day the handsome recruit distinguished himself by lassoing an escaped baboon.

The most unusual of Barnum's 1872 featured attractions, he believed, were his Fiji Islanders, "lately ransomed from King Thokambau . . . at a cost of $15,000." The Fijis were billed as converts from cannibalism, "earnestly declar[ing] their convictions that eating human flesh is wrong." Shown here posing in early 1872, the three men (right to left) are Kina Bose Yaca, Kora Tumasamora, and the warrior dwarf "General" Ra Biau. (In May 1872, while en route through Pennsylvania, Ra Biau suddenly died. Local papers had his cannibal compatriots feasting on the dead body, but Ra was in fact given a decent burial by circus friends.) Though billed as savages who spoke no English and thus needed an interpreter, the three men in the group had actually been raised in an English mission on the big island of Viti Levu. The woman in the group, described as the Fiji Princess "Otavia," and supposedly the group's interpreter, was later revealed to be a former house servant born and raised in Virginia.

Displaying weapons and dress of their native land, two Fiji warriors try to throw fear into circus-goers' hearts. Their excellent appetite for the food provided by the circus did not build up their reputation for having once banqueted on human flesh.

The Big Show Takes To the Rails

Beginning as early as the 1850s, a few small circuses had started experimenting with rail transport, but the Civil War had postponed such developments. By 1872, with more than 26,000 miles of rail now crisscrossing the country, at least eight large shows were planning the switch from horse and wagon to rail. Preeminent among these was Barnum's. "My big show leaves the city Monday morning," he wrote to his friend George Emerson in mid-April. "If it meets no R.R. accidents, the financial success will be immense." Allowing faster movement between larger cities, and opening up the rich markets of the Midwest, a rail circus could net three to four times the profits of those playing the small towns. Barnum's creation of the two-ring show, originating in 1872, was precisely in order to offer more "good seats" and thus accommodate the bigger crowds expected from the switch to rail. Much later, Coup unjustly claimed sole credit for both these new ideas, but his real contribution lay in his brilliant overseeing of the whole operation—the loading and unloading of the 65-car trains, and the complex techniques employed by 62 canvas-men in rapidly putting up and taking down the great tents. With Coup in charge of the day-to-day movements and Castello overseeing performances in the hippodrome ring, Barnum was represented by his son-in-law Samuel Hurd, the show's treasurer. From his home base in New York, Barnum himself served as chief idea person and promoter, overseeing press relations, show advertising, and the acquisition of new talent. Eager to be credited for what was turning into a monumental, million-dollar success story, even Coup had to admit that his senior partner was "the most daring manager that ever lived."

At the close of the 1872 season, Barnum's show divided. Part of it headed south to continue the tour; Barnum's name and at least one black rhino were leased to circusman Parson A. Older; and the remainder of Barnum's staff and animals returned to New York City and settled into a large wood-and-iron building on 14th Street called the Hippotheatron, purchased by Barnum as a winter quarters and performance hall. Excavating its central ring to add a second tier and gallery, and putting in 2,500 comfortable chairs, Barnum had a honeycomb of special chambers constructed for his museum curiosities and animals. Then, early on the morning of December 24, a massive fire broke out beginning in the museum's engine room. Strangely, none of the night keepers had been given keys to the cages, and once again, as in Barnum's earlier fires, almost none of the animals could be saved. Lions, tigers, bears, and sea lions, along with costumes, props, museum pieces, and cages, all were destroyed in the sickeningly familiar inferno. Within days, Barnum was ordering a dejected Coup to snap out of his despair and put some "electricity" in his "blood." Soon after, Barnum himself was placing orders with his British agents for an entire new batch of animals and supplies.

Opened on February 8, 1864, modeled after the Champs-Elysées in Paris, New York's multi-sided Hippotheatron possessed the largest horse ring in America. Not long after Barnum took it over, the building became the site of yet another disastrous fire.

P. T. BARNUM'S GREAT SHOW.

This rare view of the Barnum Show was taken on October 24, 1872, in Kalamazoo, Michigan. Showing the lineup of Barnum's big tents, funneling audiences into the huge, double-poled Big Top at the rear, the photograph also details the close proximity of the show to its rails. Seen from atop a high freight car, a string of flatbed cars reveal not only how circus wagons were transported but how they could be unloaded continuously, wheeled over steel plates that bridged the gaps between adjacent cars and then down ramps.

He Whets the Public Appetite with a Novel Secret Weapon

Barnum's idea for a regular circus newspaper was a stroke of promotion genius. At first he wrote most of it himself.

Given special billing in the *Advance Courier* for 1873 was Frenchman Monsieur D'Atalie, "The Man with the Iron Jaw," and his sidekick, Young Zephyr, "The Child Wonder." D'Atalie's sensational finale was to lift, with his teeth alone, a 40-gallon barrel filled with water upon which was seated a large man holding 200-pound weights. (When a freak fatal accident in the spring of 1873 ended D'Atalie's career, Young Zephyr filled out his contract alone.)

Barnum's name alone was priceless to Coup and Castello, and they knew it; but from the beginning the old showman rolled up sleeves and joined in the work full-time. "I don't travel with the show," Barnum admitted early on, "[though] I am looked for more than any other lion." But, from his home base in New York City and at Waldemere, Barnum concentrated on what he did best—creating huge, unprecedented public demand. Canceling his lecture schedule and working round the clock, Barnum proceeded to dream up a whole new publicity vehicle, an illustrated newspaper designed to whet public appetite in advance of his shows. "Pray don't mention my paper at present in any public way," Barnum wrote to Mark Twain, requesting an article for it; "my brother showmen may steal my thunder." Using his newspaper background and connections, and a complete familiarity with printing and engraving, Barnum soon had his new secret weapon in hand—500,000 copies of a 24-page illustrated newspaper entitled *P. T. Barnum's Advance Courier*, to be distributed free in every town a week prior to the circus's arrival. Written almost entirely by Barnum himself, with intriguing short articles on everything from the salaries of lead performers to the complexities of the tent operations, the 1871 *Advance Courier* was sprinkled throughout with free-standing jokes, endorsements from famous Americans, and lavish paid ads. On pages 16 and 17 was a 33-point countdown for why "every man, woman and child" in America had to see this greatest of all shows. Widely imitated in the years ahead, the *Courier* did much to make Barnum's new circus "the most pronounced success" of his long career.

By 1872, Barnum had taken on three full-time press agents to travel with the show, their mission to place stories in local papers and to give area journalists guided tours behind the scenes. Barnum, who never could tolerate "improper or inefficient employees," often hand-picked these special agents, and one of them, J. L. Hutchinson, later rose to full partnership in the Barnum show. By 1873, the circus had grown threefold since its inception and now boasted ten full-time bill posters and a seven-person department of "Publications and Advertisements." Overseen by W. C. Crum, the department had responsibility for the *Advance Courier* and carried out all local advertising. As for Barnum's famous autobiography, updated annually with revisions and detailed appendixes, it was now sold at the show's main gate for $1.50, in a special circus edition that included a free ticket to the show, representing an extra 50-cent value. Later, Barnum found a Buffalo, New York, printer who could produce a shortened version of the book at a cost of just a little over 9 cents a copy. Purchasing a million of them, Barnum reduced the price of the circus edition to an even dollar.

On the cover of his 1873 *Advance Courier*, against a backdrop of pyramids and icebergs and Oriental cities, Barnum seems to emerge from the fire and ashes of his museum days as a reborn impresario, promising Americans "the world in contribution."

P.T. BARNUM'S

THE WORLD IN CONTRIBUTION.

MUSEUM

CURIOSITIES ARRIVING.

BARNUM

ADVANCE COURIER.

T. BARNUM, **Editor and Proprietor.**   **1873.**   **CIRCULATION, 1,000,00**

?. T. Barnum to the Public.

D GRAND ANNUAL TOURNAMENT—

THIRTY-NINE YEARS AS MANAGER.

lthough the fire of Dec. 24, 1872, ly destroyed my third museum ding, and a magnificent collection are animals—making my losses by within fifteen years, exceed a mil- of dollars—I have emerged again the cinders and smoke, with an npaired constitution, unabated en- es, and a more earnest determina- than ever to gratify, as I have al- so successfully done, the ever-re- ing demands of the amusement- ing public. Fortunately I had sent ew-Orleans, for exhibition during holidays, duplicates of nearly all animals destroyed. And fortunate-

The Greatest Show on Earth!

A Full Menagerie, Free of Charge!

COLOSSAL WORLD'S FAIR BY RAILROAD!

20 Great Shows Consolidated !!

100,000 CURIOSITIES !

☞ **Five Railroad Trains, Four Miles Long!** 🚂

A "PHILOSOPHIC SALAMANDER" SUPERIOR TO FIRE!

4 Bands of Music ! 12 Golden Chariots ! 100 Vans !

cables enable us, in these days, to a complish more in three months tha we could formerly have done in many years. Hence, before the spar had ceased rising from my burnin museum, I had subsidized the powe of electricity to such an extent, as to e able me to start again by April, 187 with a Museum, Menagerie, Carava Ornithological Cabinet, a double Hi podrome, Polytechnic Institute, and Grand International Zoological G den combined—far more EXTENSIV NOVEL, ATTRACTIVE and DIVERSIFIE than the colossal expositions w which I had astonished, and delight the citizens of nineteen different State during the past two years.

After having successfully and sat factorily supplied the public want many years with *startling wonders*, s

POSITIVELY NO MONEY TAKEN at the DOOR.
MAIN ENTRANCE to BARNUMS
GREAT SHOW.
Children under fives Half price

In a rare view of the Barnum circus from 1873, huge sideshow banners are clearly visible in front of the large crowds. P. T. Barnum's name appears prominently on one of these, beneath portraits of the Bunnell Brothers, now owners of

his sideshow "privilege." On the far right can be seen Barnum's famous "Juno Wagon," a massively carved, mirror-studded chariot used in the daily parades, and capable of telescoping itself upward 30 feet in height.

The Sideshow Is Barnum's Special Baby

Nellie Keeler came from Indiana and always traveled with her father, who was usually on the payroll.

Barnum all but invented the sideshow. Set off from the rest of the circus, it had a lurid lure all its own and, of course, it was an additional moneymaker. Barnum had the ingredients from the start—the kind of oddity, both human and inanimate, that had been on display at his museum for years. "Representatives of the wonderful," he called them, "living curiosities such as giants, dwarfs or other freaks of nature not repulsive." From 1871 on, the museum, like the menagerie, had its own tent fitted up with 20 vans' worth of freaks, dioramas, automatons, and waxworks. Here audiences could see not only Admiral Dot and Anna Leak and "Zip," the "What Is It?," but also an "automatic trumpeter" by the German inventor Johann Nepomuk Maelzel, and Robert-Houdin's "dying zouave," from whose wound trickled a steady stream of warm, red blood. Before long, the cumbersome, lifeless exhibits were being dropped and little entertainment acts added alongside the human curiosities. Wages paid to the sideshow stars varied. Fat ladies got $15 a week and up, depending on poundage and pulchritude. A truly tiny midget could make $100 a week or more. But the best-paid of human curiosities, so said the exaggerating New York *Sun* in 1879, were female Siamese twins. "Two headed girls are very rare," stated the newspaper, "and are worth $600 a week and expenses."

The sideshow attractions having already whetted their appetites for the big show, spectators take their seats beneath the great canopy in this rare interior photograph of a Barnum circus from 1872. Note the single, walled ring.

In 1872, an armless 17-year-old from Canada approached Barnum and was hired on the spot. For more than 50 years, Charles Tripp fascinated audiences by doing with his feet what other people did with their hands—and usually doing it better, including penmanship, paper cutting, portrait painting, carpentry, and, of course, serving a genteel cup of tea.

In 1872, Barnum's favorite, giantess Anna Swan, married an equally tall exhibition, Captain M. V. Bates, who outweighed her by 65 pounds. The man at the right is the giants' agent and director, Francis M. Uffner.

The feet of Eli Bowen grew right out of his torso without the benefit of legs at all. Beautiful Mattie Haight bore Eli two towheaded daughters and a footloose son (above).

"English Jack," Barnum's frog swallower, opened his mouth wide to prove his wiggly meal was actually going down his throat. Through a controlled and mannerly act of regurgitation, "geeks" like Jack were able to recover their stunned appetizers after a few seconds.

Charity Dies, but for Barnum There Is a "Silver Lining"

Carl Hagenbeck, the noted German dealer in rare animals, was finishing up a sale with Barnum when news arrived of the death of Charity back in America.

Nancy Fish was the engaging young English woman who was distracting Barnum in 1873.

Charity Barnum grew more and more reclusive, but that did not seem to slow down her restless husband from devoting himself to his new circus work, planning travels, or becoming fascinated with a 22-year-old woman. In 1872, John Fish had returned to America, this time with Barnum's pen-pal, his younger daughter, Nancy. Over the winter of 1872–73, she was the guest of Charity's cousin Nate Beers and his wife, Emma, in New York City. Barnum's interest in the young woman, who was destined to become his second wife, appeared merely fatherly, his attentions limited to occasional visits to the Beers' Fifth Avenue home or free tickets to his show. On January 22, the 62-year-old even put his attentions in writing, letting Emma Beers know that he intended "to call in and see Miss Fish tomorrow P.M." It had all begun, of course, on that 1870 trip to Cuba, when Barnum had started reading Nancy's letters to her father. "I fell in love with my second wife before I had even seen her," admitted Barnum in later years. "Those charming letters did the work."

By March of 1873, Barnum was writing a friend that "the doctors say they think Mrs. B. will worry through, but are not *quite* sure." Charity's debilitating, nameless maladies that stretched back almost two decades finally had been diagnosed as stemming from valvular heart disease. Young Nancy returned to England sometime during the summer, and in September 1873 Barnum set sail for Europe himself, ostensibly to search for new ideas for his circus, make animal purchases, and check out the possibility of "some aeronaut" making a balloon crossing of the Atlantic. But the first person to shake his hand when he docked at Liverpool was his old friend John Fish, who took him directly to his house in Southport. After visiting there, Barnum, Fish, and daughter Nancy traveled about England. Then it was on to Cologne, Leipzig, and Dresden for Barnum, visiting museums, zoos, and circuses along the way, and finally to Vienna for a ten-day stay at the World's Fair. In November, Barnum arrived in Hamburg to deal with Carl Hagenbeck, the famed supplier of the world's menageries. "He can provide a menagerie cheaper than you can collect it in any other way," Barnum told an interviewer. "He has a dozen active agents in Asia, Africa, Australia and South America all the while. But even they don't catch the animals. The young wild animals are caught by the natives in different localities. They catch the young ones and bring them up, and sell them when the agents come around." In Hamburg, Barnum spent $15,000 on new animals—rare birds, elephants, giraffes—but Hagenbeck's ideas, which would later surface in Barnum's shows, were worth far more—"the racing elephants of India and the use of ostriches as saddle animals" were two that Hagenbeck suggested.

Then, suddenly, by telegraph on November 20, came "unlooked for" news. Charity was dead. Crushed, Barnum remained in his hotel room for days, his head bowed and tears flowing, he wrote, as he tried to imagine the funeral taking place back at Waldemere. Charity had been embalmed,

On the effect of Charity's death upon him, Barnum wrote in the 1876 edition of his autobiography: "It is difficult for those who have not had the sad experience, to imagine the degree of anguish which overwhelms one, when called to part with a beloved companion with whom he has lived forty-four years." And worse it is when the news "finds the sorrowing husband four thousand miles away from the bedside of his dead wife, alone, in a strange land. . . . I confess the 'cloud' seemed so utterly black that it was hard to realize it *could* have a silver 'lining.'"

and now her body awaited Barnum at the public receiving vault at Fairfield's Mountain Grove Cemetery, which her husband had helped found years before. But Barnum wasn't about to go right home. "After this sad blow," he confessed in his autobiography, "I yearned to be where I could meet sympathizing friends and hear my native tongue. I therefore returned to London and spent several weeks in quiet." At least some of the sympathy and solace Barnum sought was administered by Nancy Fish, who, with her father, welcomed him to their home in Lancashire. A love affair was blossoming. And blossoming fast. All previous accounts, including Barnum's own, have the showman slowly recovering his old, robust self, then returning to the U.S. in April, and finally sending for Nancy for a surprise September wedding in New York City, a full ten months after Charity's death. In actuality, as only recently discovered, Barnum and Nancy were secretly married in London on February 14, 1874—Valentine's Day—just 13 weeks and two days after Charity's death.

It is hard to believe that John Fish did not know about the union of his daughter and his great American friend. If he did, he kept it secret all the rest of his life, just as Barnum did (though Nancy may have admitted it late in her life). Not a hint of the marriage has ever been found in the records of either family, up until the discovery of the marriage certificate 120 years later. It is obvious now that the letter Barnum sent to his friend the Reverend George H. Emerson in America just a week after the secret marriage was a conscious smokescreen. The showman wrote that he had expected to be in Italy by now but it was just possible he wouldn't go at all. "I cannot enjoy sightseeing as I could before Mrs. Barnum died. Still, *time* is helping me along, & were it not for increasing years, too many cares, & a rather dizzy head, I should be all right. . . . If you were here I would surely go to Italy with you, & I want to see Rome, Naples, &c. But really my pluck and courage fail me somewhat, & I may remain in London till I sail." Then Barnum casually referred to Nancy: "You asked where you could send slip of 'Bunker Hill' to Miss Fish. Address: Miss Fish, 5 Portland St., Southport, Lancashire, England. I am sure she will be *glad* to hear from you." And then Barnum ended the letter with a reference to his energetic, headlong life-style, which had obviously been revived. "I am convinced," he wrote, "you get more happiness in your steady, sensible way of living than I do in the dash & fire which attend my way

Just weeks after Charity's death, Nancy Fish (left) secretly became Nancy Barnum, as this copy of their recently discovered marriage certificate attests. Both bride and groom gave as their residence 23 Coventry Street, an address belonging to a London luggage manufacturer.

239

Barnum's firstborn, Caroline (above), and his youngest, Pauline (below), were two of a small number who knew that their father was in the city not for the Universalist Convention, as he told most everyone, but for his wedding to an English woman 17 years younger than Caroline and four years Pauline's junior.

of living." Much later, contemplating this period, Barnum recalled, "I knew where my heart was."

Finally home in April, Barnum did nothing to stifle the rumors that he would remarry; everyone thought it was only a matter of which well-to-do, middle-aged local widow would be the lucky one. "I kept my own counsel," he remembered, getting as close to a confession as he ever would. "When I got ready I brought home my English bride."

The wedding between the already married couple was held on September 16, a day after Nancy arrived from England and almost exactly ten months after Charity's death. Present at the New York church, Barnum recorded, were "members of my family and a large gathering of gratified friends." "Startled friends" would probably have been closer to the truth, for only Barnum's daughters and sons-in-law, a sister, and his housekeeper had been let in on the secret that the old man was going to marry his young English friend. And no one, as far as we can now tell, was privy to the true state of affairs—that bride and groom were already married. Among family members who angrily disapproved of this May–September alliance were Nancy's former host and hostess Nate and Emma Beers, who had received a letter from Barnum a few days before the wedding saying they were to have Cousin Charity's hand mirror and a book to remember her by—but keeping them completely in the dark on the wedding plans. Writing again only hours after the wedding, Barnum expected "Emma was a little taken aback today," and suggested they forgive and forget—"The River *Lethe* is good to drink from sometimes." A story handed down by relatives has it that after the honeymoon the couple was greeted on Waldemere's front porch by family members dressed for a funeral.

Barnum sometimes referred to his bride as "my little wife" or "my old woman," but she was always just plain "Nancy" to his children and "Aunt Nancy" to his grandchildren. He was proud of having such a young English "girl" on his arm as they swept in and out of the best hotels, attended the opera, wintered in Virginia, or sailed on the yachts of his wealthy friends. Intelligent, a gifted pianist, and a published writer, the second Mrs. Barnum hoped not to make the same mistakes she thought her predecessor had. At 40, giving marriage advice to other wives in a magazine article, Nancy wrote: "Share his pleasures. Take your holidays together. . . . Don't spend your summer in the mountains and at the seashore, leaving him in the city; and don't stay at home in the autumn while he goes to Europe. . . . If you must be absent from him in those leisure hours in which Satan is said to provide 'some mischief still' for idle men to do, it is not incumbent of you to provide for his solace a companion of the gentler sex, younger and fairer than yourself." Strangely enough, this is just what Nancy began to do, as she slipped into the same kind of suffering and retreat as Charity had, spending more and more time at sanitoriums, and eventually persuading a young, unmarried cousin—Sarah J. Fish—to act as her husband's companion.

P. T. Barnum and his second wife, Nancy, pose at Waldemere shortly after their New York wedding. The jeweled wedding band that Barnum had worn for all 44 years of his marriage to Charity was gone now, never to be replaced by any new ring.

Now Each New Enterprise Has to Be Bigger and Better

When it traveled, the enormous hippodrome show featured not only stampedes of chariots (above) but also death-defying balloon ascensions (left).

News from the Clouds.

P. T. BARNUM'S
Great Roman Hippodrome
NEW YORK.
Ascension of the Experimental Series by
PROF. DONALDSON.

Heading off for Europe in 1873, Barnum had left Coup and Hurd in charge of finding a new fixed location for the show. In Berlin he received word that his partners had secured a lease on Vanderbilt Square, a Harlem Railroad property in New York City, which would later be the site of Madison Square Garden. With Barnum still in Europe, construction began on the New York Hippodrome, the largest amusement building ever attempted, a huge rectangular brick-and-cement edifice, 425 feet long and 28 feet high, at the center of which was an immense oval arena. Costing $150,000, with seating for 10,000 beneath a partially enclosed roof, the open-air central arena could be tented over with canvas in bad weather. Barnum, determined to make a splash in the new arena, ordered up in London exact copies of all props, costumes, and paraphernalia connected with George Sanger's highly successful "Congress of Monarchs" show. Off they were shipped to America, $50,000 worth of chariots and harnesses and suits of armor and international flags. Barnum returned to New York and the new hippodrome on April 30, 1874, and gazed out upon the largest assemblage of people ever gathered in one building in New York. It was a lavish pageant—"a dazzling half-mile of solid gold," one reporter exclaimed, followed by a bewildering array of horse races and Roman-style games.

Everything now, in this new phase of Barnum's life, had to be the

Generating anger among Barnum's partners, the notorious big-top sharpie John "Pogey" O'Brien (above) rented the Barnum name and affixed it to his own Traveling World's Fair.

Small-time circus owner P. A. Older rented Barnum's name and his rhino, not quite enough to justify the 20-word title he put on his show (P. T. Barnum's Great Traveling Museum, Menagerie, Caravan, Hippodrome, Polytechnic Institute, International Zoological Garden, and Sig. Sebastian's Royal Italian Circus).

What caused dissension among Barnum's partners was the watering down of their product by Barnum's high-handed rental of his face, name, even his ads to competing shows (right).

biggest—the longest spectacles, the largest trains, the most expensive displays. In 1874 and 1875, Barnum's hippodrome show not only played its new home, but traveled as well; the road version included a live English-style hunt with 150 riders, daily balloon ascensions by Professor W. H. Donaldson, chariot races involving "Amazon women," and a giant Western display of real Indians and buffaloes and horsemen reenacting, among other things, an Indian-Mexican battle. With a new amphitheater erected in each town along the tour—its lumber sold off at the end of each engagement—125 railroad cars were now needed, 750 horses, and sleeping and eating accommodations for 1,200 employees. "Remember," Barnum's ads read, trying to woo conservative, anti-circus audiences, "the Roman Hippodrome is not a circus." At the same time, however, a second show was being mounted, this one a true circus, with acrobats and lions and clowns, sent out under the direction of a somewhat shady circus manager named John "Pogey" O'Brien and called "P. T. Barnum's Traveling World's Fair."

To oversee this growing, multifaceted enterprise, Barnum and his partners incorporated as "The Barnum Universal Exposition Company," a million-dollar public corporation with a business plan ultimately to open as many as a dozen separate exhibitions in America and Europe. But by 1875, Barnum had become hopelessly overextended and vulnerable to an increasing string of mishaps. A two-year recession was eating away at circus revenues; Coup had had a breakdown from overwork and was absent for months at a time in Europe; a freak snowstorm in Philadelphia had destroyed the Big Top, ripping it to pieces under the snow's weight; and a flood in Iowa canceled all shows. "One accident after another followed," wrote John Dingess, a showman friend of Coup's. And then, to Barnum's dismay, over the fog-covered waters of Lake Michigan, star performer Professor Washington Donaldson and his balloon floated off to their doom. With the show costing $10,000 a day to run, and Coup deeply dissatisfied with the dividing of Barnum's name and the association with the much-hated Pogey O'Brien, Barnum made the decision to bail out of the partnership.

The New Mayor Stars on the Lecture Circuit

James Redpath established a "clearing house" for lecturers.

Julia Ward Howe helped Redpath make foreign speakers feel at home in the U.S.

A friend of Barnum's, reformer Mary Ashton Livermore was one of the most powerful Redpath speakers, and "The Queen of the Lyceum."

"[All] the beasts of the forest and jungle will roar in chorus," cheered the Buffalo *Express* upon Barnum's election to mayor. Soon he was running the city council.

During the midst of his hippodrome days, on April 5, 1875, P. T. Barnum was elected mayor of Bridgeport at the ripe age of 64. He was now by far the most well-known and popular man in the city. President of the Republican Town Committee, vice-president of the local Board of Trade, and past president of the Pequonnock Bank, Barnum was also the founder of East Bridgeport and chief sponsor and benefactor of the town's beautiful Seaside Park. In 1874, he had been lionized for his contributions at an unusual testimonial dinner. "What manner of man is Mr. Barnum," asked friend Frank Leslie in an absentee toast. "Why, just one of the kindest-hearted, public spirited men that lives." Now, in 1875, Barnum threw himself energetically into his one-year term as mayor, embarking upon a series of important local reforms. He sought improvements to the city water supply, commissioned new gaslighting for Bridgeport's streets, and supported efforts of local blacks to gain entrance into the trade unions. New police statistics linking alcohol to violent crime refired Barnum's temperance beliefs and led him to a strict enforcement of liquor licenses and Sunday saloon closures. Some felt he went too far in his crackdown on local prostitution, including an attempt to expose the identities of the men frequenting Bridgeport's whorehouses. But whatever could be said, pro or con, no one could deny Barnum's wholehearted exercise of his office. And what other city could boast of a mayor who, besides juggling a hippodrome and traveling circus with his mayoralty, also continued as one of the country's top lecturers?

In the middle of his term, in the fall of 1875, Mayor Barnum was approached by James Redpath's Lyceum Bureau in Boston and asked to deliver a series of 20 lectures throughout towns all across New England. Redpath's was the finest speakers' bureau in the country, boasting among

Charles Sumner, the contentious senator from Massachusetts, shown here cross-legged with literary monarch Henry Wadsworth Longfellow, was one of Redpath's first recruits.

Ralph Waldo Emerson started out lecturing for $5 plus three quarts of oats for his horse. Redpath helped put him in the $500 league.

Author of "A Man Without a Country," writer-preacher Edward Everett Hale was an early Redpath fixture.

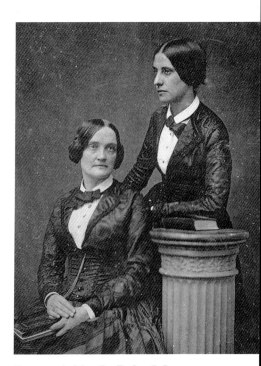

Represented by the Redpath Lyceum Bureau, Shakespearean actress Charlotte Cushman (left) did notable dramatic readings. The woman posing with her may be her longtime companion and maid, Sally Mercer.

One of Redpath's prize speakers in the mid-1870s and perhaps Barnum's personal favorite was caustic-witted humorist Samuel Clemens, or Mark Twain. Clemens had long been fascinated by Barnum. The two of them had leased a comet's tail to take a million passengers on a guided tour of outer space—or at least that's what Twain claimed in print. Highly prizing Clemens' friendship, Barnum had interested him in a project to publish a set of "Queer Letters," crazy epistles received by the showman from all over the country offering him freaky and peculiar attractions. Twain, who later went on to write about Siamese twins, refused all efforts by Barnum to enlist him as publicist, and ultimately their relationship cooled. But for a time during the 1870s, the Barnums and the Clemenses were warm friends, exchanging visits at Waldemere and at Mark Twain's Hartford home at Nook Farm.

its clients such podium giants as Henry Ward Beecher, Ralph Waldo Emerson, Mark Twain, Wendell Phillips, Julia Ward Howe, and Harriet Beecher Stowe—and virtually everybody else important. Set up in 1868 as a much-needed clearinghouse to serve both speakers and audiences, and handling all the complicated details of bookings, travel, accommodations, and fees, Redpath's could literally make a speaker's career. Barnum now joined the ranks of the most popular, the most eloquent, and the best-paid lecturers in the country.

It had not always been so easy. Back in the 1850s and '60s, Barnum had had to handle his lecture tours himself. With the same meticulous attention he had once given to the Jenny Lind tour, he set up his own engagements, sent ahead publicity materials, and negotiated terms (usually $30 a night). Giving 60 talks in a row one autumn, sometimes working so hard that a sore throat forced him to desist and recuperate, Barnum faced anti-showman prejudice in numerous locales, and at times felt like quitting the whole business, saying he preferred "showing" to "lecturing." But always he returned, routinely donating his profits to local churches and charities and organizations. His chief requirements were amazingly simple—a "good light," especially in later years, when his eyesight was weakening, and a stand to hold his outline (he used no manuscript or notes). This could be a table or a desk, he allowed, but it should be at least four feet high, with room on it for a tumbler and a pitcher of fresh water. "If there is no such thing," he wrote one host, "then take a small table, put a soap or candle box on it and cover it with a red or blue table cloth—or any color except white." This kind of economy and attention to detail was pure Barnum, part of the secret of his abiding success in life, and something everybody noticed. "He was the most prudently economical man that I have ever known," wrote J. B. Pond, assigned by Redpath to Barnum for the New England tour in October 1875. "It made no difference to him who paid the expenses. If they were unnecessary, he didn't want them incurred. Invariably he walked from the station to the hotel."

Unlike the high seriousness of other great lecturers—Emerson or Phillips or Stowe—Barnum's talks were always light-spirited and fun, peppered throughout with original Barnumisms. He liked honest, down-to-earth English. Instead of "inexpensive" he said "dog-cheap"; a giant woman was "a whopper"; reconciling himself to a failure, he said, "[S]ome pork will boil that way." He spoke in ways that made people smile—"I am happy as a clam in high water," he would say, or, "My brain is so full of all sorts of things it is *milk* and *water*." Whether it was for his "Art of Money Getting" lecture, or "Science of Humbugs," or "Success in Life," or "The World and How to Live in It," crowds everywhere roared at Barnum's racy anecdotes, chuckled away at his unique brand of wisdom, and applauded him heartily, often calling it, later, the "lecture event" of the year. But there was more to a Barnum lecture than just good humor and funny stories and an occasional magic trick thrown in for good measure. There was "thought founded on observation and experience," Barnum himself insisted. What he had to say was calculated to do good.

Abolitionist spokesman Wendell Phillips was considered the king of oratory, the "father of modern eloquence."

In the speakers' bureau, P. T. Barnum seemed a strange bedfellow for the likes of educator Horace Mann as well as most of Redpath's other clients. More similar to Barnum was gorilla expert Paul Du Chaillu, perennially popular, and Ann Elizabeth Young (above), Brigham Young's 19th wife, the "rebel of the harem," who won a wild success on the podium by castigating the Mormons.

A Formal Look at Part of Barnum's Tangled Family

Barnum's growing family consisted of numerous granddaughters, five of whom pose here, scattered among others described in the text at right. Three are results of daughter Helen's first marriage, to Samuel Hurd. To the far left sits Helen Barnum Hurd, who married Frank Rennell in 1883 and produced very acceptable "baby double-grands" for her grandfather. The next young lady is Carrie Hurd, Barnum's favorite, who died unmarried at 21. The woman standing to the right of Barnum is Julia Hurd, who would marry Henry Clark. To the right of Carrie Hurd is the child of Barnum's first daughter, Caroline, Frances Thompson, who married William Leigh. Just to the right of Barnum is the child of his youngest daughter, Pauline, Jessie Seeley, who would one day marry her brother Clinte's best friend, Wilson Marshall.

raditionally, Barnum issued invitations to members of his family to celebrate the Fourth of July at Seaside Park along with his birthday the following day. In 1875, the occasion was especially meaningful, for it was the showman's 65th, and a large family group gathered to honor him. Posing with Barnum in the family portrait at left taken for the occasion are his second wife, two daughters, three sons-in-law, five granddaughters, and two grandsons. Barnum, seated at the center, and 25-year-old Nancy, sixth from the left, had been married for less than a year and a half. Standing between them, like an odd man out, is Samuel Henry Hurd, formerly married to Barnum's second daughter, Helen. In 1871, Helen had divorced him and married Dr. William H. Buchtel, with custody of the children awarded to Hurd. Later on, a scandal-monger would circulate a story that Helen had been unfaithful to Hurd in the Barnum manse and that a terrible rift had occurred between father and daughter. Actually, Helen, who had the same looks and sense of humor as her father, remained close to Barnum, even though she and her new husband moved to far-off Colorado.

Posed third and fourth from the right are Barnum's other two surviving daughters, Caroline, the firstborn, seated, and Pauline, the fourth daughter, 13 years younger, standing beside her. (The third daughter had died in 1844, a few weeks before her second birthday.) A quarter of a century earlier, Caroline had been the young lady traveling with her father on the Jenny Lind tour; Barnum had even veiled her and used her as a decoy so the singer could slip away from the crowds unnoticed. The following year, 1852, Caroline had married David W. Thompson, a Bridgeport bookkeeper (second from right). Iranistan, the site of the nuptials, had caught fire on the day of the wedding and almost burned down, as it was destined to do five years later. Pauline, the youngest, turned out to be Barnum's pride and joy. Married on her 20th birthday to Nathan Seeley (fifth from left), Pauline had less than two years to live after she posed for this picture. It almost broke her father's heart when measles and diphtheria combined to kill her at 31.

Barnum had hoped for a male heir but got four daughters instead from Charity and no children from Nancy. Frustrated, he turned to his three grandsons. Caroline's only son was joyfully christened P. T. Barnum Thompson, but he died in 1868, not quite three years of age. The two others, offspring of Pauline, were Clinton Hallett Seeley (second from left) and his younger brother, Herbert Barnum Seeley (far right). Even though Herbert had his name, the showman preferred "Clinte" and persuaded him to change his middle name to "Barnum" after he had turned 21. Herbert was best remembered for a bachelor party he threw years later for his brother at which the notorious dancer "Little Egypt" performed on top of a table.

New Partners, New Show, and a Self-Made Curiosity

It was a small world, the circle that ran the circus in America. New Barnum partner George F. Bailey was a son-in-law of circus man Aaron Turner, for whom Barnum had once sold tickets. Bailey and his partners' nickname, "the Flatfoots," derived from a group of famous early circus men in Westchester and Putnam Counties, New York, who said they "put their foot down flat" when it came to driving away competitors.

By the end of 1875, Barnum had disposed of his entire hippodrome show, broken ties with W. C. Coup, and dissolved the Barnum Universal Exposition Company and its many enterprises. Exercising his authority as mayor, he ordered Bridgeport's bells rung on January 1 to usher in the new Centennial year. Already he was deep into the planning of an even more ambitious circus project. Not only had his agents secretly bought back many of his own items at the auction held at the demise of the hippodrome, but Barnum had now purchased the European Menagerie and Circus and taken on its owners as his new partners. And so a new team of circus men, the so-called Flatfoots, John J. Nathans, George F. Bailey, Lewis B. June, and Avery Smith, now joined Samuel Hurd to direct a special "Centennial Show." It was to be patently patriotic, filled with Continental Army troops, fireworks, a huge mounted figure of General George Washington, and at the end of the performance the singing of "America" by the entire audience.

His term as mayor now over, Barnum chose to travel with the 1876 production, often addressing audiences at his "Greatest Show on Earth." Once again, as in the early 1870s, he had one complete, undivided circus, a winning formula he would never again depart from. With separate tents for the museum and menagerie, and a Big Top containing hippodrome track and circus rings, each tent contained world-class talent. In the circus tent itself, where over 100 principal riders performed, the eight-member Carlo Family of Equestrians stood out, as well as the preeminent bareback riding of Charles Fish. In the menagerie, along with lions and elephants and a horse-riding, five-foot-tall baboon, was a newborn hippopotamus, the only living one in America, Barnum claimed, "all others advertised being base frauds." And in the sideshow or museum department, behind the bright-colored come-on banners, were Barnum's old friends Zoe Meleke, the Circassian Beauty, and William Henry Johnson, now renamed Zip, as well as a new African wild boy billed as Yeppo. Alongside Admiral Dot, Zuruby Hannum, and a new "Centennial Portrait Gallery" was a brand-new living curiosity who was by far Barnum's top act for 1876, as well as for several ensuing years—the mysterious tattooed Greek, Captain George Costentenus.

Barnum's arrangement with his new partners was similar to the old one with Coup—he got half the profits and the others split the rest. With large annual bonuses going to Barnum as well, bringing his average annual take to over $50,000, Nathans and Bailey and June were increasingly disgruntled, complaining that they did all the work and Barnum did little more than rent them his name. "I have not long to stay on this ball of dirt," Barnum warned his partners in September 1877. "I propose to receive without grumbling something like the worth of my name and powers." Barnum prevailed. The four men plus Hurd continued together for three more seasons, with Barnum pocketing, in the last of these, a stunning $87,850.

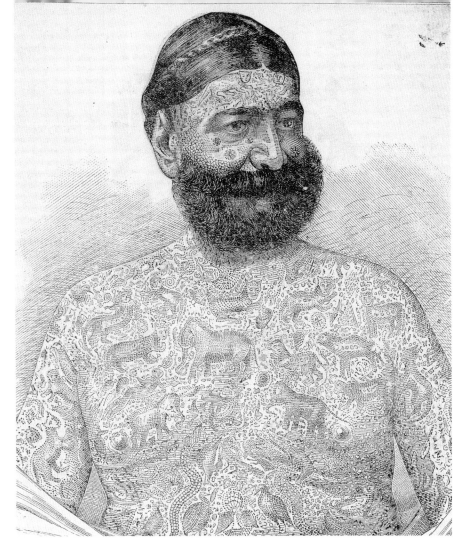

There had been tattooed exhibitors before, but no one like this. With a total of 388 designs in indigo and cinnabar, Captain George Costentenus was covered on just about every inch of his body. One list counted 2 tattoos on his forehead, 8 on his neck and throat, 50 on the chest, 37 on the back, 52 on the abdomen and buttocks, 101 on the two arms, 137 on the legs, and one on the dorsum of the penis. "It is the most perfect specimen of genuine tattooing which any of us have ever seen," attested physician Oliver Wendell Holmes. "Over seven million blood producing punctures," added Barnum. Literature circulated with the Greek's act outlined a strange and tragic past—a sensual upbringing in a Turkish harem, a love affair with the Shah of Persia's daughter, and eventually capture by the "fiendish" Khan of Kashgar. Given the choice of death by wasp stings, tiger mauling, flogging, impaling, burning, or being tattooed, Costentenus, told that if he survived the ordeal he could go free, chose the last. At the instant it began, he said, he "realized the terrible fate" in store for him. The pricks of the needles, his booklet reported, had set his "brain on fire," as if the skin had been "torn off," leaving "a sheet of bare, quivering nerves." In actuality, the eccentric Costentenus willingly obtained his own tattoos in a carefully conceived plan to become a self-made curiosity.

Acquiring the labyrinth of tattoos shown in the illustration above, Captain Costentenus claimed to have been subjected to months of blood-producing punctures (below) and to have often fainted dead away from the pain.

Arousing the Country "for Fifty Miles Around"

One of the great attractions Barnum's press agents had to publicize in the latter part of the 1870s was the famed clown Alfred Frisbie Miaco (above).

In Barnum's 1876 Centennial Circus, Harry and Leotard Carlo were the cutest elements of their eight-performer family.

Barnum's managers in the late 1870s may have begrudged his huge share of the profits, but they couldn't fault his tireless efforts in behalf of the business. With the show based no longer at the hippodrome but out of Gilmore Gardens, Barnum funneled his main energies into its publicity and promotion. Ordering up 100 new steel cars, the first ever, for his cross-country circus train, Barnum also commissioned a splendid new "Advertising Coach" that was to arrive 14 days in advance of the show and become the center of an all-out publicity blitz. Sixty-four feet long, displaying Barnum's portrait prominently on both sides, the coach was adorned with pictures of animals and circus processions, including a stunning depiction of the show's new "Trakene Stallions," painted by nationally known artist James Walker. Opened up to the public at each stop, the car was a curiosity in its own right. Its lavish, black-walnut-paneled interior housed the nerve center of a crack advertising team. A carpeted, upholstered private room served as the office for Barnum's two chiefs—F. A. Keeler, superintendent of bill posters, and Charles Gaylor, press agent. In small compartments, scattered throughout, were accommodations for Barnum's press agents and trainmen and for his poster hangers, the all-important 12-member "paste brigade." And in carefully designed work areas were the "tons of immense colored bills, programs, lithographs, photographs, electrotype cuts, etc.," as Barnum himself described the operation, all "to arouse the whole country for fifty miles around each place of exhibition to . . . P. T. Barnum's New and Greatest Show on Earth."

Barnum pioneered in the use of large-scale color lithography. As early as 1872 and 1875, his New York printers, the Torrey Brothers, were turning out 32- and 64-sheet color posters, measuring up to 10 feet tall by 50 feet wide. In 1879, never to be outdone, Barnum ordered up "the biggest and best show bill in the world." After three months of labor and a cost of $3,000, he had it—a giant poster made up of seventy 28-by-42-inch sheets, and soon covering the entire side of a large building in Newport, Rhode Island. All this was expensive. In a typical year, 1877, the cost of advertising and publicity for Barnum's circus came to over $100,000, almost a third of the total expenses. On top of this were the ever-looming, sometimes devastating unplanned-for costs—losses due to overbilling (other circuses posting bills on top of Barnum's), the poisoning of animals by competitors, and, worst of all, rail accidents. In the summer of 1877, the Barnum Advertising Coach itself was wrecked outside of Des Moines, Iowa. Occurring at night, with the crew asleep, the accident killed seven staff members outright and seriously injured another five. Within days, Barnum arrived from the East to offer sympathy to the injured and to inspect the ruined coach.

Opened to the public at each stop, Barnum's enormous hand-painted "Advertising Coach" was a draw in itself.

This lithograph trumpeting Barnum and his myriad accomplishments was typical of the fine work done by the Strobridge Lithograph Company of Cincinnati, Ohio, which for years did much of Barnum's poster work.

"It Is Our Duty to Extract the Honey"

Madame Petty, Barnum's Long Haired Woman.

The great equestrian, the pretty high-wire walker, the long-haired woman, the one-man band, the giants and midgets and bearded ladies, as well as these solemn ventriloquists with their dummies, were all testaments to Barnum's philosophy of entertainment and the spice and spirit it could add to daily human life. "I happen to be a showman," he told the *Christian Union* in 1878. "Circumstances in my early life threw me into that position. Probably if I had been a clergyman, a doctor, or a lawyer I should have exercised energy and diligence in my profession, but I honestly believe I should not have labored any more earnestly or conscientiously to make the world better than I have done as a caterer for the public recreation." Contrary to the beliefs of many a church father, laughter, Barnum was sure, was no sin. In fact, he advocated human nature taking a few "capers," and was sure that the world would be the better for it. "Amusement is not the great aim of life," he admitted, "but it gives zest to life and makes a grand improvement in human character as far as it substitutes cheerfulness for moroseness." How are noble-minded men and women to separate the pure from the impure in the amusement arena? "It is our duty, like the bee," said Barnum, "to extract the honey and reject the poison." On these pages and in the six-page portfolio of Barnum performers that follows, some of the showman's honey has been extracted.

Signor Rossi, Barnum's Italian One-Man Band.

William Morgan, equestrian.

Mlle. Victoria, "Queen of the lofty wire."

Charles Young, ventriloquist. **Harry Kennedy, ventriloquist.**

William Francis Chalet, ventriloquist.

Barnum fat lady.

Admiral Dot, the Eldorado Elf.

Hugh Murphy,
the Irish Giant.

Jack Shields,
the Texas Giant.

Monsieur Joseph,
the French Giant.

The Chinese Giant.

Bearded Lady Mrs. Meyers.

Bearded Lady Annie Jones.

The Decade Ends on a Booming Note

Rosa Richter, known as "the great Zazel," poses at the mouth of her cannon (above), and blasts forth in a supernatural version of her extraordinary act (below).

s the decade of the 1870s was closing, Barnum acquired his most spectacular act. An unlikely source was at least partly responsible. Schuyler Colfax, who had been Grant's vice-president, was an ardent circus buff, liked to give Barnum pointers, and in the summer of 1878 wrote and told him of a particularly thrilling stunt. "Your advice is excellent," Barnum replied, "and I almost think you ought to have been a showman. . . . I have seen the woman shot from the cannon and have been trying for a year to get her." The next year, an English girl named Rosa M. Richter was thrilling Barnum audiences under her stage name of Zazel. "It was an act that taxed the press agent's vocabulary to the bursting point," wrote Dexter Fellows, Barnum's publicity chief in later years. Tension was built up in the audience by "the elaborate fuss incident to bringing the cannon into the arena and adjusting it." Then, Fellows continued, "the confused murmur of apprehension" rose from "thousands of throats when Zazel, the peerless and fearless, tripped into the ring. It grew in intensity as she carefully sighted the cannon, and burst into a mighty roar when she swept off a long robe, revealing herself in pink tights." Before climbing the massive wooden cannon barrel and disappearing into its mouth, Zazel walked a wire "the size of a common knitting needle," then dived "from the very top of the tent into a net." But it was her human-cannonball finale that really stopped hearts. "Zazel was projected from the cannon by a powerful spring which also set off a charge of gunpowder," Fellows wrote. "The performer emerged in a cloud of smoke followed by a burst of flame." Zazel shot into the air and soared in an arc 40, 60, 80 feet, to a trapeze with a net beneath it. "She would catch the bar and sway back and forth while the tent reverberated with cheers and applause."

ZAZEL The BEAUTIFUL Human Cannon Ball. She is fired from a Huge Siege Gun full charged with powder 100 ft upward, where she performs Peril-defying feats on an Invisible Piano Wire, finally electrifying her audience with a HEAD-FOREMOST DIVE TO THE EARTH

Whether indicating the size of his latest midget or showing the width of a giant's toe, Barnum, in this photograph, reveals the good-natured intensity of an aging impresario.

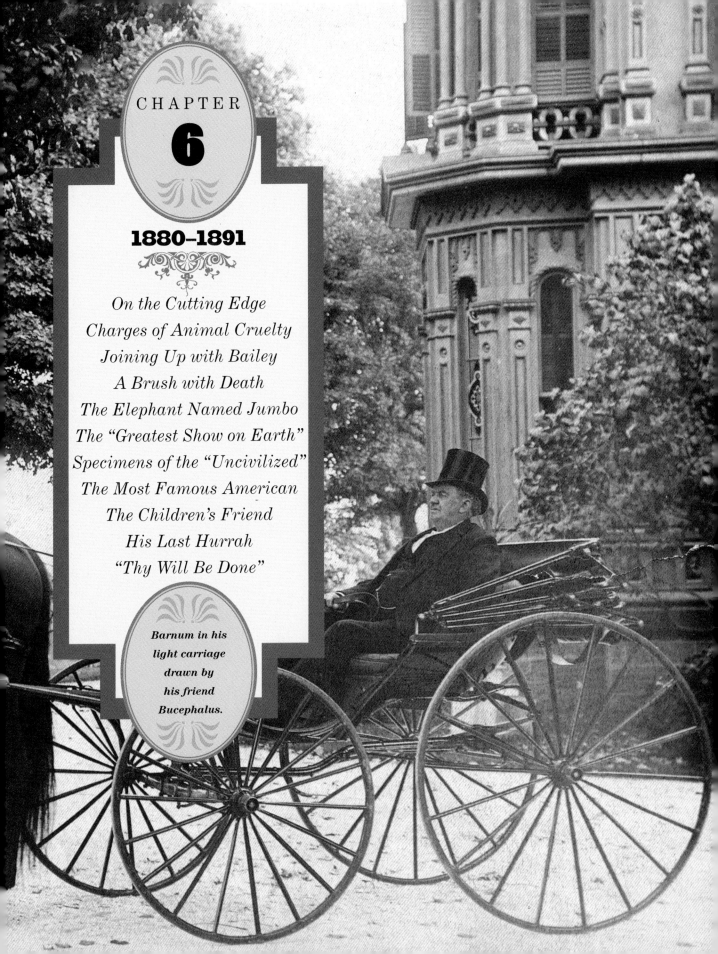

Barnum in his light carriage drawn by his friend Bucephalus.

In a Changing World, Always on the Cutting Edge

When there was still hardly a telephone in Connecticut, Barnum had two, connecting his home and downtown office.

he monster legs of the Brooklyn Bridge poking out of the East River were symbolic of the times as everywhere change swept away the old and ushered in a new world. How different was America now from the America of 1841, when Barnum first opened business in New York City. The intervening decades had seen a wealth of technological progress: the compound steam engine in 1845; a steel process in 1857 that would eventually allow skyscrapers to rise and change forever the American city; the transatlantic cable, finally completed in 1866, and the transcontinental railroad in 1869, which would make the coasts only a week apart in travel time, ensure the rapid settlement of the West, and unify the nation; the telephone in 1876; Edison's phonograph in 1877 and his electric light bulb in 1879. By the 1870s, wires were everywhere, transforming the urban landscape. Horse-drawn carriages on Broadway in the 1860s gave way to electric trains by the 1880s. Tall-masted clipper ships yielded to the age of steam. Barnum himself watched the spread of steel foundries, the rise of trestles for above-ground railroads, and advancements in the printing industry. He watched photogra-

A giant symbol of progress, the mighty Brooklyn Bridge, completed in 1883, gave the 1880s an inspiring, modernistic feel.

phy develop from the first halting images on metal and paper and glass, to the sturdy pictures available in the late 1880s to Everyman through Kodak's inexpensive hand camera.

Barnum always stayed as up-to-date as possible with changing technology—it was one of the factors that separated him from other showmen. "Certainly the two most miraculous discoveries of the age," he wrote presciently in 1845, "are . . . magnetic telegraphic communication and the *Daguerreotype*. The first brings the poles together—the last snatches nature in an instant and reflects her image upon the plate with the perfection of a mirror." Taking early advantage of both these "miraculous discoveries," Barnum had an ingenious mind that was always searching for new ways to amaze his customers and new apparatus to heighten that amazement. He pioneered the use of huge illuminated billboards, and audaciously pumped salt water all the way from the New York Harbor into his museum to keep whales alive in their giant glass tanks. He was first to incorporate steel into his circus railroad cars. The waterproof canvas he imported from France for his Big Top was the first of its kind in America, and Barnum obtained the U.S. patent for it. A huge admirer of Thomas Edison, Barnum featured the inventor's "electric letter writer" in his 1880 circus, and a decade later recorded his voice on an Edison wax cylinder. Even the usually hostile James Gordon Bennett had once been forced to admit that Barnum was a "man of the future," writing in the New York *Herald*, "He feels it, sees it rushing up to us."

As the decade of the 1880s opened, Thomas Edison was only 32, but already his inventions had helped revolutionize the world.

THROUGH FLAMING HOOPS OF BLAZING FIRE,
OVER BURNING GATES, BARS & BARRIERS,
SENSATIONAL EQUINE ANTICS WITH THE ARENA AFLAME.
THE CHARGER SCALES LITERAL WALLS OF FIRE.

THE STROBRIDGE LITH CO. CINCINNATI

In a portion of a Barnum poster, "Salamander, the Fire Horse" does exactly what was so upsetting to ASPCA President Henry W. Bergh.

Among the Charges Against Barnum Is Cruelty to Animals

In April 1880, Barnum introduced an animal trained to leap through a series of burning rings: Salamander, the Fire Horse. In the audience on opening night was an agent representing Henry W. Bergh, president of the American Society for the Prevention of Cruelty to Animals. Ever since founding his humane organization in 1866, Bergh had despised Barnum's operations. In 1867, he had called Barnum "a semi-barbarian" for keeping museum animals in cramped, dark, unventilated quarters. Worse still in Bergh's opinion was Barnum's feeding of live rabbits and pigeons to his giant boa constrictors, and the prey's resulting "terror" and "torture." Not only were "innocent creatures [being] cast alive into the dens . . . [of] disgusting reptiles," exclaimed Bergh, ascribing mammals and birds to a higher order than snakes, but feeding time itself had become a public spectacle at Barnum's, with children gathering daily to watch the carnage.

As Barnum's use of animals increased in the 1870s, Bergh watched him like a hawk, ready to swoop down with warrants at any suggestion of cruelty. Inspecting the Barnum Show in 1871, he discovered an African eland with no room to turn around in its cage, a horse being whipped on the nose by its rider, and a hyena "chained down within eight inches of the floor." In the mid-1870s, Bergh denounced the use of prods and hot irons by Barnum elephant trainers and protested the name "Roman Hippodrome" as a "repulsive" throwback to the "barbaric past." Much of it was true; the very methods of obtaining a constant supply of rare animals often involved real cruelty, such as the killing of parents to secure young, the severing of tendons to bring elephants to their knees, and the transporting of African wildlife by camelback over long distances in close, confining boxes. "Whether . . . it is humane and praiseworthy," asked Bergh, "to rescue . . . rare animals from the . . . jungle . . . and drag them through Christian lands to have peanuts and tobacco thrown at them by gaping crowds and then perish as they mostly do . . . drowned, shot or burned—is at least open to question."

Now, in April 1880, on the basis of a secondhand report, Bergh decided to exercise his authority as president of the ASPCA and close down the Fire Horse act. Barnum was appalled. "No one has a higher respect for your character, your good intentions, and the causes you represent than myself," he wrote Bergh on April 16, "but dear sir, you . . . have made a mistake." Appearing in the ring of his circus, Barnum took his complaint directly to the public. "Either Mr. Bergh or I shall run this show, and I don't think it will be Mr. Bergh." Explaining that the "fire" on his hoops was a visual effect produced by chemicals, Barnum proceeded to demonstrate their harmlessness by jumping through one of the fiery rings and then holding his hand in the flames. "I love animals too well to torture them," he said later, having won his case outright in the courts.

Sensitive, high-strung, even squeamish, ASPCA President Bergh (above) could not stand violence of any kind, whereas Barnum (below) once wrote of the overpowering excitement he had felt at a bullfight. Even so, five years after the Salamander episode, Barnum joined the ASPCA and became one of Bergh's close friends.

Bright Circus Stars in Barnum's 1880 Extravaganza

ver since the early 1870s, Barnum had worked hard to bring out one extra-special new act each year, on the level of a Costentenus or a Zazel. In 1880, it came in the form of the "Wild Men of Borneo," a pair of three-and-a-half-foot-tall, muscular, long-haired dwarfs supposedly captured off the coast of Borneo. On Barnum posters and in 25-cent pamphlets sold in the circus's new "History and Photograph Department," the brothers were depicted as powerful, bloodthirsty demons, "so wild and ferocious . . . they could easily subdue tigers." It had taken four captors to overpower them, the story went, and now, from Barnum's ring, where they performed feats of strength, males in the audience were actually challenged to fight with the tiny men. In fact, they were the retarded brothers Hiram and Barney Davis, born to English parents and raised on an Ohio farm. They were discovered in the 1850s by an itinerant showman who renamed them "Waino" and "Plutano"; under Barnum's umbrella, the pair's careers skyrocketed. With their striped shirts and leggings and with their bearded, yellowish faces, the Wild Men became one of the most famous freak acts in the world, earning over $200,000 in their lifetimes, and continuing to work into the 20th century.

Master Nino Nelton, billed as a "juggler" (below, left), and Harry Evarts, "magician" (right), both starred for Barnum at the turn of the decade. Other top 1880 performers included Miss Helen Courtland, "The Queen of Song"; J. W. Whiston, "humorist"; and Charles Betts, "pianist."

It was the last year of Barnum's partnership with the Flatfoots, but the two little men at left helped him go out in style with the biggest, most profitable year of the partners' association. They were the "Wild Men of Borneo," whose "capture" had taken nets, guns, and many strong men (below).

2 Wild Men of Borneo WAINO & PLUTANO CAPTURED ONLY AFTER A DESPERATE CONFLICT. THOUGH DWARFS IN SISE THEY EXHIBIT GREAT STRENGTH LIFTING MANY HUNDRED POUNDS IN WEIGHT or Throwing the most scientific Six-foot Athlete with Ease.

The James A. Bailey Era Begins

James A. Bailey lived and breathed the circus; born a McGinnis, he had even adopted the surname of his first circus employer, Frederick H. Bailey. Squint-eyed, perpetually nervous, pinchpenny, intensely private, fanatical about detail, he was everything the fun-loving, extroverted Barnum wasn't. His habit of chewing rubber bands was a dead giveaway to Bailey's mood. "No one went near him," wrote a performer, "until he spat the bands from his mouth."

Third partner in the newly formed triumvirate was James L. Hutchinson, a former press agent who had been running the concessions for Cooper and Bailey and now was in charge of finances. His high-handed, dictatorial ways soon earned him the nickname "Lord Hutchinson" among Barnum men.

s 1880 progressed, Barnum was increasingly aware of a major new source of competition—the Great London Show of Cooper, Bailey, and Hutchinson. For several years, this immense circus—whose titles included Sanger's British Menagerie and Howe's London Circus—had toured the world, to as far off as Australia. Now it was deliberately bearing down upon Barnum, challenging him on his own turf. In March of 1880, Cooper and Bailey had made big news when their large Indian elephant Hebe gave birth, in Philadelphia, to the first elephant ever born in America. Envious of the publicity, and eager to own "Little Columbia" for himself, Barnum offered a reputed $100,000 for her. Gleefully, the savvy owners wired back, "Will not sell at any price." Instead, they incorporated Barnum's offer into their own flyers and handbills. "I had at last met showmen 'worthy of my steel'!" wrote Barnum. "[P]leased to find comparatively young men with a business talent and energy approximating my own, I met them in friendly council . . . and we decided to join our two shows in one mammoth combination." The real story was not quite as cheery as all this; not only did Barnum first have to get rid of his present partners, but he wanted an airtight deal with Bailey and Hutchinson, James E. Cooper having decided now to drop out of the foursome. For his attorneys in the contract process, Barnum chose the most notorious, hard-playing lawyers in New York, William Howe and Abraham Hummell. With clients ranging from showgirls and madams to racetrack owners, big-time gangsters, and murderers, Howe and Hummell were infamous for winning cases and getting big cash settlements. On August 26, the new contract was signed. By it Barnum became half-owner of the show, with Bailey and Hutchinson each to own a quarter interest. Though the new operation was to be called "P. T. Barnum's and Great London Combined" (later just "Barnum and London"), it was important to Barnum that his physical presence at the circus was required only nominally. In the exchange, Barnum waived his rights to market his name independently.

There were some tensions from the beginning, to be sure. Barnum's personal representative on the show, C. P. Carey, complained of being tyrannized by "Lord Hutchinson," and reported that the managers "seem to fairly hate the sight of a Barnum man." There were also questions about the account books, especially since Bailey stacked the treasury department with his own relatives. And sometimes the partners neglected to consult with Barnum on important decisions, as the contract had specified. Nevertheless, in Bailey and Hutchinson, Barnum had finally found what had eluded him in both W. C. Coup and the Flatfoots—a secure ground for a long-term partnership. "The Great Alliance," he called it. Within a short time, he was whipping off familiar notes to his friend "Hutch," and by the end of the decade Barnum could write, in a letter to James Bailey, "You suit me exactly as a partner and as a friend."

The competition Barnum feared most was the Cooper and Bailey circus, shown here in a rare photograph taken in Ottawa, Illinois, in 1876.

The catalyst for the new partnership was Bailey's "Little Columbia," first elephant to be born in America. Barnum was so anxious to own Hebe's historic offspring (right) that, when his $100,000 offer was turned down, he decided he'd better merge circuses rather than face more of the stiff, head-to-head competition Bailey was giving him.

Main Attractions Under the Barnum and London Banner

The big surprise act of Barnum and London's first year, appearing last in the big parade in his own special chariot, and then as a finale act in the Big Top alongside Tom Thumb and his wife, was Chang Yu Sing, the Chinese Giant. Standing at least seven feet six inches, and possibly topping eight feet, Chang was the tallest man Americans had ever seen. Barnum had heard of him the previous year, when Chang was exhibiting in London, and had lured him to America by offering a phenomenal $500 a month. A favorite of the emperors of China and Russia, Chang wore varied costumes, including a French military uniform presented to him at the Palace of the Tuileries, the full armor and dress of a Mongolian warrior procured in Moscow from a Russian prince, and a huge silk mandarin robe and cap to which Chang added the two-and-a-half-pound pocket watch and nine-foot chain he had been given by Queen Victoria.

Chang was 34 years old when he arrived in New York on December 1, 1880, carrying with him his own nine-foot-long portable bed. Arriving just one year ahead of the Chinese Exclusion Act, which would ban immigration to the U.S. from China for decades, Chang represented a romanticized, exotic Orient, at once fearsome to Americans and immensely attractive. And unlike other exhibits, where Asians were often presented as sinister and demonic, Chang was offered up as an exemplar of Oriental nobility and wisdom. He had "the soul of geniality, affability and kindness," Barnum ads claimed, along with "the beauty of Apollo." He was "the urbane Chinese giant," agreed the New York *Clipper*—a chess-playing, fine-cigar-smoking scholar who not only could lift 500 pounds with ease, but spoke fluently in seven languages. Audiences everywhere marveled at the "Chinese Mastodon." And though he had come over on a strict one-year-only contract, Chang soon knew what a good thing he had found in Barnum. Appearing in the Barnum circus until as late as 1887, Chang watched his salary steadily and dramatically increase.

Upon his arrival in the U.S., Chang was visited at his hotel by a New York *Sun* reporter who was stunned by the immensity before him. "He is unquestionably the largest man in the world. He is gigantic. As he sat there smiling and nodding, his thoroughly Chinese face looked fully as broad as an ordinary man's shoulders, and as long, if not longer, than a flour barrel." Chang wore clog shoes to further increase his height.

With the Barnum and London circus in 1881 were the Boisett Brothers—three gymnasts, one playing a clown.

MR. I. W. SPRAGUE,

Age 38 years.   Height 5 feet 5½ inches.

Weight 46 pounds.

What gave Isaac W. Sprague, the "Living Skeleton," more delight than anything was showing off his normal family. Temporarily out of work after Barnum's new museum burned, Sprague courted Miss Tamar Moore of Hanson, Massachusetts, and won her hand; subsequently the couple had three boys, all "well developed, large and strong," wrote Sprague, "and to my unspeakable happiness, show[ing] no signs of the malady . . . which distinguishes me." Back with Barnum in the 1880s, Sprague was still thanking his wife for making his world "put on new garments of beauty."

In 1881, after a long absence from Barnum's side, General and Mrs. Tom Thumb joined the Barnum and London circus for what was billed as "positively their last season of exhibition." The previous three years had not been easy for the aging couple. In 1878, Lavinia's sister Minnie had died painfully while giving birth to a full-sized baby, not the miniature child she and her husband had expected. Their spirits nearly broken by the tragedy, Tom and Lavinia had to be urged by Barnum himself to stay active, and it was he who proposed their 1881 tour with his circus. Later, when fire broke out in their Milwaukee hotel on a cold night in January 1883, Tom and Lavinia's lives were saved by their manager, Sylvester Bleeker, but Bleeker's wife perished after a terrified leap from a high window. After this incident, Tom Thumb was never the same. Six months later, on July 15, alone in his Middleborough, Massachusetts, house, with Lavinia off touring, Tom died suddenly of a stroke at the age of 46. It was the end of an era. Barnum, who was in Montreal but who would soon hurry back to take part in the huge funeral service attended by 10,000, telegraphed Lavinia: "Yourself and family have my warmest sympathies. Death is as much a part of The Divine Plan as birth. The Heavenly Father finally overcomes evil with good. His will be done." *Harper's*, in its obituary, summed up the admiration of all. "It was not Tom's diminutiveness alone that put him so high up—that is, so low down—in the annals of dwarfdom, but his prettiness, brightness and grace. Above all it was his felicity in falling in with Barnum."

An Unexpected Brush with Death

As the new decade got under way, Barnum admitted he was tired. His multi-faceted, high-energy career was finally taking its toll. "Try as far as possible to relieve me from the necessity of thinking and working," he wrote to his new full-time private secretary, Henry E. Bowser. On November 16, in the midst of tying up loose ends in his association with George Bailey and J. J. Nathans, Barnum was struck by a sudden excruciating pain in his abdomen. Rushed to the New York City home of his son-in-law Samuel Hurd, he was diagnosed as having an obstruction of the intestine. He was unable to eat and plagued by vomiting; by December, his weight had dropped from 215 to 144, and Barnum was expected to die.

Six months later, finally recovered, Barnum was a changed man, "old and stiff and not as strong as Samson," he wrote to his friend George Emerson. "I don't worry about business and never shall do so again," he declared;

Depicting a figure of Triton with water spouting from an upraised horn, this bronze German-made fountain, presented by Barnum to his hometown of Bethel, Connecticut, in August 1881, may have been removed from Waldemere after causing water-pressure problems to the estate. In his speech on the day of its unveiling, Barnum not only recounted pleasant memories of his Bethel childhood, but for the first time recalled a darker past for his hometown—a legacy of public whippings, imprisonments for debt, and suicides buried at the crossroads. "How blessed are we," he concluded, showing himself a man now more of the present and future than of the past, "to live in a more charitable and enlightened age, to enjoy the comforts and conveniences of modern times and to realize that the world is continually growing wiser and better."

Photographs before and after his illness show a once forceful man now frail and ravished.

"I have had enough of it." With leisure now to look back over his life, Barnum suddenly could hardly recall a benefit he had rendered his fellow man. And so he commenced a project of letter-writing, attempting reconciliation with each of those he considered his personal adversaries. In the fall of 1881, after summering abroad, Barnum prepared for a special visit to his childhood home, Bethel. He had returned there now and again over the years—to visit his mother while she was alive, to help bury her in 1868 and then divide up her property and humble belongings, and to give an occasional lecture to benefit the local church. But this visit was to be different, and everybody knew it. Practically the whole town was out on August 19 for Barnum's official presentation of an 18-foot-tall bronze fountain. Flooded with memories, and amazed by the huge outpouring of affection for him, Barnum delivered an emotionally charged retrospective address. "Among all the varied scenes" of his long life, he told his old friends, "crowded with strange incidents of struggle and excitement, of joy and sorrow," his most "affectionate remembrance" was of the town of his birth.

The Greatest Show on Earth Gets Its Greatest Star

Extraordinary size had always been a basic Barnum staple; he was drawn to the very little and the very big. No wonder the circus showman so coveted Jumbo the elephant, the largest creature in captivity. The trouble was, the English had him.

Back in 1861, a baby elephant had been captured in the African jungles, taken to Cairo, and sold to a Paris zoo, from which it was eventually acquired by the Royal Zoological Gardens in London, swapped for a rhino. Named Jumbo by its new owners, after an African word for "elephant," the once puny creature was nursed and coddled by Matthew Scott, his keeper, as he grew over the years to the heroic size of 11½ feet in height and 6½ tons in weight. In almost two decades of service to the crown, the internationally famous Jumbo had carried hundreds of thousands of children as they flocked to the London zoo for rides.

From across the Atlantic, Barnum greedily eyed the colossal pachyderm, "but with no hope of ever getting possession of him." Nevertheless, he made an offer to the London Zoological Society of $10,000, and not long af-

terward what had been the impossible suddenly became a distinct possibility. Jumbo had thrown some uncharacteristic temper tantrums in his zoo quarters, and in 1881, fearful that it might have a potential danger on its hands, the society decided to accept Barnum's offer. Back home, the delighted showman realized he couldn't just pack up his acquisition and sail away. An international tableau had to be created first, by means of a bit of cunning, double-barrel brainwashing. In order to prove to Americans what a prize was coming their way, he set about convincing the English that they were being tricked out of a national treasure. Once the seeds of discontent were planted, loyal Britishers, from the man in the street to the Prince of Wales, were duly outraged. Like Lindmania three decades earlier, "Jumbo-mania" now swept across both countries. Jumbo souvenirs appeared by the thousands, and caricatures of Jumbo's imminent departure and projected arrival in the U.S. flooded publications. Songs and poems illuminated the controversy further, and manufacturers attached Barnum's name to their products, no matter how far-fetched the connection. Letters from England poured in to the showman, begging him to reconsider. No, Barnum would not change his mind. A deal was a deal. After all, Jumbo wasn't a born British citizen. American children deserved him, too. Now, with protest and excitement seething, an enormous, rolling, padded, boxlike cage was built of oak and iron in which the continental switch was to be made. But, try as they might, Barnum's agents were unable to persuade Jumbo to step inside. "Jumbo is lying in the garden and will not

Jumbo and his longtime keeper and friend Matthew Scott inspect each other on the grounds of the London zoo. Wrote Scott about his charge: "He has been engaged in carrying around the children of the human family almost daily for twenty years."

Whenever Jumbo bellowed, Scott came running. "He is selfish," revealed the keeper about his beloved "Jummie." "[I]f I am an hour or two overdue . . . he commences to whine and cry, and becomes very naughty, just the same as a child crying after its mother."

stir. What shall we do?" they wired home. Barnum's answer was to "let him lie there a week if he wants to. It is the best advertisement in the world."

Huge sums were now offered Barnum to relent, Parliament and the Queen practically begged, lawsuits were brought against the society's officers for making the sale, and Barnum's agent was threatened with imprisonment if any force at all was employed in Jumbo's removal. The showman stood firm. He cabled the London *Daily Telegraph*, which had asked him to name his price: "Hundred thousand pounds would be no inducement to cancel purchase." Excitement mounted in the U.S. as daily accounts of Jumbo's sit-down strike filled the papers. Finally, a resolution was hit upon. The keeper, Scott, who had uncanny influence over his charge, agreed to accompany the elephant to America. It worked. With Scott now leading the way, Jumbo willingly stepped into the six-ton box, and Barnum could write, "Jumbo [is] mine." It took 16 horses to move the cage, and "thousands followed," Scott remembered; "the grief of the children was really sorrowful." After the huge 13-ton cargo had been swung on board the *Assyrian Monarch*, the oversized passenger munched on fruit and bonbons while a goodbye dinner was held on the ship, attended by grieving lords and ladies. The cost of shipping Jumbo to the U.S. was $1,000, but Barnum had to pay for the 50 tons of freight the elephant displaced as well, plus steerage passage for 200 emigrants who normally would have been on board.

Not even Barnum knew quite what he had. America's most visible ambassador was loudly praised for taking on the British and winning, as now thousands of New Yorkers met the ship on April 9, 1882, and followed the

WHAT A TRIFLE MAY EMBROIL NATIONS!

Thomas Nast took the British side of the big Jumbo to-do with his *Harper's Weekly* picture of the English elephant crying all the way to his American fate.

In New York City, it took 16 circus horses pulling, and several elephants pushing, to roll Jumbo from the Battery up Broadway to his new home in Madison Square Garden.

procession through packed and cheering streets to the Hippodrome building—now named Madison Square Garden—where the circus was about to open. Barnum claimed the elephant had cost him $30,000 in all, but that sum would prove to be nothing beside the earning power Jumbo proceeded to demonstrate. In his first three weeks, he pulled in $3,000 a day, covering more than his entire cost. For the years ahead, astronomical receipts were credited to his presence, as Jumbo, riding in his special private car from site to site, became the most famous animal in the world—in fact, the most celebrated in history. Billed as "The Towering Monarch of His Mighty Race, Whose Like the World Will Never See Again," Jumbo never showed in America the temper that had cost him his British citizenship. Instead, he seemed to thrive on circus life, especially enjoying the bottle of beer Scotty shared with him at bedtime, a fact that led Barnum to consider merchandising a special Jumbo-shaped mug of beer. His very name soon became part of the language—the word "jumbo" being used from then on for something of true hugeness.

Always the businessman first, Barnum was forever aware of what the future might bring, and wished to be prepared. Henry A. Ward in Rochester had become his semi-official taxidermist for rare birds and animals that had died on the job, and in the summer of 1883 Ward requested, for the recognition it would bring him, that he be the one to stuff Jumbo, if and when that sad need occurred. Barnum assented: "I shall have my managers understand that if we lose Jumbo (which Heaven forbid!) you must be telegraphed to immediately, & hope you will lose no time in saving his skin and skeleton."

Jumbo Joins a Monster Show Already Crammed with Elephants

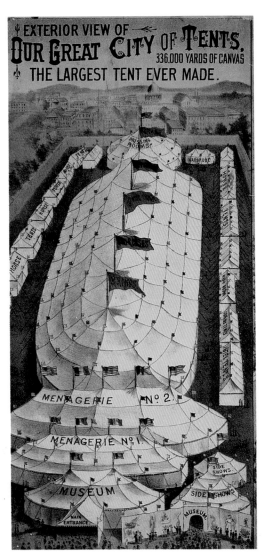

Spread across these two pages is a rare lithographic view of the "7 United Monster Shows" of 1882. In the left panel, an exterior view of the tents (above) has been separated from the cascade of acts beneath the big top.

The circus Jumbo joined, "Barnum's and London," known unofficially as the "7 United Monster Shows," was one of the first ever to employ three rings. A Strobridge and Company poster said to have been based on a photograph showed why the operation was such a "monster," and where the number "7" came from: one museum tent, two menageries, a hippodrome track, and three circuses in three rings. Beneath high-wire acts and flying trapezes, each of the rings hosted a full show in its own right, packed with clowns and stunt acts and performing horses. And on the half-mile-long hippodrome track, mounted Sioux warriors and harnessed giraffes and saddled ostriches competed against racing elephants.

Ever since he had brought ten of them over from India and amazed Americans with the country's first big elephant troupe, Barnum had kept pachyderms in the forefront of his shows. In the 1870s, he had obtained two precursors of Jumbo—Betsy, a huge 28-year-old female, and Emperor, a

Along the top of the image:

LITERAL SCENES TAKEN FROM A PHOTOGRAPH. OF THE 3 RINGS, RACING TRACK & INTERIOR VIEW OF THE 7 UNITED MONSTER *SHOWS.*

This panoramic view of the whole circus in action, three rings and hippodrome track all going at once, shows how much Barnum and Bailey and Hutchinson offered their spectators, and why some complained there was so much simultaneous amusement they didn't know where to look. Along with a few other large circuses, Barnum's pioneered the three-ring show in 1881.

giant male. In the Barnum and London circus, Jumbo joined at least 30 other elephants, including Queen, Gypsie, and Fritz, as well as Pilot, a 9,175-pound Senegalese elephant who had once killed a man in London, and Albert, an unruly male whom Barnum later wished to castrate. Also in the show, still nursing, was Barnum's own new infant elephant, his beloved Baby Bridgeport. And so Jumbo—"the biggest Elephant or Mastodon—or whatever he is—in or out of captivity"—joined a star-studded cast. Expanded in 1883 with the new title of the "8 Forever United Shows," Barnum's big circus included 32 camels, eight giant baboons, six "educated" kangaroos, and two large dromedaries. And then, as if to place his fairy tale of an elephant, Jumbo, in the proper context, Barnum added a series of stunning parade tableaux on wheels: "Cinderella's Fairy Chariot," "The Old Woman Who Lived in a Shoe," and "Santa Claus in His Merry Sleigh."

"All my thoughts and cares at present," Barnum wrote in March of 1882, "are locked up in two *trunks*—one of which belongs to *Jumbo* and the other to little 'Bridgeport.' " A month earlier, at winter quarters, Barnum's elephant Queen had given birth to a 145-pound baby, the event duly celebrated in this booklet (left).

The immense hippodrome track that encircled the three rings provided a stage
for the numerous races held during each performance—women dressed as jockeys
raced each other (above), elephants raced (left), clowns riding ostriches raced.
It was an ingenious if sometimes dangerous way to keep the pandemonium going.

As Barnum aged, a quiet thoughtfulness replaced the old noisy vitality.

Barnum still saw to it that both his circus menagerie and aquarium had dramatic
and highly promotable stocks of huge, dangerous, exotic creatures.

The All-Star Cast Includes a Giant and Two Dwarfs

One of Barnum's favorite tricks was to play off the contrasting sizes of his giants and midgets. He had done it back in his museum days, first with Tom Thumb and the Arabian Giant and later with Anna Swan and the Lilliputian King. Now he had Brustad, the Norwegian Giant (left), and Che Mah, "the only Chinese dwarf," plus Major Atom, equally tiny. How better to stimulate curiosity and draw in the people than to show the three together, two of them perched on the hands of the third (right).

Che Mah Che Sang (left) was 32 inches high, wore a braid reputedly 13 feet long, and was presented in elaborate Chinese garb, though in actuality he was a London Jew. Major Atom (right), who worked for Barnum all through the 1880s, used a cane and high hat to make himself look older.

And, Finally, Jo-Jo the Dog-Faced Boy

Having been born with skin not connected to the flesh beneath, the "Elastic Skin Man" could pull it, stretch it, or mold it at will and without pain. This may be Barnum's own James Morris, wearing a beard to cover up new scars on his face, but he has also been variously identified as Carl Haag and Felix Woerhle.

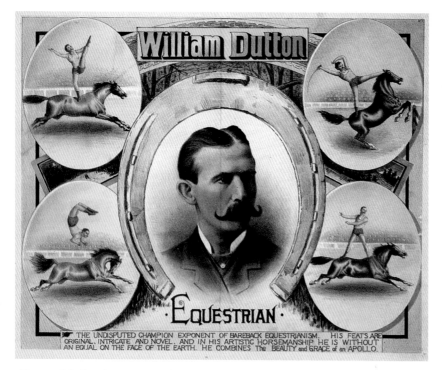

Along with the clowns, equestrian feats were the most popular circus events, and William Dutton's bareback gymnastics were considered the best in the business.

In 1884, Barnum got wind of a hairy sensation from Russia, 16-year-old Fedor Jeftichew, whom the showman soon had under contract. Jo-Jo the Dog-Faced Boy, said Barnum's lurid brochure, was found living in a cave with his father in the forests of Kostroma in central Russia. "They were subsisting at the time upon wild berries and such small game that could be killed with stones and clubs." Their origin was as unknown "as is the history of the Sphinx or the Pyramids of Egypt." The New York *Tribune* thought Barnum's latest import bore "a strong resemblance to that of a Skye Terrier," and described his face as "completely covered by a thick growth of silky yellow hair." To play up the doglike quality, the boy was taught to growl and bark in public. Jo-Jo had not only facial hair but a "scattered growth" all over his body, a quality he inherited from his father, who instead of inhabiting a cave had exhibited himself throughout Russia with his son at his side. He had died at 59 without knowing that the boy would one day become one of the most famous and memorable curiosities of all time.

Now the Charge Against Him Is Cruelty to Children

Elbridge T. Gerry was instrumental in the creation of the New York Society for the Prevention of Cruelty to Children. Family and institutional child abuse and neglect ran rampant, and the SPCC was responsible for rescuing many of the ill-treated and seeing the guilty punished. But the society was less effective in its controversial attempts to regulate public performances by children, especially when it came to Barnum.

A moment after the children appeared," wrote *The New York Times* in 1883, "the genial countenance of Mr. Barnum beamed upon the scene, and the applause which greeted him was so enthusiastic as to make Jumbo jealous." Barnum was in his element; he was being publicly challenged. The charge against him concerned children, and the case involved policemen, judges, courts, and possible imprisonment, all elements which the showman was familiar with and knew how to manipulate. Barnum had hired a family of superb child bicyclists from Portugal, the Elliotts, and now their repertoire of fast-pedaling trick turns was delighting New York audiences. They were not, however, delighting Elbridge T. Gerry, president of the Society for the Prevention of Cruelty to Children. Nine years earlier, the pitiable case of Mary Ellen, a child who was beaten day and night by her stepmother, had been brought to the attention of Henry Bergh, head of the ASPCA, and its legal adviser, Gerry. Unable at first to do anything about it, the two reformers realized that animals had more protection than abused children. A New York organization to protect children was duly originated. Now Gerry and his society were bringing charges against Barnum for cruelly using the young Elliotts. This gave Barnum the chance to appear on stage with his cyclists, ages 6 through 16, refute the charges, and set off an avalanche of publicity for himself and his circus. "Ladies and Gentlemen," Barnum intoned. "I am the last man in the world who would break the law. . . . These children make no effort. Riding their bicycles is much easier than walking, and now, unless these children and myself are arrested within three minutes, you will see the most delightful bicycle exhibition imaginable." To his dismay, no one was arrested, but Barnum managed to get himself hauled into court a few days later, just after he had presided over a special showing of the Elliotts for the physicians and judges of the city—living proof, he claimed, that he certainly was not endangering the performers' health and safety. Hearing testimony in the packed court were three justices, all of whom had watched the test performance and been treated to a tour of the menagerie as well. They did not take long to rule in Barnum's favor, and before the clapping and cheering had calmed down, the showman did what he was so good at doing, getting his adversaries to help promote him. Walking deadpan up to E. Fellows Jenkins, the person who had actually brought the charges, Barnum loudly offered him a weekly fee of $200 if he would allow himself to be exhibited as "the man who wanted to take the bread out of those children's mouths." Jenkins stuttered and fled; laughter filled the courtroom and would continue into the newspapers the next day. Typical was *The New York Times*, which had covered the whole case and now described in detail how the proceedings "against the veteran purveyor of public amusements . . . were brought . . . to a farcical conclusion."

Many children were used as entertainers practically before they could walk. With Barnum's Elliott children, bicycle riding was just as natural a means of locomotion. Tom Elliott is shown above.

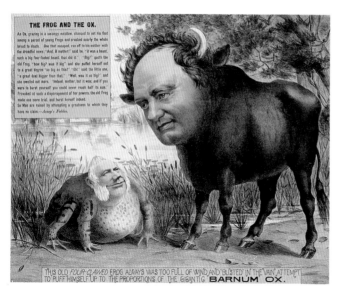

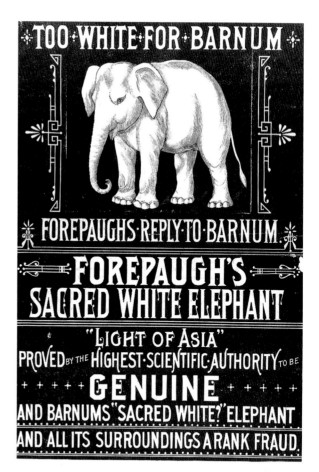

Adam Forepaugh was Barnum's chief rival, his circus and its challenging, ridiculing, and one-upping of Barnum's a constant thorn. In this Barnum-inspired poster (above), an Aesop fable is the setting for the huge and powerful Barnum ox and his vain and jealous little frog foe, Forepaugh. To compete with Barnum's real and expensively obtained sacred white elephant, Forepaugh used whitewash to make a whiter one of his own (right and below).

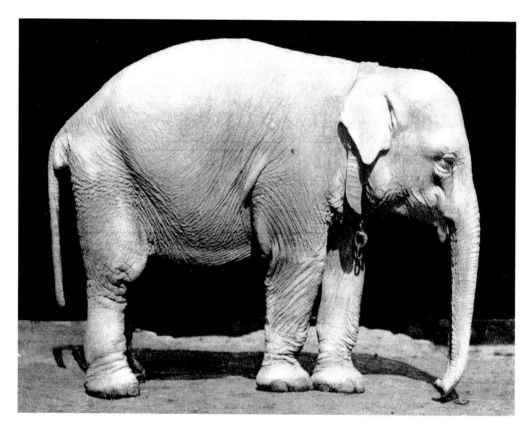

The Big To-Do over Whose Elephant Is Whiter

requently, Barnum got challenged at his own game. And when his adversary was an arch-rival, like circus man Adam Forepaugh, the showman could get downright exercised. For Barnum, 1882 had been the year of the elephant. Even before breaking Britain's heart with the acquisition of Jumbo, Barnum had written the King of Siam to lay the groundwork for one of his dreams—obtaining a real honest-to-goodness exotic white elephant from the East. These rare animals were considered sacred and therefore untouchable by Christians. Barnum commenced by trying to bribe the American minister to Siam—$10,000 if he could help obtain a specimen. Promise of much bigger money persuaded a Siamese lord to come through, but his elephant, said Barnum, "was poisoned on the eve of its departure by its attendant priests." By now Barnum's host of agents should have known better and gone home. Instead, one tried the direct approach with the King and had to get out of Siam fast for his "blasphemous presumption." Undaunted, Barnum's representatives turned to Burma, which was ruled by a detested despot, King Theebaw, whose bounteous spending had cast his country into heavy debt. Six thousand dollars sounded good to Burma's desperate prime minister, and a docile beast named Toung Taloung was selected, painted blue and red, and, thus disguised, marched past unsuspecting natives to the docks. In March of 1884, Barnum finally got his first look. "I have had my share of disappointments during my long career," he later wrote, "but I doubt whether I was ever more disgusted in all my life." The problem was, the elephant wasn't white. One ear was "pinkish" and there were a few "pale spots on the body." Nevertheless, "accompanied by a Burmese orchestra and a retinue of Buddhist priests in full ecclesiastical costume," the questionable icon was featured during the 1884 season. Now Adam Forepaugh stepped in. With so much white-elephant talk around, he had to have one, too. In order to obtain it, "4-Paws," as Barnum liked to refer to him, had a normal gray elephant whitewashed in London, shipped over, and introduced as the "Light of Asia." The masses—Barnum moved the "m" to form "them asses"—flocked to see the milk-white fake, and the war was on. In retaliation, Barnum reached back to his Cardiff Giant days, bleached one of his own elephants white, and advertised it as "an exact copy of the other whitewashed elephant." "Liar!" wrote Forepaugh. Great professors of anatomy had "made a critical and scientific examination of the animal and declared it genuine in every sense." "He is a common . . . elephant painted, & the paint renewed every week or two," responded the agitated Barnum. "Lunatic!" answered Forepaugh. "You are an old man," he continued. "And the vim, vigor and sharp wit and cunning of your youth and manhood have left you." At the end of the season, Forepaugh's white elephant conveniently died. "It was dyed already," crowed Barnum. Peace must have finally been made, for the two circuses temporarily combined in both 1886 and 1887.

Gillespie White - Washing Forepaugh's Elephant, Tiny, Renamed "Light of Asia"

BARNUM IMITATES 4-PAW

FOREPAUGH HAS BEEN IMITATING BARNUM for years. For once BARNUM will imitate FOREPAUGH.

BARNUM has had an elephant artificially colored and will show in his parade

FREE

AT EASTON THURS., MAY **15**

A WHITE ELEPHANT JUST LIKE FOREPAUGH'S WHITE-WASHED ONE

WAIT FOR BARNUM AND JUMBO !

Despite what this poster claimed, Barnum alone had the real thing—an authentic sacred white specimen from Burma. When it was mocked as not white but pink, Barnum penned a ditty in reply. "O Barnum has an elephant and advertised it 'white'; the public then supposed it was a pure snow bright. But, says Barnum, I am white and if you'll inquire and think, 'white men' and all sacred elephants are 'somewhat rather pink.' "

A Grand Collection of the World's "Uncivilized Races"

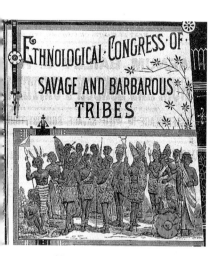

Along with Jumbo and the sacred white elephant, Barnum's Ethnological Congress got top billing in 1884. "Huge assemblage of wild, savage, superstitious and idolatrous people," claimed this Barnum booklet, "appeals directly to the intelligence of the public and the educated of all classes." On far right are some of the actual participants in the Congress.

I n 1884, the year of the white elephant, Barnum brought forth perhaps the most important spectacle of his entire career, a "Grand Ethnological Congress of Nations" made up of native "tribespersons" from all corners of the globe. He had been planning such an assemblage since at least 1860 and possibly since 1851—"a 'Congress of Nations' or 'Human Menagerie' consisting of a male and female of every race, tribe and nation that can be procured." In his 1874 hippodrome pageant he had emphasized what he called the "civilized nations"; now, in the 1880s, he wanted to show forth "the uncivilized." "I desire . . . a collection, in pairs or otherwise," he had written in August 1882, "of all the uncivilized races in existence. . . . I should be glad to receive from you description of as many such specimens as you could obtain." This letter, copied by Barnum's secretaries in batches of 50 or more at a time, had been sent out to consulates and U.S. officials all over the world. Employing agents on every continent, eventually the project began to yield the longed-for "specimens"—Zulus and Polynesians, Nubians and Hindus, Todas Indians and Afghans, Australian aborigines and Sioux Indians and Laplanders. "The remuneration of these people," Barnum wrote, "is usually minimal. I shall see that they are presented with fancy articles as are always acceptable and small allowances monthly."

Nothing of its kind had ever been seen before in America or elsewhere. The New York *Herald*, usually cool when it came to Barnum's projects, called his spectacle "a cavalcade of Orientals," using the word "Oriental" to describe anyone non-Western or nonwhite. "All kinds of black and tan personages [are here]" it continued, ". . . including the remarkable females who do not shrink from the barbarous custom of marrying a whole family." Public fascination with Barnum's "Congress" was intense; mostly white audiences howled with laughter at the "inferior" beings on display. The Chicago *Tribune* summed up Americans' attitudes by describing the Australian aborigines' "almost jet black skin" and "gorillaish features."

As for Barnum, he saw himself as a kind of father figure to all these assembled "child-like" peoples of the world. Believing with other Universalists that "God looks with an equal eye upon all his children," Barnum also, in 19th-century fashion, felt that non-Christian peoples needed to be brought under the sway of "superior" Western culture and religion. To the end of his life, he could never shake this prejudice against non-Christians. And yet, introduced on the circus hippodrome track, and praised by New York's august Ethnological Society, Barnum's Grand Ethnological Congress became an eye-opening introduction for audiences all across America to the wondrous diversity of the human family.

A band of Nubians from the Sudan.

Zulu warriors, including princess and child.

Specimens of high-caste Hindus.

"Todas Indians," billed as the "lost children of Israel."

Jumbo Is Killed by a Thundering Train in the Night

Barnum was in a New York City hotel at the time Jumbo was killed.

In less than four short seasons, Jumbo had achieved unheard-of success. He was Barnum's pride and joy, the favorite out of all the extraordinary creatures in a long career. Beloved by millions of children and adults all across America, "dear Jumbo" could make the old showman misty like nobody else. On the night of September 15, 1885, the Greatest Show on Earth was playing the town of St. Thomas, Ontario. Twenty-nine elephants had already finished their routines and had been led down the railroad tracks to their waiting cars. Only the smallest, named after Tom Thumb, and the largest, Jumbo, remained to close the show. As keeper Matthew Scott finally guided the two mismatched performers along the tracks, he heard a whistle. The unscheduled express train hit Tom Thumb first, scooping him up on its cowcatcher and knocking him down a steep embankment, breaking his leg. Not willing to attempt the embankment and hemmed in by the circus train on the other side, the fleeing Jumbo was hit from the rear. The locomotive was derailed but Jumbo was crushed, his skull broken in over a hundred places. Still conscious and groaning, the dying elephant was comforted in his final moments by Scott. It took 160 men to drag the immense body to the edge of the embankment and roll it down. Overcome, Scott lay down upon his old friend and lapsed into a deep sleep while souvenir hunters approached with their knives.

Barnum was taking breakfast at the Murray Hill Hotel in New York when the news was brought to him. "The loss is tremendous," he gasped, then quickly remembered his standard role in tragedies and continued, "but such a trifle never disturbs my nerves." It took two days for the Rochester-based taxidermist Henry Ward to arrive on the scene. After measuring every last detail of the animal, he and six local butchers fought through the heavy fat and the thick odor to recover the 1,538-pound hide and 2,400 pounds of bone, for Barnum was determined to have two Jumbos to replace the flesh-and-blood model, one made of skin, the other a skeleton. When Barnum heard that the hide could be stretched to make an even bigger beast than Jumbo had been, he wrote Ward, "[B]y all means let that show as large as possible. Let him show like a mountain." Fearful that his gruesome display would not be ready for the next season, Barnum warned Ward of the March 1, 1886, deadline stipulated in their contract. "We must have both Jumbos complete and as strong as thunder," he emphasized. Now the showman set out to kindle public interest in his "Double-Jumbo." Barnum's version of Jumbo's death was bound to help. As the locomotive bore down, Jumbo had "snatched the little elephant from in front of the thundering train and hurled the little fellow twenty yards to safety." Then "the mountain of bone and brawn," in Barnum's terminology, took on "the leviathan of the rail" in a terrifying clash as Jumbo met death "with a becoming dignity and fortitude."

In Barnum's own version of the accident, the heroic Jumbo first saved a small colleague, then actually did battle with the evil locomotive.

Circus personnel pose with Jumbo's body before the taxidermist starts his work. At the elephant's head is his devastated keeper, Matthew Scott. The man in the middle is Barnum and Bailey partner James L. Hutchinson—"Hutch," as Barnum called him.

JUMBO AFRICANUS. Mounted at W.

THE TREMENDOUS SKELETON
OF
JUMBO, LORD OF BEASTS,
PREPARED BY THE DISTINGUISHED SCIENTIST AND
NATURALIST, PROF. HENRY A. WARD OF ROCHESTER, N.Y.

A MOST PRODIGIOUS SIGHT,
EXHIBITED WITHOUT EXTRA CHARGE IN
THE GREAT BARNUM AND LONDON UNITED SHOWS,
THEIR POSITIVELY GRANDEST TOUR.

When the circus opened in April 1886, spectators were in for a morbid treat, Jumbo in two
versions, skin as well as skeleton (left). In the
grand parade both mammoth reconstructions
were mounted on special springed wagons and
were followed by Jumbo's "widow," Alice, an
old colleague from the London Zoo brought
quickly across the Atlantic. Alice was followed
by a long line of the circus's regular elephants
playing the widow's attendants, all of which
had been carefully trained to carry black-
bordered sheets with their trunks and every
few steps to wipe their eyes.

The Stunning Stars and Lavish Show
That Double-Jumbo Joins

During the summer of 1886, the mighty Barnum and London parade stomps, rolls, and toots its way down the main street of Janesville, Wisconsin.

The seven Sutherland sisters claimed the longest hair on record, seven feet of "luxuriant" mane. This, tossed about and swished seven times over and combined with some lively singing, made the sisters a top attraction with Barnum in 1886. On the side the Sutherlands sold hair grower and scalp cleaner that could be found in better hairdressing parlors everywhere.

The great Siegrist Family, including child gymnasts Louis, Toto, and Willie, appeared regularly in Barnum's show during the late 1880s.

They Make Barnum's Other Dwarfs Look Like Giants

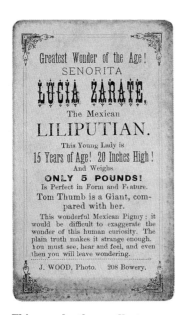

This may be the smallest midget who ever lived, certainly the most diminutive Barnum exhibited. Lucia Zarate was born in San Carlos, Mexico, in 1864. At birth she was seven inches long and weighed eight ounces. At 17 she measured only 20 inches and weighed a mere five pounds. Appearing at Barnum's in 1886, this bright, animated little lady became one of the highest-paid midgets in history. She was well on her way to amassing a small fortune, but at 26 she froze to death in a snowstorm that stalled her train high in the mountains. At right and above are the front and back of a carte de visite that Lucia sold on stage.

**General Mite was not quite as
tiny as Lucia, with whom he
often exhibited, but at nine
pounds he still weighed in
mighty small. Born Francis
Joseph Flynn in Greene, New
York, in 1864, Mite liked to
boast that the top of his head
had come barely up to the first
button on Tom Thumb's vest.**

Touch Them for Luck

Throughout the 1880s, again and again Barnum attempted to outdo himself in his special surprise acts. But in 1887, with his introduction of the "Sacred Hairy Family of Burmah," he rose to new heights of uniqueness. Never mind that Jo-Jo had been of similar description; in the Hairy Family, Barnum had reached his hand into far-off "mysterious Asia," the supposed birthplace of the human race, and had discovered there a primordial wonder. "They do not come heralded as freaks or monstrosities," Barnum insisted, "but as pure, long-established types of the most weird, peculiar, distinct race of mankind of whom there is any trace or record." Consisting of two members, a 30-year-old man, Moung-Phoset, and his adored, 70-year-old mother, Mah-Phoon, the pair had been obtained by Barnum probably at a fraction of his claimed expenditure of $100,000. Said to be descended from hair-covered parents and grandparents, and known in Burma as the "hairy luck givers," Barnum's pair had served as court mascots to King Theebaw and were said to have proved a source of good luck to all who touched them. Drawings made at the time of Barnum's engagement, such as the one above, showed the pair as utterly hirsute, possessing a thick, dark, shaggy coat completely covering their arms, legs, chests, backs, shoulders, hands, faces, and feet. But photographs show their hands to have in fact been smooth and hairless (opposite page); and one rare image of a shirtless Moung reveals that his chest and arms were only faintly covered by a fine, light-colored fuzz. It was their faces where the real wonder lay, and here no exaggeration was ever needed. Long hair grew out of almost every pore—out of ears, nose, forehead, and cheeks. Only by combing it sideways could they reveal to the public their sparkling eyes. Visitors to Barnum's show in 1887 were permitted the closest inspection—were even encouraged to touch them and try to obtain some of the good luck that they had once given to Burmese royalty.

The "Weird Hairy Family of Burmah," as circus programs called them, consisted of a mother and her son. "If . . . 'a woman's hair is her glory,'" one Barnum ad declared, quoting the Bible, "then is Mah-Phoon glorious, far beyond all the daughters of Eve."

One of the most unique ads for a Barnum act was this odd but compelling "bird's-eye view" of a twisting river with adventurer Captain Paul Boyton popping up at different points (left). Boyton had spent years taming rivers, waterfalls, whirlpools—anything wet and dangerous. He had navigated the Mississippi when it was filled with grinding ice. Abroad, he had been attacked by sharks in the Straits of Messina. He had conquered the Thames, the Rhine, the Danube, the Tiber, the Arno. All this in preparation for his tour with the great Barnum and London United Monster Shows, for which Barnum admitted paying Boyton a "princely salary" for an undertaking that "would severely tax even our enormous resources," the daily construction of a miniature lake (right) in which the Captain could revel in his rubber suit.

An Extraordinary Aquatic Act Underneath the Big Top

n act to remember from the 1887 show was Captain Paul Boyton's survival demonstrations in an "artificial lake" beneath the Big Top. At each stop the excavation had to be made anew and enough water pumped to the site "for the realistic presentation of Captain Boyton's amazing and novel nautical exhibitions." The Captain had single-handedly navigated both the Yellowstone and Missouri rivers, sluicing his way down 3,580 miles of often dangerous water in 64 days. During his adventure he had been fired on by Indians and encountered "quicksand, whirlpools, caving banks, snags and mud sucks." To demonstrate how he managed to live through it all, Boyton donned the ingenious rubber suit he invented, then plunged into the "lake" to show the enormous audience how he had shaded himself from the sun, shot birds, fished, raised sails, and even set himself a handsome table on his raft. A few years later, at Coney Island, Boyton fathered the country's first amusement-park water rides, culminating in his famous "Shoot the Chute."

DIGGING THE ARTIFICIAL LAKE SIX DAYS IN ADVANCE FOR CAPT. BOYTON'S EXHIBITIONS.

CAPT. PAUL BOYTON
THE KNIGHT-ERRANT OF THE DEEP

FORCING THE WATER FROM CITY RESERVOIR INTO CAPT. BOYTON'S ARTIFICIAL LAKE.

Key Men of the Far-Flung Circus Staff

Commenting on Barnum's nose, staff member George Conklin wrote that behind his back "the boys" claimed he "had quite a snitch on him."

By the mid-1880s, Barnum's full-time circus staff had grown to over 700. The tent operations alone required 117 canvas-men in 1886, most of them attached to the Big Top. In that same year, route books listed 19 trainmen, 17 ushers, 7 ticket sellers, 11 confectioners, 2 barbers, 2 laundrymen, a tailor, a watch repairer, a shoemaker, and a 26-piece circus band. On top of this, the "Hotel Barnum," as it was called, providing meals for a traveling army of employees, was staffed by 10 cooks and 26 waiters. The immense tent city even required its own postmaster. Most of these employees were never photographed and have long been forgotten. Even at the time, most of the top department directors and officers seemed literally to vanish behind the bright light of Barnum's all-encompassing glow. But there they were, doing the important, not always glamorous, behind-the-scenes work. Here was J. B. Gaylord, "foreign agent"; and Frank Hyatt, Barnum's hardworking assistant manager, who climbed his way up to superintendent; and Byron V. Rose, the pompous, disliked, not entirely honest "Master of Transportation," who always seemed just barely to hold on to his job. Some of the middle-management staff members were relatives of one of the top partners, such as Merrit F. Young, a Bailey relative who served as show treasurer in the mid-1880s; and Joseph T. McCaddon, Bailey's brother-in-law, who as assistant treasurer helped set up Bailey's complete dominance over financial records. In reaction, Barnum brought over from England his wife's cousin Benjamin Fish and installed him as his new personal representative on the show, with full access to the books.

Other key players in Barnum's circus machine included George Conklin, "Superintendent of the Menagerie," and a brilliant trainer of hippos, big cats, and monkeys; William Ducrow, a former bareback rider who rose in the ranks to both equestrian director and ringmaster; and George Arstingstall, the show's elephant trainer in the mid-1880s, who was said to rule his animals "through fear, and not affection." But the group with perhaps the highest status among all the various departments remained Barnum's advertising corps. Though it was headed up by W. H. Gardner, after 1883 its star member was Richard F. Hamilton, affectionately known to all simply as "Tody." By 1886, he was listed as both press agent and advertising director, and not without reason. A former writer for the New York *Herald*, Hamilton was a verbal conjurer in the tradition of Barnum himself. A master of alliteration and effective repetition, Hamilton produced torrents of ad copy as exciting as the events they described, often more so. Defending the fine art of exaggeration, he once said, "[T]o state a fact in ordinary language is to permit doubt concerning the statement." Hamilton was credited with getting circus news finally accepted by the general press, and became involved in every big Barnum promotion from Jumbo on. According to Dexter Fellows, a circus press agent in the 1890s, Barnum once declared he "owed more of his success to Tody Hamilton than to any other man."

Known as "Professor," George Arstingstall was in charge of Barnum's elephants in the early 1880s and taught them to play musical instruments.

Partner James A. Bailey tried to stack the staff with his relatives. His brother-in-law, Joseph T. McCaddon (above), was the show's assistant treasurer.

W. H. Gardner was in charge of the press corps in the 1880s and headed up the advance team that inundated each city with circus propaganda before the Big Top arrived.

Each time George Conklin, in charge of the menagerie, led the white hippo around the arena in the big parade, Barnum would call to him from his front-row box to "make her open her mouth." Invariably this would give the old showman a chuckle.

A wizard with words and exaggeration, Tody Hamilton became Barnum and Bailey's most celebrated press agent, creating a magically magnified circus world with his extraordinary descriptions of its inhabitants and their talents.

J. B. Gaylord was Barnum's foremost "foreign agent," who twice reached into a corner of mysterious Asia to acquire from the hated Burmese oppressor King Theebaw first the sacred white elephant and later the King's pets, the Sacred Hairy Family.

311

In the 1880s the constant hum of deals being made, rents collected, construction under way, figures calculated, books balanced, and money pouring in at 269 Main Street in Bridgeport came largely from a hive of activity appropriately called the "Busy B's" and consisting primarily of Barnum and his two most important personal assistants, Henry Eugene Bowser and Charles R. Brothwell. They even had their own joke picture (above), which included three other B's among the inner circle.

In 1880, on the recommendation of a Bridgeport bank clerk, Barnum hired a 42-year-old Canadian accountant from a local lumber company to help oversee his financial empire. Barnum's dealings were so complex, and the trusted Bowser's involvement with all the strands soon grew so intimate, that to protect himself from the possibility of Bowser's sudden departure, Barnum had eventually to hire a second accountant just to keep track of what the first was doing.

Charles Brothwell supervised the complicated web of Barnum real-estate holdings, the chief hiding place and source of the showman's wealth. A construction expert who dealt in landfills, grading, and sidewalk construction as well as new buildings, Brothwell also bought and sold lots for Barnum, collected rents, and maintained the hundreds of properties Barnum owned. One whose construction he supervised was a large three-story Bridgeport establishment Barnum called "Recreation Hall," a combination of gym, skating rink, shooting gallery, bowling alley, bike track, dance hall, and restaurant.

The Two "Busy B's" of His Personal Business Staff

In the decade of the 1880s, with his business and real-estate affairs at their most complex ever, Barnum made extra efforts to procure top-notch, personal staff support. He had been long used to having a chief personal assistant—in the early years of the museum, it had been Parson Hitchcock; in the 1860s, it was John Greenwood; and during the 1870s, Julius Gorham had filled the bill, hired on as private secretary, bookkeeper, and "agent" with authority to sign Barnum's name on letters and documents. But whereas Gorham had been impeccably honest, he had turned out to be a poor accountant, and so, in a secret night meeting at Waldemere, Barnum had offered the job to a Bridgeport lumber-company employee named Henry Eugene Bowser. Joining the staff in early 1880, Bowser found himself in charge of the finances of a private empire. His job was to collect all rents, pay the salaries of Barnum's five domestic servants, monitor all circus receipts, and issue regular, eventually monthly, financial reports. On top of this he was to distribute "pin money," as Barnum called it, to Nancy Barnum ($500 a year), take charge of the showman's constantly amended will and codicils, and serve as Barnum's personal financial adviser. "Never fail to give me your opinion about the propriety or impropriety of my expending money," Barnum wrote him early in his tenure, and soon it was clear how well Bowser understood his tasks. Pleased with his way of doing business, Barnum praised Bowser's "system," his "promptness," and his *push*." Before long, to assist Bowser in the vast real-estate portion of his job, Barnum added another assistant to his staff, the Bridgeport local Charles R. Brothwell. Calling the two men his "watchdogs," Barnum urged their total "vigilance" and a single-minded pursuit of his "interests." These alone, he said, could put him at ease and add much-desired years to his life. And so the "Busy B's" were born—Barnum, Bowser, and Brothwell—with their beehive located in a new Bridgeport office building at 269 Main Street.

Insisting on a strict separation of business and home life, Barnum appeared daily at these offices whenever in town, setting up regular hours as well at the circus' Winter Quarters in Bridgeport, and later at the Murray Hill Hotel in New York. Once he was freed from financial concerns by the work of the "Busy B's," Barnum's health rebounded. Interviewers in the mid- and late 1880s found him "plump" and "ruddy," as if he had shed years of his life. Barnum wrote Bowser and Brothwell into his will, for $5,000 each, and by late in the decade, he was filled with praise for both men, and especially for Bowser. "Millions of my dollars have passed through your hands, almost unwatched and unchecked," he wrote admiringly to his chief assistant. "[A]nd auditors have found the accounts of your books perfectly correct." Though never once mentioned in Barnum's autobiography—in which almost everyone and everything else was mentioned—Bowser was an all-important behind-the-scenes force during the last decade of Barnum's life.

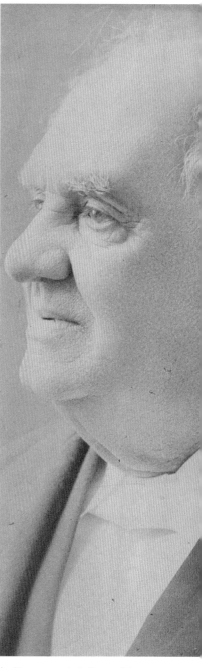

As Barnum aged, he could relax, knowing Bowser was watching his money and Brothwell was tending his buildings.

Just How Much Was Barnum Worth?

By any standard, P. T. Barnum was a very rich man. Some even calculated that by the 1850s he was the second-richest man in New York, a city of riches. Of course, the huge fortunes of future tycoons like J. P. Morgan and Andrew Carnegie had not yet been made. Apart from John Jacob Astor, the fur merchant, whose estate surpassed $20 million, $250,000 defined the domain of New York's "super-rich." The very word "millionaire" was still new, an import from France used for the first time in America possibly by Barnum himself, writing from Paris in the mid-1840s. Whether he knew it or not, the brash showman would become an early example of what the new word described. In its first three years his museum had grossed over $100,000, and to this enormous cash flow was added hundreds of thousands of pure profit from the Tom Thumb tour. With the 1850s came Jenny Lind and the half-million or so dollars pocketed by Barnum through his venturesome use of her nightingale voice. This may well have been Barnum's wealthiest period, for in an era of 20-cent gourmet dinners and $200 annual salaries, Barnum's early fortune, in terms of today's dollar, was worth tens of millions. These were the Iranistan years, and by Barnum's admission the most materialistic days of his life. Once, while patting his pocket, he told a dismayed Jenny Lind, "the only music I like is the ring of American silver dollars." Forty years later, when his estate was figured at over $4 million, Barnum's total worth was still astronomical. It even frightened him a bit, all that real estate he had invested in, all that profit, up to $300,000 a year, that streamed in from his circus. What would his heirs think if they knew he was giving some of it away to a college or a church? And so Barnum was secretive, even furtive when it came to writing checks, transferring funds. He needn't have been. No one in his family was about to challenge the wise old man whose feel for the pulse of America had been so successfully translated into gold.

Barnum was so eager to have his name carried on that he wrote into his will a bequest of $25,000 to grandson Clinton Hallett Seeley (above) if the boy would legally change his middle name to Barnum. He did.

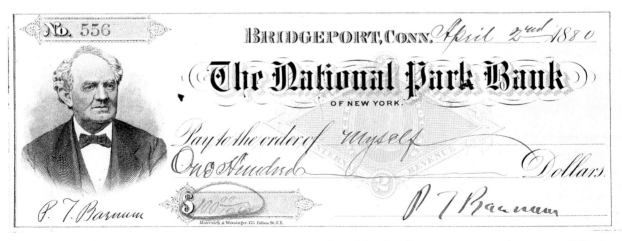

"As a business man," Barnum wrote back in the 1840s, "my prime object has been to put money in my purse." By the time this check was written out to himself 40 years later, Barnum had declared otherwise. "I would abandon the show business if cash was my only reward. . . . Travelling exhibitions . . . are an important power for good."

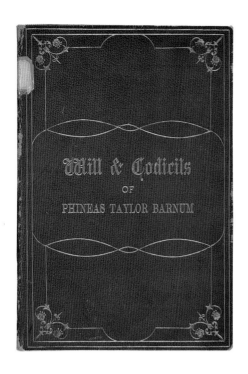

Barnum's last will and testament, with codicils, ran 53 pages and outlined in detail gifts to family members and friends—his "best piano," his stereoscopic-slide collection, his marble bust of Jenny Lind, his silver tea-set, his gold Iranistan ring. There were also large cash gifts to individuals and charities. The figures below are from page 37 of the Salmagundi Account Book, a large-size ledger in which private secretary Bowser kept many of Barnum's financial records. This one lists certain receipts from the circus in 1878, broken down to admissions, programs, candy, and sales of books and pictures. Barnum got half of the profits plus a bonus figured at 5 percent of the first $200,000, 6 percent of anything over.

Receipts

From	Admissions	446.077.64
"	Programmes	800.
"	Candy Stand	4.212.90
"	Side Show	8.427.04
"	Sale of Animal Books	721.42
"	do of Song Books	869.82
"	do of Tattoo's Pictures	100.
		461.208.82

Due P. S. Barnum	
5% on 200.000	10.000
6% on 261.208.82	15.672.52
	25.672.52

More Famous Than Any of His Famous Friends

The elder statesman pauses before scribbling in his notebook.

Barnum had early on made it his ambition to climb into the circles of the rich and the famous. Leaving behind his working-class roots and his youthful rebelliousness, he had learned how to curry royal favor, amass his own personal fortune, and then recast himself as a serious patron of the arts. Insisting that his personal tastes ran to high culture, and not to the fare of his mass-marketed shows, Barnum had finally entered high society, in part on Horace Greeley's coattails. By the 1880s, he was being counted among America's most successful capitalists, alongside Vanderbilts, Carnegies, and Rockefellers. Among the steady stream of famous guests pouring into Lindencroft and then Waldemere were not only Greeley and Twain and the Cary sisters, but Edwin Booth, George Sala, Colonel George Custer, and Matthew Arnold. Barnum's name and personality and boundless energy appealed to the likes of Tennyson and Whittier, Louis Agassiz and Joseph Henry, Robert Lincoln and William Tecumseh Sherman and Spencer F. Baird, all supporters. He once claimed he had been on personal terms with every U.S. president since Andrew Jackson, which was somewhat of an exaggeration; Barnum's ties to many of them were minimal at best. He had met Jackson in Nashville, Tennessee, in 1837, at the former president's cotton plantation, The Hermitage; he had petitioned Franklin Pierce in 1853 for a job for his uncle, Edward Taylor; and he had tried, unsuccessfully, to involve Andrew Johnson in a scheme to build a huge national free museum. He had been a supporter, but no particular friend, of Democrats Harrison, Polk, Taylor, and Pierce, visiting at least some of them in the White House. But only after his switch to the party of Lincoln did real friendships blossom: with Lincoln himself, with James A. Garfield, who dubbed Barnum affectionately the "Kris Kringle of America," and most of all, with Ulysses S. Grant.

Barnum had admired General Grant intensely during the Civil War, and had afterward received the gift of his military hat for display at the new museum. As president, Grant became a Barnum ally, welcoming him to the White House in 1870, and later, in 1874, attending Barnum's new hippodrome show. When Barnum ran for the Connecticut Senate in 1880, Grant traveled to the state to rally behind him, joining in a grand festive dinner in both of their honors. Just months before the old war hero's death, Barnum called on President Grant in his home. After an intimate visit, Barnum turned to his friend and said, "General, since your journey around the world you are the best known man on the globe." "By no means," Grant shot back without a pause. "You beat me sky-high; for where ever I went—in China, Japan, the Indies, etc.—the constant inquiry was 'Do you know Barnum?' I think, Barnum, you are the best known man in the world." And it was true.

Barnum made it his business to court the famous; not only did he bask in their light, but often friendships could sell tickets. In 1881, he wrote to President James A. Garfield (above) urging him to come to his circus. This happened just four months before Garfield was shot, and the letter opened on a strangely prophetic note: "My dear Mr. President, About all the favor I ask from you is, do please have the kindness to live. . . ."

To Oliver Wendell Holmes, Barnum wrote on behalf of his "40-year-old English wife" to ask for the good doctor's autographed photo. He added that he could now taunt the admiring Nancy, for he had experienced the inside of the Holmes residence in Boston when he had called and "begged" his way in to the library.

Remembering the people who had rallied behind him during his bankruptcy, Barnum made Ulysses S. Grant a kind and generous offer of assistance when the General and former President was suffering similar financial woes.

This page from Barnum's 1889 address book lists newspapers and editors who were known to be friendly to him. Other pages contain the addresses of showmen, ministers, photographers, taxidermists, and publishers useful to Barnum. And then there was a host of famous friends—Miss Greeley of Chappaqua, New York; Robert Lincoln; Mary Livermore; plus John Greenleaf Whittier, "poet"; and Thomas Edison, "inventor." Barnum's tailor was Brooks Brothers, Broadway and 22nd Street.

On his first trips abroad, in the 1840s, Barnum was entertained by the English actor Henry Irving (above), who 45 years later helped organize a welcoming banquet for the old showman on his final visit to England.

He Is Drawn to Ministers as His Closest Companions

The Reverend Edwin H. Chapin "married" P. T. and Nancy in 1874. Affectionately referring to each other as "Chang" and "Eng," the two men shared a constant barrage of puns and jokes.

Well-known Universalist editor and writer George H. Emerson provided chess games and important friendship for the last 30 years of Barnum's life.

Lewis B. Fisher, Barnum's final pastor in Bridgeport, would one day preside, along with the Reverend Robert Collyer, over Barnum's funeral.

Perhaps the most surprising aspect of Barnum's oft-misrepresented life was his intense devotion to religion and his deep friendships within the church. Early on rejecting Calvinist doctrines of hell and damnation, Barnum had joined others in the bold new Universalist faith, whose central teaching was the love of God for all God's children. "It is [a] doctrine which distinguishes us from all other sects [and] gives us a wondrous power for good," wrote Bridgeport pastor Olympia Brown, and Barnum agreed. "If God is a consuming fire," he pondered in a carefully reasoned theological essay, then "He consumes man as the refiner's fire does the ore, burning the dross and bringing forth the good." Though he faithfully kept up ties to early friends like Moses Kimball, increasingly Barnum turned to persons of the cloth for his most intimate friendships: to New York pastor Edwin H. Chapin, one of the great preachers of the age; to Presbyterian minister Theodore Cuyler, who once described Barnum as having "a big warm heart that bound all his friends to him with hooks of steel"; to Abel C. Thomas, at whose Pennsylvania home Barnum was often a visitor. For 40 years, Barnum remained an active member of Bridgeport's Universalist Church, helping bring to it Olympia Brown, the nation's first denominationally ordained woman, and sometimes even climbing into the high pulpit there to preach sermons himself. As the decades passed, he became more and more generous in his churchly support. A life member of the Chapin Home for the Aged and Infirm, he helped build churches in Bethel and Bridgeport, sponsored a theological student, Isaac Coddington, through college and seminary, willed thousands to the Universalist Publishing House in Boston, and in 1887 deeded to his local church a house and lot valued at $10,000.

One by one, as the years went by, he saw himself outlive his closest clergy friends: Chapin, Barnum's favorite, died in 1880; Abel Thomas, in some ways even closer to Barnum than Chapin, in that same year; and Henry Ward Beecher, once described as "eternally young"—gone in 1887.

But even as old clergy friends slipped away, Barnum gravitated to new: to the Reverend George H. Emerson, a former disciple of Abel Thomas; to Robert Collyer, pastor of New York City's Unitarian Church of the Messiah, whom (shades of Edwin Chapin) Barnum had placed in charge of a white-elephant poetry-writing contest; to Lewis B. Fisher, the family's last minister in Bridgeport, whom Barnum once addressed as "beloved pastor—the Fisher of Men (and Women)." Fisher, who liked to ride with Barnum behind the showman's fast horse, Bucephalus, seemed to see into the old showman's soul almost better than anyone. "If being made for a thing is a divine call to that thing," he once claimed, "then Mr. Barnum was divinely called to be a showman." And Barnum agreed. "If I had been a clergyman," he wrote, "I should not have labored any more earnestly."

Henry Ward Beecher, pastor of Brooklyn's Plymouth Congregational Church, first used his silver tongue to blast the likes of Barnum but ended up endorsing Barnum's circus.

To Abel C. Thomas, who buried Charity, Barnum reflected: "[T]ime rolls on, troubles come and go, but . . . high above all is . . . everlasting quietude."

Her sermons drew Barnum's praise, but Olympia Brown, the first woman ever ordained to her own parish, was forced out of her Bridgeport church in part because of her feminist views.

A former blacksmith, the famous white-haired Unitarian minister Robert Collyer was the showman's closest friend in the 1880s. Here, in 1885, he visits the Barnums, whose Bridgeport pastor, John Lyon, stands at top right, just above Nancy.

Alongside Fires, Railroad Wrecks Are Dreaded Most

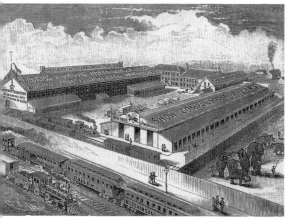

By the mid-1880s, Barnum's Winter Quarters in Bridgeport, Connecticut, was one of the largest animal-training grounds in the world. Steam-heated by its own power plant, it contained special accommodations for hippopotami, sea lions, monkeys, giraffes, big cats, and elephants. Bedecked with colorful depictions of Barnum's diverse animals, the Main Building contained a room large enough for 20 elephants in rehearsal. Besides a Chariot House, numerous workshop buildings, and dining facilities for 150 full-time permanent employees, there was a 350-foot-long Railroad Building housing Barnum's more than 100 circus cars and wagons. The atmosphere of the Winter Quarters was a happy one, and Barnum often brought private guests in to tour the grounds. Elephants sported outdoors in a large, enclosed yard, wild birds ambled loose over the property, a constant din of activity arose from the repair shops and costume rooms and sawdust rings, and townspeople found excitement in the occasional escape of animals into the community.

Then, on November 20, 1887, Barnum was hit by what would become known as his "fifth great fire." Breaking out in the main animal building at 10 p.m., the flames were unstoppable. It was as if part of a terrible, recurring nightmare; once again almost all of the animals were either burned or boiled alive. Only the elephants could be saved, escaping out of the burning building en masse into the night, so that only four out of a total of 34 perished.

Fire had plagued Barnum's entire career, so much so that wisecracks were made about "Barnum the arsonist." But by the late 1880s there was a new concern—train wrecks. One of the worst of these occurred just a year and a half after his big Winter Quarters fire outside Potsdam, New York, on the night of August 22, 1889. With attendants fast asleep, and the animal-packed cars hurtling through the darkness, suddenly an axle under a forward car snapped in two. As the car was sent grinding into and under the car behind it, a giant smashup occurred. Cars telescoped over one another, flew off the tracks, piled up crosswise. Miraculously, most of the animals were saved. The worst losses were among the horses: 28 were killed outright or trampled in the panic, including a costly Arabian stallion. Barnum received the news in the Adirondacks, where he had gone on a summer outing with Nancy. Once again his public stance was one of dispassion and calm, but in reality Barnum was troubled. "If we should somehow kill 50 persons instead of 30 horses," he wrote James Bailey on August 26th, "it might cost us a quarter million dollars." And so the man who had never fully insured his enterprises now suggested creating a public stock company, whose primary purpose would be to protect Barnum and Bailey's personal liability in the event of future disasters.

Before their partnership, Bailey's circus wintered in Philadelphia, and Barnum kept his on the road or boarded the animals at zoos or local farms. But when the two shows combined in 1880, a huge Winter Quarters complex was built on Barnum land in Bridgeport, its 500-foot-long railroad-car barn harboring eight tracks that connected directly to the commercial lines. In late 1887, the whole place went up in flames.

An old, patched photograph shows the smoking ruins of the Bridgeport Winter Quarters. Though he pretended his usual calm resignation, Barnum later wrote of the "thrilling incidents of that night," including the wild night swim of Gracie the elephant, who made it out to Bridgeport's lighthouse before finally succumbing.

Barnum's worst train wreck (above) occurred in northern New York in 1889, when the carnage included more than two dozen horses. Menagerie chief George Conklin recalled the moment when an axle of the elephant car broke. "When the crash came my end of the car was thrown up on top of the car next ahead, and the elephant car was driven under it in such a way that it killed my horse and the twelve camels, but did not hurt one of the twenty-eight men who were asleep in the car. . . ."

An Equal Partnership Leads to the Circus We Know Today

Multiple partnerships no longer worked for Barnum.

Dissolving his cumbersome four-way partnership, Barnum asked Bailey to join him in an equal collaboration, whence sprung the not entirely new title "Greatest Show on Earth."

James A. Bailey suffered from insomnia and nervousness. Orphaned at eight, and nicknamed "Cinderella," for years he had driven himself to the edge of exhaustion. At the close of the big 1884 season, with circus profits eaten up by the huge expenses of procuring Barnum's Ethnological Congress, he had simply collapsed. "[I]t comes from too much thinking," Barnum wrote Bailey's wife in July 1885, after Bailey had obtained a leave of absence. "I beg you and him to remember that our business *will not suffer* this season in his absence." But at the close of the 1885 season, instead of extending his temporary leave, Bailey wanted out of the partnership permanently. Disappointed, Barnum and Hutchinson moved quickly to replace him, turning to Chicago circus man W. W. Cole and to Bailey's old partner and friend, James E. Cooper. And so, throughout 1886 and 1887, Bailey was forced to watch from the sidelines, gradually recovering his health and more and more missing his old partner and his old role, even as Barnum chafed under the bit of a new four-way partnership which had reduced his stake in the enterprise to a minority position for the first time ever. Sometime during 1887, the year of the Hairy Family, Barnum and Bailey met privately for a fateful discussion. Then, at the close of the 1887 season, Barnum dissolved his four-way partnership, and invited James A. Bailey to rejoin him as equal partner in a new

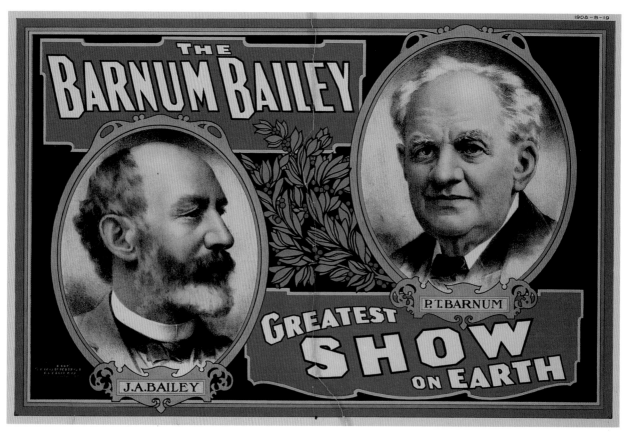

THE BARNUM BAILEY

GREATEST SHOW ON EARTH

J.A.BAILEY

P.T.BARNUM

In 1888, with P. T. Barnum and James A. Bailey finally as sole owners and equal proprietors, the Big Top, with its five central poles already set and etched against the sky, goes up in this rare and dramatic picture.

"Barnum and Bailey Circus." For Barnum, nothing better could have taken place. Seventy-seven years old now, he could no longer be expected to ride herd over a rebellious multiple partnership. More than ever he needed the intensely well-organized, time-proven loyalty of James Bailey. Here was a man who liked to wake up his employees personally on Sunday mornings and get them to work, and who considered Fridays lucky and a good day to start new projects, and who thought no task too humble for himself to get involved in. "I shall never cease to admire . . . your manliness or integrity," Barnum had once written to Bailey, "nor your marvelous perception of how to hit public taste and to do it in the best way." Now, in 1888, the first year of the new team, Barnum wrote his partner once again. "[A] man of my age cannot stand much worry or work, and he cannot reasonably expect to live much longer. I try to impress on the public that we are prepared to keep the show at the top of the heap for generations to come and I hope it will be so. . . . You manage it ten times better than I could do it." And as the big show was increasingly placed in the able hands of James A. Bailey, P. T. Barnum settled back to reap the harvest of his years.

Candid Scenes from an 1888 Barnum and Bailey Scrapbook

In these early candid circus pictures, elephants and zebras pass the same shutterbug on a street in Milwaukee (above), and a more firmly held camera in a South Bend, Indiana, window captures the horse-drawn tableau wagon (below).

A spectator with a camera in the sideshow crowd must have called out for a pose, for the barker has his eyes on the photographer and the charmer is shaking her snake in the direction of the lens (above). The next big show is not yet under way: Barnum and Bailey's rolling ticket office is still closed up tight (below).

A Potpourri of Top Acts in the Eighties

Mrs. William H. Batchellor, whose gymnast husband was also a Barnum circus employee, specialized in open-air balloon ascensions.

There were other "lady riders" of note in Barnum's shows over the years—Annie Yates, Jeanette Watson, Katie Stokes, Linda Jeal, and Viola Rivers to name just five. But few could match the longevity or audience-pleasing pizzazz of Madame Eliza Dockrill, Barnum's "Empress of the Arena" (above).

Flora Stirk, part of a large circus family at Barnum's, bicycled and juggled her way through the big 1888 show.

The big hit in the museum department for 1888 and 1889 was a group of Arab performers from the Paris Hippodrome, led by Ali Ben Dib, shown at left battling a swordswoman, possibly his daughter. Miss Ben Dib also appeared inside Barnum's "Black Tent" of supernatural wonders, offering an illusion entitled "The Decapitated Turk."

In an informal lineup from 1888, Barnum and Bailey sideshow performers are displayed by manager William Henshaw, sitting front and center. To the right, also seated, is "moss haired" Circassian snake charmer Alma Janata and then two "Aztec People." To the right of the six-legged cow and his bowlered attendant is Thin Man John Coffee in top hat, then Elastic Skin Man William Morris, Armless Wonders Charles Tripp and Anna Leak, Annie Jones with coiffured beard, and two albinos, the Martin sisters. Behind these are the four uniformed Texas giants, the Shields Brothers, and in the back is magician and Punch and Judy performer Professor McNulty, standing next to Signor and Signora Galletti, who had a bird-and-animal act.

A Final Mansion to Make Life Easier for Nancy

Barnum had three more years to live when, in 1888, he moved into his fourth and final mansion—Marina—which, to preserve the magnificent ocean view of Waldemere, had been built on a site only three feet east of its predecessor. The reason for a new dwelling was simple—Barnum wanted Nancy to have a compact, modern place that she could personally run after he was gone, one with conveniences like electric lighting and sanitary plumbing that were not available when Waldemere had been built. As soon as all their possessions had been moved to the new, Queen Anne–style "ideal" of brick and stone, Waldemere was razed, its cellar filled in, and the old site covered with grass sod and large trees.

The new mansion contained a music room, a library, a fine dining room, and, upstairs, a domed art gallery and a series of elaborate guestrooms. But P. T.'s favorite section of the house was the extravagant private first-floor office, which he nicknamed his "growler." Designed around a large open fireplace, and hung with mirrors and portraits of leading journalists and framed Barnum treasures, the room looked out upon the estate's splendid gardens. Connected to a generous storage room, the office also had its own lavatory, as well as a side chamber with hot and cold running water where each day Barnum was carefully shaved.

No longer with either a town house or an office in New York, Barnum often did business now at the Murray Hill Hotel. In Chicago he held court at the Auditorium Hotel, in Boston at the Parker or Tremont House, in London at the Hotel Victoria. During winter he sometimes sought warmth at the Hygeia Hotel in Old Point Comfort, Virginia, and in summertime he escaped the heat of Bridgeport on Block Island, at the Crawford House in the White Mountains, or at Paul Smith's Adirondack retreats, with a plan of one day getting to Mount Desert Island. One summer, after a vacation in the Adirondacks, he was writing his favorite great-grandson, little Henry Rennell, his "dear Baby Double-Grand." "Don't get married before Grandma Barnum and I get home," he jokingly told the lad. As his years progressed, Barnum thought of himself more and more as the Pied Piper of the world. In 1890, from Marina, he wrote James Bailey of his wishes for their 1891 *Courier*: "Hope you will print under my portrait next season *The Children's Friend*." From the comfort of his final manse, in his final year, Barnum also wrote down his no-nonsense feelings about children's education and training. He believed a mother should tell her child stories "in plain, pure, grammatical English, and he should be taught at the first to pronounce words correctly. Too much 'pootsy-tootsy,' namby-pamby baby talk is undesirable." Barnum thought the child's mind "should be sacredly respected." He believed that natural inclinations should be followed. He wrote that "the true end of culture is to make people as unselfish as possible, and hence easier to live with." And he felt a sense of humor was a child's most important attribute.

As Barnum's last mansion went up in 1888 (right), it pushed aside his previous one, Waldemere, soon vacant and ready to be knocked down.

This picture of Barnum relaxing by his Waldemere hearth comes from the period at mid-decade when he was beginning to formulate ideas for a simpler house that Nancy could more easily live in after his death.

This photograph of Nancy is from a group she had taken to show people back in England how gracious was her life as Barnum's wife.

With Age Comes a Craving for a Personal Monument

Able fund-raiser that he was, the Reverend Elmer H. Capen, president of Tufts College, knew what chords to play to get big Barnum gifts for his college.

arly on, Barnum had promoted his youthful, self-inflicted title "Prince of Humbugs," but that was long ago, and as age crept up on him, he began to encourage the new label he had coined for himself, "The Children's Friend." It fitted him well. He not only considered himself grand entertainer to the world's children; on a more personal level, he took pleasure in and spoiled his own grandchildren and great-grandchildren, and also aided Bridgeport's Boys' Club and Girls' Club, took great interest in the local orphan asylum, and on at least one occasion supported a speech contest at the Bridgeport High School, presenting special Tiffany medals to the winners. "Humbug" would not have sat well on one so willing to share at least a part of his fortune with the Bridgeport Public Library, the Bridgeport Hospital, Seaside Park, the Actors' Fund of America, and the Universalist Church, to name but a few of the many causes Barnum supported. His dearest project, though, was the endowing of a museum of natural history at Tufts College in Medford, Massachusetts. The negotiations were strange and revealing, filled with secrecy, paranoia, and a sudden craving for a personal monument, as exhibited in the 1880s correspondence between Barnum and the persuasive Reverend Elmer H. Capen, then president of Tufts. In the 1850s, Barnum had been a trustee of the college, but he had paid little attention to it since, until Capen put the arm on him by letter in 1883. "My dear Mr. Capen," Barnum answered. "It is not likely that I can do as you suggest, for I have but a short time to stay here, being nearly 73." Almost immediately Barnum changed his mind, but he wanted Capen to "keep mum" about it. Within a week, he had promised $50,000, "with the understanding the museum be evermore called the Barnum Museum of Natural History." Days later, Barnum was hoping that "a niche for a full-length statue or bust could be introduced over the door," and it was not long before he had made an appointment with a famous sculptor. But Barnum was fearful that if word got out about his generosity every church in the country needing money would come pounding on his door, and that his heirs might raise a fuss about how he was decreasing the estate they would one day inherit. "You shall have bank drafts in which my name shall not appear," he told Capen. "I hope you will address me in a plain envelope." When he was finally persuaded to allow the announcement of the donor's name at the museum's dedication, he at first agreed to be there and speak—but only a few words, for "it tires me to stand and talk much." Then he became "nervous in bed alone under gaslight" and finally could not make the opening after all. Nevertheless, anxious lest his wife and the rest of his heirs learn about what he had done in the newspapers, he told Capen he trusted that accomplished reporters would be on the scene to tell the story straight. "Heirs may as well know," he said, feeling his old independence again, "I do what I like with my own."

An important deposit is made in 1889 as Jumbo's mounted hide
is delivered to the Barnum Museum of Natural History at Tufts.

The Mellowing of a Bridgeport Fixture

Enjoying life on a trip to Virginia with the founder of the Warner Corset Company and party, Barnum and Nancy take the driver's seat of a local ox cart.

or some time now, Barnum had felt the years flying away from him. "I hope you will come soon and visit me at my . . . sea-shore home," he wrote one old friend, "for if you don't, our next meeting will be in that shoreless sphere where there is 'no sea.' " His near-fatal illness in 1880 had turned out to be a solitary occurrence, however, paradoxically giving him the sense of a new "lease on life." It mellowed him, too. And though Nancy was not faring well, her regular stays in sanitoriums to help calm her nerves increasing to a month or more at a time now, for the rest of the decade Barnum's health was robust—his worst problem a case of "mashed fingers," making it impossible to hold a pen for a time.

In Bridgeport, Barnum continued to serve on local boards—the water company, the Pequonnock Bank, the Parks Commission, and a new steam-boat-line company. He continued to put out books; *The Wild Beasts, Birds and Reptiles of the World* appeared in 1888, and an anthology of humorous anecdotes collected over a lifetime was readied under the title of *Funny Stories*. And in 1888, at age 78, Barnum surprised everyone by seriously considering a run for the presidency, against Democrat Grover Cleveland, going so far as to contemplate an Illinois running mate. But the Republican Party fell behind Benjamin Harrison instead, who went on to win the election and receive Barnum's congratulations and condolences.

"He grew more charitable and gentle as he grew older," wrote a friend. Here "Grandpop" poses with young Harry Rennell, his favorite great-grandson.

In 1888, as usual shunning publicity, Barnum, standing behind the fourth panel of railing with Mayor Patrick Coughlin to his left, secretly tests a Bridgeport bridge with the weight of 11 elephants.

To England for the Showman's Last Hurrah

I t was Barnum's last hurrah. Even though he had contemplated sending a circus to Europe for almost a decade, only now did his dream become a reality. At first Barnum worried that the tremendous investment involved in taking the Greatest Show on Earth to London for a 100-day engagement might result in financial disaster, but he was also concerned with what kind of reception awaited the once despised Jumbo-napper. The logistics for the journey were staggering—it would take a small fleet to cross the Atlantic with a menagerie, carfuls of equipment and gear, bandwagons, an enormous herd of horses, Roman chariots, costumes galore, eight tons of posters and ads, and 1,240 performers. But that was Bailey's job, exactly the kind of complex management he was skilled at. It was Bailey's task to construct slings that would lift elephants and camels aboard, to measure every cage and wagon so all would fit snugly, to dream up the idea of freezing the meat for all the flesh-eating animals. It was the job of Bailey's 79-year-old, white-haired partner to make sure that for three months a man named Barnum was on the tip of every last Britisher's tongue. On September 5, 1889, Barnum wrote the American Museum of Natural History in New York, which was now the proud recipient of Jumbo's bones, "Mr. Bailey writes me that he will take the skeleton of Jumbo with us to England soon and return it to you in the spring." The figure made out of Jumbo's hide would go, too, even though this seemed like a double rub of salt into an old English wound. But nothing seemed to matter; Barnum was given a royal reception and Jumbo was wel-

It was pure magic, what Barnum and Bailey brought to England in 1889, the "supernatural illusions" being a wondrous new feature of the big show.

MATCHLESS WORKS OF MAGIC

MIRTHFUL AND ASTOUNDING VISIONS

The united enchantments, delusions and displays of all ancient and modern magicians of every clime, are common-place and puerile, compared with the

SUPERNATURAL ILLUSIONS

Now for the first time exhibited, without extra charge, in the Great Show's

ELECTRIC-LIGHTED WIZARD'S TEMPLE

And which Messrs. Barnum & Bailey have ransacked the whole world, and employed for many months the first of all living inventors and mechanical experts in collecting and creating

STRANGE SPIRITUAL MANIFESTATIONS

Of apparent Miracle, which the superstitious pronounce living realities; a point we shall not argue, but content ourselves with defying any one to discover wherein they differ from tangible being and existence. Mighty Merlin, Michæl Scott or the Witch of Endor

NEVER PRODUCED THE SEMBLANCE OF SUCH WITCHING POWER

Under the resistless spell of whose enchantment tens of thousands in America have already gazed in boundless wonder and fascination. We can only here refer, in the briefest manner, to but a few of

THESE ASTOUNDING BLACK ART TRIUMPHS

THE BIRTH OF APHRODITE.—This magic triumph opens with a view of the ocean ; the horizon illuminated by the prismatic, shooting rays of the Northern Lights. The life-size *Apparition of Venus*, bathed in the rosy tints of the Aurora Borealis, rises from the waves, ascends into airy space, and after assuming a number of bewitching poses, disappears, by diving head-long into the deep.

PYGMALION'S DREAM.—The audience is permitted to inspect a marble statue of *GALATÉA*, which is then placed in full view on its pedestal, when, wonder of wonders, its cheeks slowly redden, the hair assumes natural color, the marble warms into dainty flesh, the eyes are illuminated with intelligence, and the lovely creation lives and speaks. The last and most startling transformation is that of the beautiful Nymph back into stone, which finally assumes the form of a skeleton.

THE WITCH'S HEAD.—In this incredible achievement a square box is placed upon an ordinary table in full view. The box is then opened at the front, and a *LIVING, SPEAKING HUMAN HEAD* is shown. The box is then taken from the table and exhibited to the audience with the head still in it.

FLORA.—A most beautiful revelation, in which the head and bust of a lovely living woman appears in a basket of flowers.

THE HEADLESS TROOPER.—In this marvelous mystery, a Soldier is revealed lying on the ground, with his living head resting on a tray several feet above the body.

" SHE."—Here the mysterious heroine of Haggard's strange romance is made a spiritual reality ; seen through its misty veil.

THE MERMAID.—This mythologic miracle presents a beautiful amphibious being, *HALF WOMAN AND HALF FISH*, disporting in a miniature lake of living water.

THE WIZARD'S AQUARIUM.—In this amazing creation an empty fish bowl is first shown, and then magically filled with living fish.

THE PEACOCK MYSTERY.—The blending of a beautiful woman's living head and shoulders with the body of a Peacock, is one of the prettiest of these necromantic transformations. In this vision the Peacock's gorgeous tail unfolds and closes at will.

NARCISSE.—In this aerial marvel the upper half of a young lady's person is shown on the seat of the swing, which oscillates in open space.

FATIMA.—Reveals the upper part of an Oriental Beauty's body resting on a stool, which in turn rests on an undraped table.

THE BOTTLE IMP.—A living human head seen in a narrow-necked, transparent glass bottle.

THE FAIRY BOUQUET.—A most beautiful and bewildering illustration of the birth and death of the flowers; which bud, blossom, wither and die in their few moments of magic life.

METEORA.—A star-born sprite, dancing, revolving and disporting like a bird in mid-air.

The Alaska Wonder, Neptune's Bride, The Centaur, The Transmigrations of Indus, Grecian Metamorphoses, The Gnome's Carnival, and many other equally novel, droll, incomprehensible and indescribable spectacles.

One of the three ships used to transport the enormous circus to England held its share of the tons of gear, the 380 horses, the 16,000 pounds of posters, and the 1,240 people—including 38 uniformed hangers who were to plaster the posters all over London.

Celebrities who partook of the Greatest Show on Earth in England included the Prince of Wales and his Princess (shown above with her baby son), the Queen's daughter Princess Victoria, the Duke and Duchess of Edinburgh, the Right Honorable W. E. Gladstone, Lord Churchill, and Robert Lincoln.

Even though it was Barnum's vision to include an extravaganza like "Nero, or The Destruction of Rome," the production of the mammoth confection of Christian heroism and heathen decadence belonged to the Hungarian impresario Imre Kiralfy (above).

comed back twice over. Not only did the show get rave reviews as 12,000 packed the Olympia auditorium twice a day, but Barnum himself was greeted as a venerable and beloved celebrity. The press poured forth articles about him. Many of the city's distinguished clubs pressed honorary memberships upon him. Madame Tussaud's did him in wax. His voice was recorded on a new phonograph machine of Edison's. At a special banquet in his honor, committeed by the likes of Randolph Churchill, Henry Irving, and Oscar Wilde and attended by 150 of London's finest, toastmaster George A. Sala likened Barnum in impact to Caesar, Alexander the Great, and Napoleon, the only difference being that the American showman had used innocent pleasure as his weapon instead of armies. At almost every performance at Olympia, the frenzied activity in the three rings and on the high wires above would suddenly cease as the major attraction appeared in an open carriage that would slowly circle the arena. The distinguished, ruddy occupant would rise and bow at intervals, repeating each time to the audience, "I suppose you all come to see Barnum. Wa-al, I'm Barnum." Queen Victoria was away on the Isle of Wight, but just about every other member of British royalty visited the show, first officially and then, for a second and third time, disguised as commoners. The Prince of Wales brought his young son George to the royal box, where Barnum visited them and asked the boy whether he planned to stay until the performance was over. The youngster, who would one day become George V, replied, "Mr. Barnum, I shall remain here until they sing God Save Grandmother." That meant the young Prince would be awed like everybody else by the grand finale—"Nero, or The Destruction of Rome"—an epic extravaganza played out on an enormous stage by a cast of over a thousand, along with most of the show's animals, as Christians and pagans clashed in pantomime to dizzying lights and waves of music. The English had never seen anything like it before. The critic for the London *Evening News and Post* was overcome by the sheer numbers. "Imagine a line of stage about half a mile long, backed by a vista of lordly palaces and temples, and of blue sea and sky; people it with five hundred ballet girls . . . and as many men in splendid classic garb. . . . A gladiatorial combat is shown . . . and the stage is presently strewn with enough corpses to keep all the coroners in England busy for a month." But that was not all. Now the stage was filled with vestal virgins, now with elephants and camels, now with orgy, now with barbarism, and now with the final, uplifting pageant of Christian victory. It was the work of the Hungarian stage genius Imre Kiralfy, the Cecil B. DeMille of his day, but Barnum got all the credit. "He has one idea—the show, the whole show and nothing but the show," the *News and Post* completed its paean on the grand spectacle. "The audience does not matter, nor the stage, nor the expense. He piles on crowds on crowds, throws in a dozen of elephants here, a hundred ballet girls there, with a splendid audacity worthy of Nero himself."

This is the cover of the *Advance Courier* for the spectacular 1889–90 Barnum and Bailey offering in London.

With hat and without, the distinguished visitor from America was photographed in London. Before returning home his voice, too, was immortalized. After thanking the British for their kindness and generosity, he spoke these words which we can still hear today: "I thus address the world through the medium of the latest wonderful invention, Edison's phonograph, so that my voice, like my great show, will reach future generations and be heard centuries after I have joined the great and, as I believe, happy majority."

"Thy Will Be Done"

Throughout the 1880s, Barnum's New York headquarters had been at his old Hippodrome Building, known since 1879 as Madison Square Garden. In August 1889, demolition began on it, to make way for a new, modern building in its place. With its stockholders headed up by J. P. Morgan and its architects the fashionable firm of McKim, Mead and White, the new Madison Square Garden was, by contract, to be ready in time for Barnum's triumphant return from England. But when Barnum and Bailey discovered that it would seat only 4,400, not their usual 10,000, and that it lacked adequate space for their giant new stage, they balked. And so the 1890 show opened not at Madison Square Garden but under canvas at 110th Street and Fifth Avenue, on the site of the old Polo Grounds. The show's main feature, as in London, was the Kiralfy spectacle "Nero." Presented on a 450-foot-long stage, with a cast of 1,200 persons, it boasted of $250,000 worth of costumery and $75,000 worth of scenery, the most money ever spent on any show. There was a hippodrome, a horse fair, 80 circus acts, 20 clowns, two herds of elephants, and of course the famous three rings. Barnum's mysterious "Black Tent" was back as well, for a second year, its darkened interiors holding a series of "mystifying illusions" and "spectral exhibits." To bring the crowds up to the top of Central Park, special trains were set up from Grand Central Station, with runs before and after each of the two big daily performances.

By June, Nancy, who had remained behind sick in England for three long months after Barnum's departure, was finally arriving home. She later described Barnum meeting her ship at the New York City wharves, his "kindly face" smiling up at her from over a big bouquet of flowers. On July 4, Nancy helped Barnum celebrate his 80th birthday, with 200 guests gathering at Marina for a clambake on the shore. "He seemed on this day unusually anxious that none should be missing," observed Nancy, "unusually tender to every one present—child, grandchild and great grandchild." After dinner, Barnum made a special address to a gathering of his employees, his voice faltering with emotion as he looked back on their many years together. "It was as if he had some prescience that it was for the last time," Nancy wrote.

In late July, Barnum and Nancy were back in the Adirondacks, at Paul Smith's cabins. "Take your holidays together," Nancy advised wives in an upcoming article called "Moths of Modern Marriages." "It is an ominous state of things when husband and wife can really enjoy separate pleasures." In the fall, the couple set out for Colorado, "in fulfillment of his great desire to show me the West," explained Nancy. October in Denver was a time of "flawless happiness" she wrote, with her husband showing "boyish eagerness" and exuberantly throwing himself into their outdoor activities. "I eat, sleep and walk like a boy of sixteen," Barnum exclaimed. But then, suddenly, he asked to come home. In early November, he suffered a stroke.

Barnum spent his last months confined to his home. At Thanksgiving, he gave a parsonage to his Bridgeport church; at Christmastime, he redoubled his contributions to local charities. Even when he was sickest, he insisted on dressing each day. In early 1891, he seemed to rally a bit, becoming strong enough to wander about the house and even receive visitors. "I sleep well," he told magazine writer Edith Sessions Tupper in a mid-March interview. "I eat everything and anything, but I have no strength." His attention was now focused on the opening of the 1891 circus season—the big torchlight parade scheduled for March 26 in New York City. "I want to ride around with the procession once more," Barnum told Tupper, his eyes "glistening," she said, with a kind of "fire." But it was never to be. On March 24, the New York *Evening Sun*, breaking all tradition as a final favor to Barnum, actually published his obituary in advance. "Great and Only Barnum," its title ran, "He Wanted to Read His Obituary; Here it is."

As Barnum's world closed in more and more on him, he continued to read avidly—poetry, magazines, newspapers, especially his old favorite, the New York *Tribune*. Finding comfort in looking out his windows at the sea, he had food put out for the gulls so he could watch them congregate and wheel through the sky. When special friends arrived to visit, he often pulled out rare remaining copies of his 1854 autobiography and gave them as gifts. In one such volume, given to Nancy, he inscribed "with love forevermore." "[He] was always cheerful, often merry," Nancy wrote. "His room was the one bright spot in a sad house, and his hearty laugh was often heard." In a rare moment, speaking about death in the abstract, Barnum once said to her, "It is a good thing, a beautiful thing, just as much so as life."

As he had done for years, Barnum continued his daily readings in the Universalist handbook, *Manna: Daily Worship*, each morning meditating on a selection of Bible lessons and special prayers. He taught himself the New Testament by heart during these days, and at night Nancy would hear him whisper, just before sleep, "Thy Will be done." The last day Barnum could move about the house was Thursday, April 2, when he sat up at his desk to

In the spring of 1890, the Barnum and Bailey Circus appeared under canvas at 110th Street and Fifth Avenue, at the top of Central Park (left).

"I am prouder of my title 'The Children's Friend' than if I were to be called 'The King of the World.'"

This ribbon, issued at the time of the unveiling of Barnum's statue in Bridgeport, became a precious keepsake for all who loved the great showman.

write an extraordinary letter to his well-loved James Bailey. It was an out-and-out last letter, in which he set down his final beliefs about his lifelong business. "You must have always a great and progressive show and also one which is clean, pure, moral and instructive. Never cater to the baser instincts of humanity . . . and always remember that the children have ever been our best patrons. . . . I wish to assure you of my unalterable esteem, affection, and trust in you, and to bestow a fatherly blessing upon one who is in every way so worthy to become my successor." On this same day, Nancy noticed that Barnum's hands were trembling heavily.

Children and grandchildren now began to gather around at the house and in Barnum's bedroom, receiving from him faint words of tenderness as he greeted each one. On Sunday, April 5, Barnum asked his wife not to leave his side. "I want you with me every moment of the little time that is left," he whispered. Then, on Monday night, after telling Nancy that his last thoughts were of her, he sank into a deep sleep which lasted, almost unbroken, until the following evening. "Death was kind," Nancy recorded. "[N]o physical pain disturbed the quiet figure on the little bed. . . . [A]t 6:34 . . . passed out of this . . . life, one of the most remarkable and best-loved men of his country."

It was true. Barnum had outlived all the ridicule, all the bias against him. The Boston *Herald* now proclaimed him "the foremost showman of all time," and *The New York Times*, remembering how Barnum had "beamed on the public with . . . a broad geniality," called him "the connecting link between children . . . and the land of their storybooks." In France, he was named "the character of our century," "the great Barnum," whose fame was "as wide as the Universe." And in England, where he was described as "an almost classical figure," it was said that his death would be "regretted by millions."

In Bridgeport, a wreath made of roses was hung on Marina's front door to inform neighbors of Barnum's end. The April 11 service had been planned by Barnum himself. Held at South Church (Congregationalist) because it alone was large enough to hold the expected guests, the funeral attracted thousands of others as well. Unable to get in, they crowded the sidewalks outdoors, under a cold, gray sky. Robert Collyer, Barnum's robust, white-headed friend, was to deliver the funeral address. In the midst of it, his strong voice suddenly became "husky," wrote family friend Joel Benton, "and tears streamed down his wrinkled cheeks." Barnum's pastor, Lewis Fisher, called out the names of hymns selected by Barnum—one by Whittier and another by Holmes, each filled with Barnum's own sun-filled Universalist philosophy and faith. And then, following the singing of "Auld Lang Syne," so emotional that during it all broke down in tears, the lily-of-the-valley–covered casket was carried out to Mountain Grove Cemetery, placed in a cedar box, lowered into a deep brick vault, and then covered by a two-ton slab of stone.

This huge statue of Barnum, shown here with its maker, Thomas Ball, was completed in 1888, but ordered hidden in a warehouse by Barnum until after his death. It was finally erected in Bridgeport by his circus partners and neighbors in 1893.

he authors are committed to the twin effort of creating books and their companion television documentaries. Therefore, it is not by chance that our first acknowledgment goes to the Discovery Channel, without whose backing this Barnum project would not have been possible. Our three-hour documentary on the great showman has had the enthusiastic support of Greg Moyer, Mike Quattrone, Chuck Gingold, Suzy Geller, and Peter McKelvy, and we thank them all for having the faith in us to produce lasting television for Discovery's tenth anniversary.

Our thanks go to Esther Newberg of ICM for believing in *Barnum* from the beginning and for once again bringing us together with Knopf, where Jane Friedman was enthusiastically behind the project almost immediately. We have worked before with Ashbel Green, our editor at Knopf, so we already knew why his trust, judgment, and fine hand with words and history have left such a mark on his industry. With Jennifer Bernstein assisting Ash, Debra Helfand in charge of the copy editing, Virginia Tan overseeing design, and Andy Hughes in command of production, our book, we knew, was always well served.

Over the course of this project, many scores of individuals have lent a hand. Chief among them are three from Barnum's own home territory in Connecticut: Bob Pelton of the Barnum Museum, Mary Witkowski of the Bridgeport Public Library, and Arthur H. Saxon, Barnum biographer. "I want to see both the book and the television series as perfect as they can be," wrote Arthur—who carefully checked our manuscript—in one of his many letters. Bob Pelton, along with colleagues Ben Ortiz and Linda Altshuler, has made available to us the rich resources of the Barnum Museum in Bridgeport, Connecticut. Housed in a Barnumesque building that was bequeathed by Barnum himself, the museum is a unique showcase of the renowned entertainer's career. Just a short walk away is the Bridgeport Public Library, to which Barnum left both money and many of his own books. The finest Barnum collection in the world resides here, under the able care of curator Mary Witkowski. We spent many long, enjoyable days in an upper room working with Mary and her assistant, Diane Kurtz.

A third great Barnum collection resides in Baraboo, Wisconsin, home of Circus World Museum and the finest circus archives anywhere. Curator Fred Dahlinger and his assistant, Tim Spindler, enthusiastically opened up their enormous files and provided us with research and photographs. Thanks go to them and to Phil Mueller of Maple Plain, Minnesota, who spent a week at the museum meticulously copying photographs, newspaper ads, and color posters. His work, as well as that of Marc Jaffe, rounded out the enormous job of copying and printing done for us by the Time-Life photo lab in New York City. This great lab worked not only with Meserve-Kunhardt material but also with numerous daguerreotypes, glass negatives, prints, paintings, and memorabilia loaned to us by other archives. Here special thanks are due Hanns Kohl, chief of the lab, and Tom Stone for giving such special care to all the archival materials.

In our search to flesh out the Barnum story, we investigated, of course, the major archives of New York City, especially those of the New-York Historical Society and the Museum of the City of New York. At the former, Dale Neighbors helped steer us through the rich holdings of the Prints and Photographs Department. At the latter, we spent pleasant days with curator Leslie Nolan and with Marty Jacobs, who oversees the Theater Collection. At the New York Public Library's Theater Collection, we received enthusiastic help from Bob Marx, Bob Taylor, and Kevin Winkler. A bit farther away from our Mt. Kisco, New York, offices was Princeton University's McCaddon Collection of the Barnum and Bailey Circus, through which Mary Ann Jensen and Alice V. Clark were our helpful guides. The Shelburne Museum in Shelburne, Vermont, provided a rich source of Barnum pictorial material, as did the Becker Collection of Syracuse University. At the Harvard Theater Collection, where Barbara Harrison conducted picture research for us, we received guidance and help from Dr. Jeanne T. Newlin, curator, and from curatorial assistant Michael T. Dumas. And right around the corner from us in Westchester County was the unassuming yet treasure-filled circus collection of the Somers Historical Society with its kindly curator, Florence Oliver. Helpful as well were Alan Seaburg of the Harvard Divinity School archives, Stephen Z. Nonack of the Boston Athenaeum, and Patrick Wild, the committed town historian of Barnum's birthplace and childhood home, Bethel, Connecticut. Richard Flint, Russell Norton, and John Skutel were sources for several hard-to-find Barnum photographs. Too numerous to single out by name, but appreciated none the less, are the curators of the 40 public and private archives from which we obtained copies of Barnum's personal and business correspondence. We learned much from each of the experts who appeared on camera in our documentary, among them Jean Ashton of Columbia University, Ron Walters of Georgetown University, Neil Harris of the University of Chicago, and Bluford Adams of Ohio State University, whose interesting Ph.D. thesis on Barnum is scheduled for publication as a book. But we must give special emphasis to Fred Pfening III, editor of *Bandwagon* magazine, who not only read and commented on our circus chapters but also offered numerous suggestions throughout the course of the project. Deserving special recognition as well is the staff of the Mt. Kisco Public Library, in particular Juliana Biro and Wendy Bloom, with whom we have been in almost weekly communication for two years.

We would like to thank Robert Gold for his careful, behind-the-scenes legal work, which has certainly made our lives easier. And thanks, too, to Edwin London and his staff at Gelfand, Rennert and Feldman for their financial skills and business advice.

We must especially single out the man responsible for the overall design of this book—Elton Robinson. A good friend, Elton had a long and celebrated career in the magazine and corporate worlds and now runs his own design business in Croton, New York. Authors formerly accustomed to old-fashioned cut-and-paste methods, we have been brought into the computer age by Elton. We thank him.

Inside our own offices many have helped, including Michael Kunhardt, who served as our cameraman and assistant on the television series, and research assistants Dyllan McGee and Kathleen Toner. Nancy Malin and Jamie Edgar both contributed greatly during the past two years. But the member of our staff who deserves chief recognition is Joan Caron, who not only had the full responsibility for typing and correcting our manuscript but also served as overall project assistant, helped with research, oversaw picture acquisition, and always kept her cool.

We have paid tribute to Frederick Hill Meserve and his daughter Dorothy Kunhardt in our introduction. We would like to mention here Meserve's other two children, Helen Meserve Paton and Frederick Leighton Meserve, who, after their father's death in 1962, presented their sister with their respective one-third interests in the Meserve Collection, thereby allowing it to remain as a working whole in the hands of the next family expert. All these people are gone now, as is Josephine Cobb, for decades the iconographic expert at the National Archives who helped generation after generation of our family in our quests into the American past and whose private files, through the generosity of her friend and executor, Pauline Piro, are now a part of the Meserve-Kunhardt Collection. In Washington, D.C., we are indebted not only to the National Archives, the Library of Congress, and the Smithsonian Institution and its curator of photographs, Paula Fleming, but to the National Portrait Gallery, which in 1981, by a special act of Congress, acquired Meserve's 5,420 life negatives taken by Mathew Brady and his staff. As well as overseeing the good care of these negatives, the Portrait Gallery's director, Alan Fern, and the curator of photographs, Mary Panzer, provided us with the stunning portrait of Barnum and Tom Thumb that appears on our book's cover, a daguerreotype the gallery recently obtained at auction.

We cannot end without mentioning our wives—Katharine, Margie, and Suzy—and thanking them for putting up with our long hours, our preoccupations, and our humbug. Barnum felt that his appeal to children was his greatest legacy. Possibly he does not appeal quite so much at present to our children and grandchildren, especially the younger ones, who have had anything but a circus for the past couple of years. So, finally, to Jessie, Philip, Harry, Peter, Abby, Teddy, and George, a jumbo thanks to each and every one of you.

Notes on Sources

The two modern starting places for the study of P. T. Barnum are A. H. Saxon's *P. T. Barnum: The Legend and The Man* (1989) and Neil Harris's *Humbug: The Art of P. T. Barnum* (1973). Both contain detailed bibliographies and critical notes, and each served as an important early guide in our research. Harris's groundbreaking work focuses on Barnum's showmanship and sets him in cultural context; Saxon's deals with the whole man and meticulously sorts out fact from error. Of the dozens of published Barnum biographies, it alone can be called definitive. Saxon, who served as our primary consultant, reading every page of this book and giving us detailed notes and suggested corrections, is also the editor of the only published collection of Barnum's letters, a selection of 303. In addition to these, we gathered almost 1,000 unpublished letters from 40 public and private archives.

Primary research into Barnum's life begins with the letters and moves to his published autobiographies, of which there are three main versions: the original 1855 edition, published in December 1854 by J. S. Redfield; the completely rewritten 1869 edition, published by J. B. Burr & Co., for sale by subscription only; and the much-abridged 1876 edition, with its many later appendixes and additions. Barnum's other published works are listed in our bibliography, but special mention must be made of the 100 or so letters he wrote between March 1844 and April 1846 as a foreign correspondent for the New York *Atlas*. Saucy, honest, sparkling, and sometimes crude, these "letters home" from the Tom Thumb tour in Europe have an off-the-cuff authenticity and bite sometimes lacking in the autobiographies. The most significant collections of letters to or about Barnum came to us from the Henry Bergh papers, housed at the ASPCA, and from the Henry Ward papers, at the University of Rochester.

Contemporary newspapers and magazines are essential to the study of a man so immersed in publicity and promotion. We followed several closely, in particular the New York *Atlas* for the 1840s, *Leslie's Weekly* for the late 1850s, and *Leslie's* and *Harper's Weekly* for the 1860s. Important articles and notices were also found in the Danbury *Times*, the New York *Herald*, *Gleason's Pictorial*, the New York *Sun*, *The New York Times*, *Packard's Monthly*, *Century Magazine*, *The Christian Leader*, and numerous other journals, including Barnum's own *Herald of Freedom* and his short-lived *Illustrated News*. For the circus era we turned to circus "route books" as well as to Barnum's own *Advance Couriers*, each group containing a wealth of information and available for study at the Bridgeport Public Library and

at Circus World Museum. These institutions also allowed us to sift through their vast files of manuscripts, newspaper clippings, and photographs, from which we gleaned and used much. Many of Barnum's performers had small, supposedly autobiographical pamphlets published about them. We gathered 31 of these from institutions across the country, and learned much from them about Barnum's presentation of his "living curiosities." Numerous extant contracts and deeds helped fill out the picture of Barnum's personal and business-related ventures.

From early on, we decided to follow a chronological, decade-by-decade approach to Barnum's life. Too many past treatments, we felt, did not carefully enough document the unfolding, ever-changing character of Barnum's career. Using five chief sources—contemporary playbills, Barnum newspaper ads, published obituaries, and two fine theatrical dictionaries, those of T. Allston Brown (1870) and George C. D. Odell (1927–49)—we assembled the names of over 800 performers known to have been employed by Barnum at his two museums. This research allowed us to reconstruct the pattern of Barnum's evolving theatrical career. Our picture research, linked to study in the so-called Draper and vertical files at Circus World Museum, as well as in the route books, helped us to periodize Barnum's circus career. In both cases, we concentrated not only on Barnum's performers, but on his equally vital but usually overlooked behind-the-scenes staff.

We paid special attention to describing the evolution of Barnum's American Museum in New York City. To this end, contemporary playbills, newspaper ads, published pamphlets, and eyewitness accounts helped us to add texture to Barnum's own published accounts of the museum, in particular his 112-page *Guide Book* from the early 1860s. Materials in the Scudder Collection at the Museum of the City of New York, focusing on the American Museum as it existed under previous management, helped us pinpoint Barnum's precise innovations and expansions. And illustrations collected from numerous sources, most notably from the New-York Historical Society, helped us to chronicle the museum building's own history, as well as the changing tenor of Barnum's New York. In the New York *Clipper*, an important source for theatrical and circus history, we discovered little-known eyewitness accounts of Barnum's 1865 museum fire, leading us to interpret that event as a case of arson.

Barnum shared a close personal friendship with some of his era's most notable figures. Neither Horace Greeley nor Mark Twain chose even to mention him in their memoirs, but valuable firsthand accounts,

from individuals willing to acknowledge friendship with the showman publicly, include those of Charles Godfrey Leland, George Emerson, Lavinia Stratton, Joel Benton, L. B. Fisher, and Albert Smith. Personal interviews with Barnum, conducted in 1864, 1884, and 1891 for *Leslie's Weekly*, for the New York *Sun*, and for the New York *World*, respectively, contain additional, revealing insights.

Barnum's career spanned the range of early photography, and it is not surprising that portraits of him exist in most formats, from daguerreotypes to collodion glass negatives, from cartes de visite and stereoviews to cabinet cards and imperial prints. Beginning with the two dozen Barnum portraits in the Meserve-Kunhardt Collection, and moving to the 20 or so pictures of a mostly older Barnum housed in the Bridgeport collections, we gathered a total of 80 distinct images of the great showman, including some that are exceedingly rare. The earliest known view is the Barnum and Tom Thumb daguerreotype that appears on our book's cover and on pages 28–29. Now owned by the National Portrait Gallery, it is believed to be the work of either Marcus or Samuel Root, who was also responsible for the image that Barnum used on the engraved frontispiece of his 1854 autobiography (see page 120). The National Portrait Gallery believes that its daguerreotype was taken from life with the aid of a reversing lens, which would explain why it shows Barnum as he looked and not in the reversed fashion typical of a daguerreotype portrait. A cabinet card at the Harvard Theatre Collection (see page 91) bearing the handwritten inscription "From Daguerreotype taken 1851" may also derive from one of the Root brothers, though in this case the image has not been corrected. Amongst the scores of other portraits that have been unearthed in this study, dozens are previously unpublished images. They include rare Barnum group scenes, both indoors and out; little-known Barnum family pictures; and the only known portrait of P. T. Barnum wearing a beard.

Following Arthur Saxon's lead, and that of the earlier biographer Irving Wallace, we have concentrated on Barnum's private life as well as his public. It was in the course of this research that information from Mary Witkowski at the Bridgeport Public Library, based on her conversations with a descendant of a cousin of Nancy Fish Barnum, led us to the previously unknown record of Barnum's second marriage that puts the date fully nine months earlier than previously known. This secret Barnum took to his grave, his last great humbug.

Selected Bibliography

Albion, Robert Greenhalgh, *The Rise of the New York Port, 1815–1860*. New York, 1939.

American Literary Manuscripts, 2nd ed. Athens, Georgia, 1977.

Appleton, William W., "The Marvelous Museum of P. T. Barnum." In *Le Merveilleux et les Arts du Spectacle*, pp. 57–62. Paris, 1963.

Barnum, Nancy, *"The Last Chapter": In Memoriam, P. T. Barnum*. New York, 1893.

Barnum, Nancy Fish, "Moths of Modern Marriages." *Ladies' Home Journal*, March 1891.

Barnum, P. T., *Funny Stories Told by P. T. Barnum*. New York and London, 1890.

Barnum, P. T., *The Humbugs of the World: An Account of Humbugs, Delusions, Impositions, Quackeries, Deceits and Deceivers Generally, in All Ages*. New York, 1865.

Barnum, P. T., *The Life of P. T. Barnum, Written by Himself*. New York, 1855.

Barnum, P. T., *Struggles and Triumphs; or Forty Years' Recollections of P. T. Barnum, Written by Himself*. Hartford, Connecticut, 1869.

Barnum, P. T., *Struggles and Triumphs; or, Sixty Years' Recollections of P. T. Barnum, Including His Golden Rules for Money-Making, Illustrated and Brought Up to 1889, Written by Himself*. Buffalo, New York, 1889.

Barnum, P. T., *Why I Am a Universalist*. Boston and Chicago, n.d.

Barnum, P. T., *Will & Codicils of Phineas Taylor Barnum*. Admitted to Probate April 11th, 1891. Bridgeport, Connecticut, 1891.

Basso, Hamilton, *Mainstream*. New York, 1943.

Bennett, James Gordon, *Memoirs of James Gordon Bennett and His Times by a Journalist*. New York, 1855.

Benton, Joel, "P. T. Barnum, Showman and Humorist." *Century Magazine*, August 1902, pp. 580–92.

Betts, John Rickards, "P. T. Barnum and the Popularization of Natural History." *Journal of the History of Ideas* 20, 1959, pp. 353–68.

Birdoff, Harry, *The World's Greatest Hit—Uncle Tom's Cabin*. New York, 1947.

Bleeker, Sylvester, *Gen. Tom Thumb's Three Years' Tour Around the World, Accompanied by His Wife—Lavinia Warren Stratton, Commodore Nutt, Minnie Warren, and Party*. New York, 1872.

Bode, Carl, *The Anatomy of American Popular Culture 1840–61*. Berkeley and Los Angeles, 1960.

Bogdan, Robert, *Freak Show: Presenting Human Oddities for Amusement and Profit*. Chicago, 1988.

Boxell, Paul J., "P. T. Barnum's Lectures for Londoners." *Quarterly Journal of Speech* 54, 1968, pp. 140–46.

Bradford, Gamaliel, *Damaged Souls*. Boston, 1923.

Brown, Henry Collins, *Book of Old New York*. New York, 1913.

Brown, Henry Collins, *Valentine's Manual of Old New York*. New York, 1924.

Brown, T. Allston, *History of the American Stage, Containing Biographical Sketches of Nearly Every Member of the Profession That Has Appeared on the American Stage from 1733 to 1870*. 1870; reprint, New York, 1969.

Brown, T. Allston, *A History of the New York Stage*, 3 vols. New York, 1903.

Bryan, George S., ed., *Struggles and Triumphs; Or the Life of P. T. Barnum, Written by Himself*, 2 vols. New York and London, 1927.

Bulman, Joan, *Jenny Lind: A Biography*. London, 1956.

Bunn, Alfred, *Old England and New England, in a Series of Views Taken on the Spot*, 2 vols. London, 1853.

[Butler, William], *Barnum's Parnassus*. New York, 1850.

Chindahl, George L., *A History of the Circus in America*. Caldwell, Idaho, 1959.

Complimentary Banquet to P. T. Barnum, from Citizens of Bridgeport, Connecticut, Atlantic House, June 25th, 1874. Bridgeport, Connecticut, 1874.

Conklin, George, *The Ways of the Circus, Being the Memories and Adventures of George Conklin, Tamer of Lions*, ed. Harvey W. Root. New York, 1921.

Coup, W. C., *Sawdust & Spangles: Stories & Secrets of the Circus*. 1901; reprint, Washington, D.C., 1961.

Crum, W. C., *History of Animals and Leading Curiosities Contained in P. T. Barnum's World's Fair and Coliseum of Natural History and Art*. New York, 1873.

Deems, Charles F., "Alice & Phoebe Cary: Their Home and Friends." *Packard's Monthly* 3, no. 2 (February 1870), pp. 49–52.

Desmond, Alice Curtis, *Barnum Presents General Tom Thumb*. New York, 1954.

Durant, John, and Alice Durant, *Pictorial History of the American Circus*. New York, 1957.

Fellows, Dexter W., and Andrew A. Freeman, *This Way to the Big Show: The Life of Dexter Fellows*. New York, 1936.

Fiedler, Leslie, *Freaks: Myths and Images of the Secret Self*. New York, 1978.

Fisher, L. B., "Recollections of P. T. Barnum." *The Christian Leader*, November 16, 1929, pp. 1457–58.

Fitzsimons, Raymond, *Barnum in London*. London, 1969.

Frith, W. P., *My Autobiography & Reminiscences*. New York, 1885.

Haberly, Lloyd, "The American Museum from Baker to Barnum." *NYHS Quarterly* 43, 1959, pp. 273–87.

Harris, Neil, *Humbug: The Art of P. T. Barnum*. Boston, 1973.

Harrison, Harry P., as told to Karl Detzer. *Culture Under Canvas: The Story of Tent Chautauqua*. New York, 1958.

Holloway, Laura C., *Famous American Fortunes and the Men Who Have Made Them*. Philadelphia, 1884.

Hone, Philip, *Diary of Philip Hone, 1828–1851*, 2 vols., ed. Allan Nevins. New York, 1927.

Horner, Charles F., *The Life of James Redpath and the Development of the Modern Lyceum*. New York, 1926.

An Illustrated Catalogue and Guide Book to Barnum's American Museum. New York, n.d.

Jerome, Chauncey, *History of the American Clock Business for the Past Sixty Years, and Life of Chauncey Jerome*. New Haven, 1860.

Kouwenhoven, John A., *The Arts in Modern American Civilization*. New York, 1907.

Lanigan, Alice Graham, "Mrs. Phineas T. Barnum," part of the series "Unknown Wives of Well-Known Men." *Ladies' Home Journal*, February 1891.

Larrabee, Eric, "The Old Showman's Last Triumph." In *American Heritage*, December 1961.

Leland, Charles Godfrey, *Memoirs*, 2 vols. London, 1893.

Levine, Lawrence W., *Highbrow/Lowbrow: The Emergence of Cultural Hierarchy in America*. Cambridge, Massachusetts, 1988.

Lindberg, Gary, *The Confidence Man in American Literature*. New York, 1982.

Mathews, Cornelius, *A Pen and Ink Panorama of New York City*. New York, 1853.

McGlinchee, Claire, *The First Decade of the Boston Museum*. Boston, 1940.

Morinni, Clara de, "P. T. Barnum's Second Wife." *The New Yorker*, April 11, 1936.

"Moses Kimball." In *National Cyclopedia of American Biography*, vol. 20, p. 70.

"Moses Kimball." In the *New England Historical and Genealogical Register*, vol. 56, 1902, pp. 335–40.

Nevins, Allan, *America Through British Eyes*. New York, 1948.

Odell, George C. D., *Annals of the New York Stage*, 15 vols. New York, 1927–1949.

Orcutt, Samuel, *History of the Old Town of Stratford and the City of Bridgeport, Connecticut*, 2 vols. New Haven, 1892.

Palmquist, David W., *Bridgeport: A Pictorial History*, rev. ed. Norfolk, Virginia, 1985.

Peterson, A. Everett, ed., *Landmarks of New York: An Historical Guide to the Metropolis*. New York, 1923.

Pond, J. B., *Eccentricities of Genius: Memories of Famous Men and Women of the Platform and Stage*. New York, 1900.

Presbrey, Frank, *The History and Development of Advertising*. Garden City, New York, 1929.

Robert-Houdin, Jean-Eugene, *Memoirs of Robert Houdin, Ambassador, Author, and Conjurer: Written by Himself*, 2 vols. London, 1859.

Romaine, Mertie E., *General Tom Thumb and His Lady*. Taunton, Massachusetts, 1976.

Root, Harvey W., *The Unknown Barnum*. New York, 1927.

Rosenberg, C. G., *Jenny Lind in America*. New York, 1851.

Rourke, Constance Mayfield, *Trumpets of Jubilee: Henry Ward Beecher, Harriet Beecher Stowe, Lyman Beecher, Horace Greeley, P. T. Barnum*. New York, 1927.

Russell, George W. E., ed., *Letters of Matthew Arnold*. New York, 1900.

Saxon, A. H., *P. T. Barnum: The Legend and the Man*. New York, 1989.

Saxon, A. H., ed., *The Autobiography of Mrs. Tom Thumb (Some of My Life Experiences) by Countess M. Lavinia Magri*. Hamden, Connecticut, 1979.

Saxon, A. H., ed., *Selected Letters of P. T. Barnum*. New York, 1983.

Scott, Matthew, *Autobiography of Matthew Scott, Jumbo's Keeper, Formerly of the Zoological Society's Gardens, London, and Receiver of Sir Edwin Landseer Medal in 1866*. Bridgeport, Connecticut, 1885.

Sellers, Charles Coleman, *Mr. Peale's Museum*. New York, 1980.

Shultz, Gladys Denny, *Jenny Lind: The Swedish Nightingale*. Philadelphia and New York, 1962.

Sketch of the Life, Personal Appearance, Character and Manners of Charles S. Stratton. New York, 1863, 1874.

Skinner, J. E. Hilary, *After the Storm; or Jonathan and His Neighbors in 1865–6*, 2 vols. London, 1866.

Smith, Albert, "A Go-A-Head Day with Barnum." In *Bentley's Miscellany*, vol. 21, 1847, pp. 522–27, 623–28.

Speaight, George, *A History of the Circus*. London, 1980.

Stedman, Edmund Clarence, and George Edward Woodberry, eds., "Diddling Considered as One of the Exact Sciences." In *The Works of Edgar Allan Poe*, vol. 4, pp. 234–38. New York, 1894, 1914.

Stoddard, Richard Henry, *Recollections Personal & Literary*. New York, 1903.

Strong, George Templeton, *The Diary of George Templeton Strong*, 4 vols., ed.

Allan Nevins and Milton Halsey Thomas. New York, 1952.

Toole-Stott, Raymond, *Circus and Allied Arts: A World Bibliography*, 5 vols. Derby, England, 1958–71; Liverpool, England, 1992.

Trollope, Mrs., *Domestic Manners of the Americans*. London, 1836.

Tupper, Edith Sessions, "P. T. Barnum at Home." *New York World*, March 15, 1891.

Vail, R. W. G., *Random Notes on the History of the Early American Circus*. Barre, Massachusetts, 1956.

Wallace, Irving, *The Fabulous Showman: The Life and Times of P. T. Barnum*. New York, 1959.

Ward, Henry A. *The Life and Death of Jumbo*. Philadelphia, 1886.

Ware, W. Porter, and Thaddeus C. Lockard, Jr., *P. T. Barnum Presents Jenny Lind: The American Tour of the Swedish Nightingale*. Baton Rouge, Louisiana, 1980.

Wemyss, Francis Courtney, *Twenty-Six Years of Life as an Actor and Manager*. New York, 1847.

Werner, M. R., *Barnum*. New York, 1923.

Whitehouse, Roger, *New York: Sunlight and Shadow*. New York, 1974.

Willis, Nathaniel Parker, *Famous Persons and Famous Places*. London, 1854.

Willis, Nathaniel Parker, *Memoranda of the Life of Jenny Lind*. Philadelphia, 1851.

Wilmeth, Don B., *Variety Entertainment and Outdoor Amusements: A Reference Guide*. Westport, Connecticut, 1982.

Index

Italicized page numbers indicate photographs, paintings, and drawings.

Picture Sources

Whenever a picture is not listed here, it comes from the Meserve-Kunhardt Collection, owned by the authors. All other pictures were obtained from the outside sources that are credited here.

The trademarks and names BARNUM & BAILEY and THE GREATEST SHOW ON EARTH are owned by, and reproductions in this book which include these names and marks are used by permission of, Ringling Bros. Barnum & Bailey Combined Shows, Inc.

Cover: National Portrait Gallery. **ii:** Robert Gould Shaw Collection, Harvard Theatre Collection. **2–3:** Bridgeport Public Library. **6:** The Barnum Museum, Bridgeport, Conn. **8:** Danbury Town Clerk's Office (top right); Bridgeport Public Library (center left and lower left). **9:** Somers Historical Society (top left); Bridgeport Public Library (bottom). **10:** Danbury Scott-Fanton Museum and Historical Society (bottom). **11:** Bridgeport Public Library (top right); Danbury Scott-Fanton Museum and Historical Society (bottom left). **12–13:** New York Public Library. **14:** The Barnum Museum, Bridgeport, Conn. **15:** The Barnum Museum, Bridgeport, Conn. **16:** Bridgeport Public Library (top). **17:** The Barnum Museum, Bridgeport, Conn. (top). **18:** Museum of Fine Arts, Boston, Gift of Mrs. J. D. Cameron Bradley (top right). **20:** Fred D. Pfening III Collection. **21:** Somers Historical Society. **22:** Circus World Museum, Baraboo, Wisc. **23:** Bridgeport Public Library (top). **24:** Somers Historical Society. **25:** Bridgeport Public Library (top). **27:** Historic New Orleans Collection. **28–29:** National Portrait Gallery, Smithsonian Institution/Art Resource, N.Y. **31:** Missouri Historical Society, St. Louis. **34–35:** Museum of the City of New York, the J. Clarence Davies Collection. **36:** Museum of the City of New York (bottom). **37:** Pennsylvania Academy of Fine Arts, Philadelphia, Gift of Mrs. Sarah Harrison (the Joseph Harrison, Jr., Collection). **38–39:** Collection of the New-York Historical Society. **43:** Peabody Museum of Archaeology and Ethnology, Harvard University. **44:** Boston Athenaeum. **45:** Society for the Preservation of New England Antiquities. **47:** Bridgeport Public Library. **48–49:** Fred D. Pfening III Collection (top center). **49:** The Barnum Museum, Bridgeport, Conn. **50:** The Barnum Museum, Bridgeport, Conn. **51:** Harvard Theatre Collection (bottom). **53:** Bridgeport Public Library; Collections of the Harvard Divinity School Library (bottom). **54:** The Barnum Museum, Bridgeport, Conn. (top). **57:** Bridgeport Public Library (top left). **58:** The Barnum Museum, Bridgeport, Conn. (left). **60:** Russell Norton (top); Somers Historical Society (bottom). **61:** Charles Schwartz Photography. **62:** National Portrait Gallery, Smithsonian Institution/Art Resource, N.Y. **63:** Shelburne Museum, Shelburne, Vt., Photograph by Ken Burris (top). **69:** The Hulton Deutsch Collection (bottom). **70:** Robert Coe. **72:** Griswold Collection, Harvard Theatre Collection. **76:** Collection of the New-York Historical Society (left); Library of Congress (center). **77:** Collection of the New-York Historical Society (left). **78:** The Barnum Museum, Bridgeport, Conn. **81:** The Barnum Museum, Bridgeport, Conn. (bottom). **85:** Bridgeport Public Library. **86–87:** Russell Norton Collection. **88:** Brander Matthews, Dramatic Museum, Rare Book and Manuscript Library, Columbia University (top); Tufts University Archives and Special Collections (bottom). **89:** Library of Congress. **90:** Bridgeport Public Library. **91:** Robert Gould Shaw Collection, Harvard Theatre Collection. **92:** Bridgeport Public Library. **95:** Bridgeport Public Library (left). **96:** Museum of the City of New York (bottom). **97:** Bridgeport Public Library (top right and bottom). **100:** Maryland Historical Society, Baltimore. **101:** Missouri Historical Society, St. Louis (top); Tennessee State Library and Archives (bottom). **103:** Collection of the New-York Historical Society. **104–105:** The Barnum Museum, Bridgeport, Conn. **107:** Harvard Theatre Collection, Bequest of Evert Jansen Wendell (center). **109:** Bridgeport Public Library (top left). **110:** Bridgeport Public Library. **111:** Collection of the New-York Historical Society (top left and bottom). **112:** Collection of the New-York Historical Society (left); Missouri Historical Society, St. Louis (right). **113:** Somers Historical Society (right). **114:** Museum of the City of New York (bottom left). **115:** Bridgeport Public Library. **117:** Circus World Museum, Baraboo, Wisc. (top right). **119:** Bridgeport Public Library (bottom left and right). **120:** Bridgeport Public Library (bottom). **122–123:** Bridgeport Public Library (bottom). **123:** Bridgeport Public Library (top). **126:** The Barnum Museum, Bridgeport, Conn. **129:** The Barnum Museum, Bridgeport, Conn. **131:** Russell Norton Collection. **134:** The Barnum Museum, Bridgeport, Conn. **135:** The Barnum Museum, Bridgeport, Conn. **138:** Bridgeport Public Library. **139:** Bridgeport Public Library. **140:** Bridgeport Public Library. **141:** Bridgeport Public Library (top and bottom). **144:** Bridgeport Public Library. **146:** Ronald G. Becker Collection, Syracuse University Library, Department of Special Collections (bottom). **149:** Somers Historical Society (bottom). **151:** National Portrait Gallery (left); Somers Historical Society (upper right); Ronald G. Becker Collection, Syracuse University Library, Department of Spe- cial Collections (bottom). **152:** Bridgeport Public Library (top). **158:** Floyd and Marion Rinhart Collection, the Ohio State University Cartoon, Graphic, and Photographic Arts Research Library. **159:** Bridgeport Public Library (top and bottom). **160:** National Portrait Gallery, Smithsonian Institution/Art Resource, N.Y. (top). **164:** Bridgeport Public Library (top right and bottom right). **165:** Bridgeport Public Library (bottom). **166:** Bridgeport Public Library (top). **172:** Harvard Theatre Collection, Bequest of Evert Jansen Wendell (lower left); Patrick Wild (top right). **175:** Ronald G. Becker Collection, Syracuse University Library, Department of Special Collections (top). **176:** Circus World Museum, Baraboo, Wisc. **191:** Memorial Art Gallery of the University of Rochester. **192:** Bridgeport Public Library. **196:** Circus World Museum, Baraboo, Wisc. **197:** Somers Historical Society (top left); Fred D. Pfening III Collection (lower left). **200:** Bridgeport Public Library. **209:** Bridgeport Public Library (upper left). **211:** The Barnum Museum, Bridgeport, Conn. **212:** The Barnum Museum, Bridgeport, Conn. **213:** Bridgeport Public Library (top); The Barnum Museum, Bridgeport, Conn. (lower left and right). **215:** New York State Historical Association, Cooperstown. **216–217:** Ronald G. Becker Collection, Syracuse University Library, Department of Special Collections. **218:** Bridgeport Public Library. **222:** Circus World Museum, Baraboo, Wisc. (top and bottom). **223:** Bridgeport Public Library (top); The Barnum Museum, Bridgeport, Conn. (bottom left); Collection of Richard W. Flint, Baltimore (bottom right). **224:** Circus World Museum, Baraboo, Wisc. **229:** Pfening Archives (upper left); The Barnum Museum, Bridgeport, Conn. (upper right); Circus World Museum, Baraboo, Wisc. (bottom). **231:** Bridgeport Public Library. **232–233:** Circus World Museum, Baraboo, Wisc. **234:** Collection of Richard W. Flint, Baltimore (bottom). **236:** Bridgeport Public Library (top); Somers Historical Society (bottom). **238:** Bridgeport Public Library. **240:** The Barnum Museum, Bridgeport, Conn. (top). **242:** Circus World Museum, Baraboo, Wisc. (left); Bridgeport Public Library (right). **243:** Circus World Museum, Baraboo, Wisc. (all three). **244:** Bridgeport Public Library (top right). **248:** The Barnum Museum, Bridgeport, Conn. **250:** Circus World Museum, Baraboo, Wisc. **251:** Bridgeport Public Library (top and bottom). **253:** Collection of Richard W. Flint, Baltimore (top); The Barnum Museum, Bridgeport, Conn. (bottom). **262:** Circus World Museum, Baraboo, Wisc. (top); Bridgeport Public Library (bottom). **264–265:** Bridgeport Public Library. **266:** Missouri Historical Society, St.

Louis (top). **268**: Circus World Museum, Baraboo, Wisc. **271**: Bridgeport Public Library (bottom). **272**: Circus World Museum, Baraboo, Wisc. (top and bottom). **273**: Howard Tibbals (top); McCaddon Collection of the Barnum and Bailey Circus. Theatre Collections. Visual Materials Division. Princeton University Libraries (bottom). **276**: Bridgeport Public Library. **277**: Fred D. Pfening III Collection (left and right). **278**: Bridgeport Public Library. **278–279**: Circus World Museum, Baraboo, Wisc. **280**: The Barnum Museum, Bridgeport, Conn. **281**: Bridgeport Public Library (top). **282–283**: Somers Historical Society. **284**: Bridgeport Public Library (top and bottom). **285**: Circus World Museum, Baraboo, Wisc. **286**: Museum of the City of New York. **287**: Bridgeport Public Library (top); Circus World Museum, Baraboo, Wisc. (bottom). **289**: Bridgeport Public Library (bottom). **290**: Ronald G. Becker Collection, Syracuse University Library, Department of Special Collections (top); Bridgeport Public Library (bottom). **291**: Ronald G. Becker Collection, Syracuse University Library, Department of Special Collections. **292**: New York Society for the Prevention of Cruelty to Children. **293**: McCaddon Collection of the Barnum and Bailey Circus. Theatre Collections. Visual Materials Division. Princeton University Libraries (bottom center). **294**: Bridgeport Public Library (top left); McCaddon Collection of the Barnum and Bailey Circus. Theatre Collections. Visual Materials Division. Princeton University Libraries (top right); Fred D. Pfening III Collection (bottom). **295**: Circus World Museum, Baraboo, Wisc. **296**: Pfening Archives. **297**: McCaddon Collection of the Barnum and Bailey Circus. Theatre Collections. Visual Materials Division. Princeton University Libraries (top left and bottom right); Ronald G. Becker Collection, Syracuse University Library, Department of Special Collections (top right and bottom left). **298**: Bridgeport Public Library. **299**: Bridge-port Public Library (top and bottom). **300–301**: Circus World Museum, Baraboo, Wisc. **301**: Bridgeport Public Library (inset). **302**: Albert Conover Collection. **306**: Bridgeport Public Library. **308**: Collection of the New-York Historical Society. **309**: Bridgeport Public Library. **310**: The Barnum Museum, Bridgeport, Conn. **311**: Circus World Museum, Baraboo, Wisc. (top left, top right, and bottom center); McCaddon Collection of the Barnum and Bailey Circus. Theatre Collections. Visual Materials Division. Princeton University Libraries (center left, bottom left, and bottom right). **312**: Fred D. Pfening III Collection (left); McCaddon Collection of the Barnum and Bailey Circus. Theatre Collections. Visual Materials Division. Princeton University Libraries (center); Bridgeport Public Library (right). **313**: The Barnum Museum, Bridgeport, Conn. **314**: The Barnum Museum, Bridgeport, Conn. (top and bottom). **315**: The Barnum Museum, Bridgeport, Conn. (top); Bridgeport Public Library (bottom). **317**: The Barnum Museum, Bridgeport, Conn. (lower left). **318**: Collections of the Harvard Divinity School Library (center and bottom). **319**: Collections of the Harvard Divinity School Library (top center); Archives, St. Lawrence University (top right); Tufts University (bottom). **321**: McCaddon Collection of the Barnum and Bailey Circus. Theatre Collections. Visual Materials Division. Princeton University Libraries (top left); Bridgeport Public Library (top right); Circus World Museum, Baraboo, Wisc. (bottom). **322**: McCaddon Collection of the Barnum and Bailey Circus. Theatre Collections. Visual Materials Division. Princeton University Libraries (top); Bridgeport Public Library (bottom). **323**: Howard Tibbals. **324**: Circus World Museum, Baraboo, Wisc. (all three). **325**: Circus World Museum, Baraboo, Wisc. (top and bottom). **326**: McCad-don Collection of the Barnum and Bailey Circus. Theatre Collections. Visual Materials Division. Princeton University Libraries. **327**: McCaddon Collection of the Barnum and Bailey Circus. Theatre Collections. Visual Materials Division. Princeton University Libraries (top); Circus World Museum, Baraboo, Wisc. (bottom). **329**: Bridgeport Public Library (top); The Barnum Museum, Bridgeport, Conn. (bottom, left and right). **330**: Tufts University Archives and Special Collections. **331**: Tufts University Archives and Special Collections. **332**: McCaddon Collection of the Barnum and Bailey Circus. Theatre Collections. Visual Materials Division. Princeton University Libraries. **333**: The Barnum Museum, Bridgeport, Conn. **334–335**: Bridgeport Public Library. **336–337**: Bridgeport Public Library. **337**: Bridgeport Public Library (top). **338**: McCaddon Collection of the Barnum and Bailey Circus. Theatre Collections. Visual Materials Division. Princeton University Libraries (bottom). **339**: Bridgeport Public Library. **340**: The Barnum Museum, Bridgeport, Conn. **341**: The Barnum Museum, Bridgeport, Conn. **342**: McCaddon Collection of the Barnum and Bailey Circus. Theatre Collections. Visual Materials Division. Princeton University Libraries (top); Fred D. Pfening III Collection (bottom). **344**: Bridgeport Public Library. **345**: Fred D. Pfening III Collection. **346**: Circus World Museum, Baraboo, Wisc. **367**: Circus World Museum, Baraboo, Wisc.

BARNUM'S MUSEUM.

OVER 100,000 CURIOSITIES!

Mammoth Ox, Re-union,

The largest ever exhibited in America.

AN AFRICAN VULTURE. THE ADJUTANT.

GOLD & SILVER PHEASANTS.

AUSTRALIAN OPOSSUM & YOUNG.

To be seen at all hours,

THE CAROLINA TWINS,

Aged 13 Years.

Although inseparably joined, yet their individual movements are easy and graceful.
They are lively and vivacious, and are pronounced by all who have seen them as the
Greatest Curiosity in the World.

300 Living Australian Birds,

Specimens of which are for sale.

3,000 Specimens of Native Birds.

WOODROFFE'S BOHEMIAN GLASS BLOWERS,
WILL EXHIBIT A GLASS STEAM ENGINE

In full operation.   They also manufacture an endless variety of charming ornaments.

The SMALLEST DWARFS in the World,
Gen. GRANT, Jr., aged 14 years, 27 inches high, and weighing only 18 pounds.
Master WILLIAM WALLACE, Scotch Dwarf, aged 15 years, 21 inches high, weighing 22 pounds.